THE KIDS
GOT IT
RIGHT

ALSO BY JIM DENT

Monster of the Midway
The Undefeated
The Junction Boys
You're Out and You're Ugly, Too!
    (with Durwood Merrill)
King of the Cowboys
Twelve Mighty Orphans
Resurrection
Super Bowl Texas Style
Courage Beyond the Game

THE KIDS GOT IT RIGHT

How the Texas All-Stars
Kicked Down Racial Walls

Jim Dent

Thomas Dunne Books
St. Martin's Press
New York

THOMAS DUNNE BOOKS.
An imprint of St. Martin's Press.

THE KIDS GOT IT RIGHT. Copyright © 2013 by Jim Dent. All rights reserved.
Printed in the United States of America. For information, address St. Martin's
Press, 175 Fifth Avenue, New York, N.Y. 10010.

www.thomasdunnebooks.com
www.stmartins.com

Book design by Omar Chapa

ISBN 978-1-250-00785-8 (hardcover)
ISBN 978-1-250-01789-5 (e-book)

St. Martin's Press books may be purchased for educational, business, or promotional
use. For information on bulk purchases, please contact Macmillan Corporate
and Premium Sales Department at 1-800-221-7945, extension 5442, or write
specialmarkets@macmillan.com.

First Edition: August 2013

10 9 8 7 6 5 4 3 2 1

To Kathryn Shrum

The love of my life and a terrific proofreader; you have made my life complete the past three years, and I look forward to spending the rest of my time with you.

CONTENTS

PREFACE

A high school all-star game staged in the medium-sized central Pennsylvania town of Hershey captured the nation's attention in August of 1965. For one week, Hershey was the center of the American sports universe. It was common in this era for high school football to dominate the daily sports pages. Fertile states like Texas and Pennsylvania, with football-crazy towns like Odessa, Altoona, Abilene, and Johnstown, packed the high school stadiums every Friday night and Saturday afternoon.

Before the advent of the Super Bowl, ESPN, the Internet, and football glut, fans were enamored of Joe Willie Namath of Beaver Falls (Pennsylvania) High School. They knew more about Bill Bradley of Palestine (Texas) High School than Bill Howton of the Dallas Cowboys. They went to the games to feel the raw excitement and to smell the fresh-cut grass, not to drink a twelve-dollar margarita and to tweet about the proud ownership of a new six-figure Jaguar.

In Texas, they turned out in droves to see the Italy Gladiators, the Hereford Whitefaces, the Hutto Hippos, and the Winters Blizzards. Pennsylvania fans adored the Franklin Electronics, the Punxsutawney Chucks, the Aliquippa Quips, and the Boiling Springs Bubblers.

High school football in the mid-1960s was just more fun. The NFL was not yet the darling of Park Avenue. The NBA could count only a handful of stars in spite of seven straight league titles by the Boston Celtics. Major League Baseball was still the national pastime, but it thrived because of one powerful club, the New York Yankees.

Big-time sports in 1965 lacked the glitz, the megamillions, and the idolization that would come later. The NFL championship game matching Green Bay versus Cleveland at Lambeau Field was a mud-slog that was about as exciting as ice fishing. The Packers roared from ahead to win 23–12. That year, the Yankees did not reach the World Series for the first time in six years and were replaced by the forget-table Minnesota Twins, who lost to the Los Angeles Dodgers. The de facto college football national championship game was played on January 1, 1966, at the Orange Bowl between third-ranked Nebraska and No. 4 Alabama. With a 39–28 victory, Alabama, 9-1-1, leapfrogged to No. 1, thanks to bowl-game losses by No. 1 Michigan State and No. 2 Arkansas. The 1965 NCAA basketball tournament was composed of only twenty-three teams, and the Final Four was not even televised.

Meanwhile, the Big 33 game would be beamed to forty-two cities in Texas and Pennsylvania, along with several closed-circuit sites.

In 1965, the Big 33 drew more than a hundred newspaper report-ers during a time when NFL teams were lucky to receive twenty cre-dential requests. Just three years earlier, Wilt Chamberlain had scored 100 points to smash the NBA record with not a single newspaperman or TV camera in the arena.

Sports Illustrated had been trumpeting the Texas-Pennsylvania Big 33 game for two years. Also coming to town were writers from the *Saturday Evening Post* and photographers from *Life*. Every journal-ist in town knew he could fill up a notebook with quotes from Texas coach and former All-Pro quarterback Bobby Layne, who led the De-troit Lions to back-to-back NFL titles in 1952 and 1953. Layne was one of the most colorful characters in the history of American sports.

So fascinating was the Texas-Pennsylvania game that Browns owner Art Modell wanted to bring the game to Cleveland to be part of a preseason double-header involving his club. The high schoolers might have drawn more interest than the pros. In Houston, the

Astrodome was offering big money for a Texas-Pennsylvania matchup. Judge Roy Hofheinz pledged to fill every one of the 46,000 seats in the "Eighth Wonder of the World."

The 1965 game featured a cast of all-stars whose future successes would be almost immeasurable. Three stars from the '65 game would finish among the top 10 Heisman Trophy vote-getters in 1968. Pennsylvania quarterback Terry Hanratty (Notre Dame) finished third and tight end Ted Kwalick (Penn State) fourth. Chris Gilbert (Texas) finished ninth. Hanratty also led Notre Dame to the 1966 national title. In 1969, Pennsylvania defensive tackle Mike Reid (Penn State) finished fifth in the Heisman race while winning the Outland Trophy as the country's best interior lineman and the Maxwell Award as the College Player of the Year. Jerry LeVias made All-Southwest Conference for three straight seasons and became a unanimous All American his senior year. The most decorated of the NFL players to come out of the Big 33 was Bill Bradley, who made All-Pro three straight years with a mediocre Philadelphia team. He still shares the club record with 34 interceptions and was inducted into the Eagles Hall of Fame in 1993.

With so many great players on both rosters, it was little wonder that the August 14 game in Hershey had been a sellout for several months. Tickets with a face value of two and three dollars were already being scalped for ten times that amount. College football coaches had arrived from all parts of the country to get a closer look at sixty-six of the biggest football studs in America.

No one could have scripted a better matchup than Texas versus Pennsylvania. The Keystone State boasted a robust history from the steel mills to the coal towns to the Catholic Leagues of Philadelphia and Pittsburgh. The steelworkers around Pittsburgh and Bethlehem produced hard-nosed sons who made a seamless transition into a physically demanding game. Four Heisman Trophy winners had already been produced by Pennsylvania, including Ernie Davis of Syracuse in 1961. Included among the countless stars were Mike Ditka and Lenny Moore. In the early part of the century, the University of Pennsylvania alone produced sixty-three All Americans. Penn was the university of John Heisman, whose name is on the trophy given each year to college football's best player.

The enormous popularity of Texas high school football was hard to explain. When Texas was more of a rural state, the start of the football season in September marked the end of the growing season. The idle farmers, needing something to do, headed straight to the football stadium. As the temperatures dropped, the ranchers would follow. In those days, especially in places like Abilene and Breckenridge, it was one team, one town. A dusty old pickup truck could get you to all of the district games, home and away.

As early as the 1920s, the state's football powerhouses were held in the utmost esteem by some of America's best football minds. Waco High School coach Paul Tyson made the state championship game each year from 1922 through 1927, losing only 2 games. His team scored more than 100 points nine times. He introduced the "spinner series," an offense where the backs would spin and cross paths. One day, Tyson received a letter from Notre Dame coach Knute Rockne saying he was coming to Texas to learn the offense. Tyson laughed it off, only to receive a telegram with instructions on when to meet Rockne's train. The result of picking Tyson's brain would become the "Notre Dame Box." Rockne once called Tyson "the greatest mind in football." Tyson had been hired as a Notre Dame assistant coach for the 1931 season when Rockne's plane crashed in a wheat field near Bazaar, Kansas. The plan was for Tyson to coach in South Bend for a few years, then replace Rockne when he retired. After the crash, Tyson changed his mind and stayed in Texas.

One of Texas's most famous coaches was O. A. "Bum" Phillips, who excelled at the high school level in Nederland, Port Neches, Jacksonville, and Amarillo before gaining national fame as the head coach of the Houston Oilers and New Orleans Saints. His Oilers missed the Super Bowl by one game in 1979. Writing in the foreword to *Pigskin Pulpit*, a comprehensive social history of Texas high school football, Phillips explained the phenomenon. He wrote, "There is something about high school football in Texas that captures the essence of what the sport is all about. It's about pride; it's about boys playing for the love of the game; it's about communities coming together for the common cause. In college and pro football, you lose some of that."

Nothing was lost at the Big 33 game of 1965. Texas was desperately trying to avenge a 12–6 defeat from the previous year. Meanwhile, Pennsylvanians clung to the belief that they were the leading producers of high school football talent in America. The result was a weeklong battle of words that led to a dramatic come-from-behind victory. It rivaled some of the biggest sporting events of the year. No, it was not the World Series or the NFL championship game, but it contained elements of emotion, drama, and loyalty that are lacking in today's sports.

It was a story for the ages.

THE KIDS
GOT IT
RIGHT

1

The Blond Bomber

That steamy August night in the faraway hills of central Pennsylvania, Bobby Layne stomped the ground like a man snuffing out a grass fire. His full-throated Texas twang sounded like the whine of a distant crop duster. He yanked the spent Marlboro from his lips and fired it into the grass.

Unfolding before his eyes was the horror of losing the biggest game of his coaching life. Never mind it was his coaching debut. On August 1, 1964, Layne's team of Texas high school all-stars was faltering against a bunch of overfed, heavy-legged Pennsylvania boys by the score of 12–6. The scene in Hershey grew more hopeless with each tick of the scoreboard clock.

The Texas team had traveled fourteen hundred miles to participate in the Big 33 Football Classic. It was called the Big 33 because thirty-three players were selected for each team. Weeks earlier, the all-stars from both Texas and Pennsylvania had graduated from high school. The vast majority were about to embark on college football careers. The contest had been arranged by a group of Pennsylvania promoters who were dead set on proving their state played a better brand of high school football than the arrogant Texans. A few months earlier, *Sports Illustrated* had ranked Texas as the No. 1 high school football state in America, followed by California and Pennsylvania.

Bobby Layne sets up to pass for the
Pittsburgh Steelers.
　　　　　—*Texas Sports Hall of Fame*

This was not surprising. After all, Texas high schools bragged of more football teams than all of America's colleges combined. Texas was known for cattle and oil, but the state's most prominent identity was derived from the Friday night lights that glowed from Dalhart to McAllen, and from Orange to El Paso.

So much was at stake in the final two minutes of the inaugural Big 33 game between Texas and Pennsylvania that Bobby Layne had worked himself into a menacing mixture of foot stomping and foul language. Nothing revealed the madman inside Layne like failure. His longtime friend Doak Walker once said, "Bobby never lost a game in his life. Time just ran out on him."

Just three years earlier, Layne had walked away from a legendary fifteen-year NFL quarterbacking career that included back-to-back championships in 1952 and 1953 with the Detroit Lions. From 1950 to 1955, Layne was reunited with Walker, his best friend since high school days at Dallas Highland Park. Fans in the Motor City once considered Bobby Layne bigger than General Motors. His worshippers compared him to Mickey Cochrane, the catcher/manager who led the Detroit Tigers to their first World Series title in 1935. In an era when stars were measured more by magazine covers than TV exposure, Layne was the first football star to grace the cover of *Time*. The story read, "The best quarterback in the world is Robert Lawrence Layne, a blond-haired, bandy-legged Texan with a prairie squint in his narrow blue eyes and a athletic paunch on his ample, 6-1, 195-pound frame."

Before Layne, the pro game ranked just a notch above championship wrestling. There were only fifteen million television sets in America in 1952, and the players operated in a sea of electric snow. Those in the stadium, though, knew that Layne was cocky and fun to watch. He played with a constant chatter that pleased the crowd and angered opponents. More than anyone else, he delivered the pro game into the golden age that officially began with the 1958 Colts-Giants championship game that went into overtime and almost sent America into cardiac arrest. Johnny Unitas was standing on Layne's shoulders late that afternoon as he drove the Colts down the field in the shadows at

Yankee Stadium. Alan Ameche's 1-yard touchdown burst in sudden death overtime won the championship for Baltimore and changed the game for all time. They all could thank Bobby Layne for wallowing in the muddy trenches before the game was finally delivered to the masses on a clear Sylvania screen.

Before retiring in 1962, Layne held NFL passing records for attempts (3,700), completions (1,814), yards gained (26,768), and touchdowns (196). He was also credited with starting the two-minute offense. If he had thrived during the sports TV boom of the 1960s, he would have been Roger Staubach with a drinking problem.

After leading the Lions to a third straight NFL title game in 1954, and losing to the Browns, Layne began to battle injuries that included a torn labrum in his right shoulder. Still, no one was surprised that he stared down the pain. By 1957, his loosely hinged throwing shoulder felt like it had been stuck with a hot poker. He often medicated himself in the locker room with shots of straight whiskey. Baltimore tackle Art Donovan once sacked Layne and upon smelling his breath asked, "Bobby, have you been drinking?" "Hell yes," Layne snapped, "and I plan to have a few more at halftime."

Bob Hope once quipped, "He's the only football player who had a water bucket on the sideline with a head on it."

As the late nights took their toll, Layne's football mystique began to fade in 1957. Still, he led the Lions to the brink of yet another NFL title game before shattering his right ankle in a late-season game against the Browns. He was viciously high-lowed by tackles Don Colo and Paul Wiggin. The lower right leg and ankle collapsed with a cracking sound, three bones breaking at once. His replacement, Tobin Rote, steered the Lions all the way to the NFL championship game, where they pounded the Cleveland Browns 59–14. The third league championship of the decade should have belonged to Layne, but the toast of the town turned out to be Rote.

When Layne was no longer the brightest star in Detroit, his drinking accelerated. The wary Lions traded him to the Pittsburgh Steelers after the second game of the 1958 season. The Steelers were the doormat of the NFL before Layne arrived. Pittsburgh turned out to be no place to send a thirsty man like Bobby Layne. The town was cold and lonely, and the Steelers were a hopeless bunch. Boos roared down on Pitt Stadium like a blizzard off the Monongahela River. Still, Layne cobbled together three winning seasons in five years.

Layne's drinkathons were as famous as the binges of Babe Ruth and Mickey Mantle. Not surprisingly, Mantle and Layne hit the bars at full speed when their off-seasons overlapped back home in Texas.

When his controversial career ended in 1962, Layne still firmly believed he would become the next great head coach in the NFL. It was the same trap that Babe Ruth had fallen into during the mid-1930s. Ruth believed he could eat, drink, and chase women until dawn and still wind up a manager. He found out the hard way. "Ruth, you can't even mange your own life," Yankees owner Jacob Ruppert told him. "How can you manage a baseball team?"

Not a single NFL team was willing to roll the dice on Layne. He could not outrun his own reputation. His friendship with renowned football fixer Donald "Dice" Dawson had set in motion rumors that Layne bet on his team during the glory years of the 1950s. Dawson once admitted to fixing thirty games. There was no way that a competitor like Layne fixed games, but NFL players gambling on games in the 1950s was as common as helmets without face masks. Average salaries ranged from $8,000 to $10,000. Players could make mortgage money by betting on or against their own teams.

Layne's friendship with Dawson was widely known. They spent time together in Detroit, and Dawson traveled to Lubbock during the off-season and stayed at Layne's house.

During the late 1950s, Layne struck up a friendship with Green Bay running back Paul Hornung, who would be suspended by the NFL in 1963 for betting on games. Hornung and Layne were known for their carousing, and both loved to gamble. In a book titled *Golden Boy* that was published in 2004, Hornung wrote, "Bobby gambled more than anybody who ever played football, period. How did the league go all those years without ever getting him?"

Layne denied ever gambling on games. He wrote in his 1962 autobiography, *Always on Sunday*, "I know that I've been accused of gambling, especially when the team loses . . . But I would have to be crazy to endanger my livelihood for a few thousand dollars."

The official crackdown on gambling began with the hiring of Pete Rozelle as the NFL commissioner in 1960. The game would have to be cleaned up if the league was ever to make megamillions off the TV networks. One of the first players to be summoned to Rozelle's New York office to discuss gambling rumors was Layne. No action was ever taken against him, but the rumors still persisted.

As part of the cleansing, the commissioner suspended two of the league's best players, Detroit tackle Alex Karras and Hornung. Ironically, Karras spent a good portion of his rookie training camp partying with Bobby Layne and learning the ropes.

Upon Layne's retirement, the atmosphere was not right for his ascension to the head coaching ranks. When no one hired him, Layne took a part-time job with the Steelers, working the press-box phones and relaying information to coaches on the sideline. Not exactly the kind of job you would expect a two-time NFL championship quarterback to have.

For two long years, Layne did not receive a single call from an NFL owner. So he telephoned Buddy Parker, his former coach in Detroit and Pittsburgh, to ask why.

"Bobby, I hate to tell you this," Parker said, "but Rozelle is trying to purify the game. You're one helluva competitor, but you've got a bad reputation. Nobody is looking to hire you."

Never in his life had Layne faced a challenge he could not conquer. He was the dogged street hustler. In the spring of 1964, though, Layne was on the outside looking in.

No one was surprised when he jumped at the chance to coach the Texas Big 33 all-star team. Men like Layne are forever searching for redemption. Old jocks do not readily adjust to life after football, especially when your name is Bobby Layne. He was pushing forty when he got his first coaching offer and a whopping $500 to lead the Texas high school all-stars into the biggest game of their lives.

Layne believed the Big 33 game before 25,000 fans at Hershey Stadium would be his ticket back to pro football. He visualized the national sporting press converging on Hershey for the single purpose of trumpeting his return to the national stage. He would buy the writers fresh drinks and regale them with old stories. Surely they would be smart enough to recognize the promise of his coaching prowess.

The Big 33 game was a grand experiment cooked up by a Harrisburg sportswriter and a team of promoters in central Pennsylvania. The Pennsys were pissed off that they were a distant third behind Texas in the most recent *Sports Illustrated* high school rankings. How could a state that had bred and reared such players as Joe Namath, John Unitas, and Johnny Lujack not be No. 1? The Pennsylvania promoters were itching to call out the Texans.

During the winter of 1963, the Pennsy organizers decided to contact Texas sportswriter Fred Cervelli and proffer a game. Cervelli was baffled to receive the Western Union wire, along with a phone call from *Harrisburg Patriot-News* sports editor Al Clark. Cervelli was just a small-town sportswriter from Orange, deep in the southeast corner of Texas. He was a kindhearted man without an arrogant bone in his body. He loved every high school kid he covered.

Clark asked Cervelli if he would pick the best thirty-three players in the state to represent Texas against Pennsylvania. He would also be in charge of hiring a head coach.

"I guess I can handle it," Cervelli said. "But here's my question for you, Al. Why didn't you call one of the big-time writers from Houston or Dallas?"

"Because you know high school football better than anyone in Texas," Clark said.

Having grown up in Texas, Cervelli could smell bullshit upwind or downwind. He knew Clark was not telling him the whole truth.

Without delay, Cervelli contacted Layne, his childhood hero, to ask if he would coach the team. The two had never met, but the sportswriter was certain that Layne was the right man for the job.

"Hell, yes, Fred, I'm your man," Layne said.

To Layne, the Big 33 all-star game between Texas and Pennsylvania seemed larger than an NFL title game. He quickly picked Doak Walker, the Heisman Trophy winner at SMU in 1948, to be his No. 1 assistant. The two had been best friends since high school playing days at Highland Park High in Dallas and played together for several years in Detroit.

The giddiness of it all lasted two full days before Cervelli called Layne with the bad news. As it turned out, the Texans had been hornswoggled. The date of the Big 33 game, August 1, was the same as the Texas North-South All-Star Game. The Pennsylvanians had intentionally set the August 1 date to make sure the Texans would *not* be bringing their best players north. In effect, Layne would be coaching Texas's junior varsity.

"Bobby," Cervelli said to his new coach, "the Pennslvania promoters took advantage of me. I could smell a rat when they called. They already knew our all-star game was on August 1. I should have seen it coming. I'm real sorry, Bobby."

"Hell, Fred, we all get caught with our panties down," Layne said. "Your panties just happen to be bigger than most. Don't worry, Freddie boy. We'll still whip their asses with the fourth stringers if we have to."

When the team traveled north in late July, Layne's trademark cockiness never slept. He swaggered into his first press conference and said, "We came up here with our second stringers, but we'll still whip these lard-ass boys from Pennsylvania. We've got speed and they don't. Wait till those fat boys from Altoona see our quick little rabbits."

On Layne's roster was some decent talent. Still, his only bluechipper was Palestine halfback David Dickey. (The town is pronounced *Pal*-uhsteen.) Layne had big plans for the swift, agile, and powerful Dickey until he tore two ligaments in his right knee on the first play of the game.

Layne's playbook might have been thicker than a Baptist hymnal, but it was shredded before halftime. His pro-set passing offense was hapless without a strong-armed quarterback. *Sports Illustrated* writer Robert H. Boyle described the action as "three yards and a mushroom cloud." He also wrote, "The teams played as though they were fighting over a bone instead of a ball."

The Texans crossed the 6-yard line three times and came away with only 6 points. The game might have ended in a 6–6 tie if not for a breakdown in the Texas kicking game. With 5:30 to play, Texas punter Ken Hebert sent a high, 43-yard punt down the middle that was fielded by Ben Gregory at the 20-yard line. Gregory took two steps upfield, rammed into a Texas defender, then bounced to the outside. Gregory found his picket line of blockers down the left sideline and dashed 80 yards to the end zone.

After the game, Layne stormed off the field and dog-cussed everyone in his wake. The Hershey PA announcer bellowed, "Hey, Texas, do you want a rematch?"

Layne glared into the press box and wagged the dirty finger at the man. "Hell, yes!" he yelled. "We'll be back next year with our *real* team!"

Layne would never forget the catcalls rumbling down from the overwhelmingly partisan crowd. The Hershey fans even blamed the Texas players for the assassination of President John F. Kennedy nine months earlier.

"Hey, Texas, you killed our president," they yelled. Layne almost climbed into the stands, but Walker stopped him.

For weeks, Layne could barely sleep. The loss had been nothing short of blasphemy in a state where football outranked religion. Even more disheartening was the wild celebration in Hershey and the chest thumping that followed.

"We knew all along that we were the best football state in America, a *lot* better than those braggarts from Texas," Pennsylvania governor William Scranton said.

No doubt, Texans had invented the art of full-blown bragging. So hearing a windbag like Scranton chattering on about planetary supremacy was a bit unsettling. Since the advent of the leather helmet, Texas had billed itself as the Cadillac of high school football.

Layne blamed himself for the defeat. "Doaker," he said, "I feel so danged bad. Hell, I couldn't coach frogs to jump."

He promised himself that he would return in exactly one year with a better team and a superior game plan. He would win next time, even if it killed him.

2

Political Football

Five months later, Bobby Layne and Doak Walker paused on the bottom step of the state capitol in Austin and looked up. They were on a mission to right a terrible wrong. The telegram from Fred Cervelli had arrived a few days earlier with disturbing news.

"Penn has set the 1965 game for August 14. Same date as our North-South game. No way we can change the date. We're going to Hershey again with our second stringers."

Layne wadded up the telegram and threw a trash can rattling down a long stairwell. His office on the eighth floor of the Citizens Tower in downtown Lubbock looked like the work of a Texas twister. He jumped into his cherry red Cadillac and drove across town like a madman. Roaring into the valet parking entrance at the Lubbock Country Club, he slammed on the brakes, jumped out of the car, marched straight into the bar, ordered a drink, and asked the bartender for the phone. He placed a long distance call to Denver, where Doak Walker had moved from Dallas.

"Meet me in Austin in two days, Doaker," Layne said. "We're going to see the governor. This time, we mean business."

As they climbed the steps to the capitol entrance that day, Layne leaned toward his best friend since high school and said, "Doaker, this is it. Our last chance."

Only a gambling man could have dreamed up such a scheme. In early January of 1965, Layne and Walker were on their way to the office of John Connally. The governor and the former quarterback were old friends. Connally, a law student at the University of Texas in the early 1940s just ahead of Layne's arrival, witnessed firsthand the relentless drive inside Layne, who quarterbacked the Longhorns back to national prominence and was named All-Southwest Conference four straight years. He also saw Walker star at SMU in the same period.

The men's cowboy boots thundered on the marble floors as they marched down the capitol corridors. Taking the lead was Layne, whose face was so famous that legislators, lobbyists, and clerks stopped to call out his name. He paid no attention. Behind him, Walker smiled broadly. He was also quickly recognized. Going back to his Heisman days at SMU, Walker's handsome profile had appeared on forty-seven magazine covers, from *Collier's* to *Life* to *Look* to *Sports Illustrated*. His good friend and SMU teammate Kyle Rote once saw a fan buying a football magazine and stopped him. "Don't buy that one," he said. "It's not official. It doesn't have Doak Walker's photo on it."

Layne once said, "Doak got quite a lot of publicity, especially when he was in Dallas. Hell, if he took his cat for a walk, somebody would take a picture of it."

So good-looking was Walker at SMU that when he strolled the campus quadrangle, he made the coeds bite their necklaces and twirl their hair.

No one could ever overestimate the value of Walker's friendship to Layne. Walker came along at a time when Layne needed the companionship. They were united at Dallas Highland Park High School in 1942 during a *perfect storm*.

As Layne was arriving, and Walker was blooming into a star running back, the Scots hired Rusty Russell as coach. The school district had been trying to lure Russell away for several years from the Masonic Home, a small orphanage on the east side of Fort Worth. Highland Park was the wealthiest of all the Dallas suburbs, and the

Bobby Layne wearing his Highland Park
letter jacket in 1944.
—*Texas Sports Hall of Fame*

folks from the Neiman Marcus crowd were tired of losing to Russell and the Mighty Mites. The Scots were 0-4 against Russell's little band of orphans.

Ironically, the Highland Park fans had raised money in 1938 to buy the ragtag orphans new uniforms as they headed into the state high school playoffs. They did this in spite of the fact that the Mighty Mites had knocked the Scots out of playoff contention with a tie-breaking win at Ownby Stadium.

With Russell coming to Highland Park four years later, Walker and Layne were in the right spot to win a state title. Russell was the best high school coach in Texas. He had launched the Masonic Home football program in 1927 with only six leather helmets and no football to practice with. Five years later, Russell led the Mighty Mites to a share of the state championship. They would reach the state semi-finals three more times by 1940. Russell was considered a genius in Texas coaching circles, having invented the spread offense. He did this out of necessity since his little orphans, averaging 135 pounds per man, were not physically equipped to play power football.

What Russell found at Highland Park was two of the best football players in the state. The coach could not remember seeing a faster running back than Walker, or a kid with more confidence than Layne. He would not forget the first day of practice at Highland Park when the two best friends proceeded to beat the hell out of each other.

"I lined up 80 boys for a hitting drill and they went to work," Russell recalled. "Bobby and Doak decided to go after each other. They were like a couple of boxers—Boom! Boom! Boom! They were laughing and giggling and just trying to kill each other. They were having a good time trying to beat each other up."

They instantly bonded as best friends in spite of vast differences in their personalities. Even their teammates at Highland Park were amazed at how quickly the friendship grew. Walker seldom talked, and Layne's mouth rarely stopped motoring. When Layne talked, Walker normally just grinned and nodded. Walker was a serious-minded youngster, while Layne liked to live on the edge.

"Bobby and I were different people right from the start," Walker recalled. "We came from different backgrounds. I had such a wonderful childhood, and Bobby lived a hard life. There had been problems in his life, and he was raised by an aunt and uncle. But we always managed to remain good friends, and we were always an inspiration to each other."

Walker would never have been caught down on Harry Hines Boulevard at a seedy hotel in the sinful section of Dallas, but that was where Russell found Layne rolling the dice one night. Russell was a kind and gentle man who rarely raised his voice, but he demanded a high standard of behavior. When he walked into the hotel room and found Layne down on his knees shooting craps, Russell grabbed him by the collar and dragged him away. Before the sun rose the next morning, Layne would be running stadium steps as punishment.

Ewell Doak Walker Jr. rarely got into trouble. He came from a rock-solid family. His father, Ewell Sr., was a teacher and coach at North Dallas High School. He began tossing a baseball underhanded to his son at the age of three. Doak grew up in the shadows of SMU's Ownby Stadium. On Friday night, he went to the Highland Park High School games with his mother. On Saturday, he attended the SMU games with his dad.

Layne barely knew his mother and father. When he was eight, the family was driving from their small farm near Santa Anna to Brownwood. His mother, Beatrice, was behind the wheel. Bobby sat next to his dad, a large man named Sherman. Along the way, thirty-six-year-old Sherman suffered a massive heart attack. Racked with convulsions, he lurched forward, fell back, and landed on top of his small son, jamming him back into the seat. It took several minutes for Beatrice to get the body off her son. Stuck behind his dead father, the youngster almost suffocated. The horrible incident led to recurring nightmares. Bobby had trouble sleeping, a condition that would stay with him for the rest of his life.

Two months later, Bobby was sent to Brownwood to live with his grandparents. He was told the arrangement would be temporary and that he would soon be reunited with his mother. A few months later, though, he was informed that his mother had moved away to Dallas with his two sisters and was not coming back. Losing his mother and father in such a short span of time traumatized the youngster. He grew quiet and retreated into himself.

Brownwood was boring. Bobby soon asked his favorite aunt and uncle in Fort Worth if he could move in with them. Aunt Lavinia and Uncle Wade Hampton loved Bobby and had always wanted a son. They adopted him but did not change his name because he was the last male child in the family.

The three lived happily together in a small home situated in a modest neighborhood. They were not wealthy, but it did not matter. Bobby became the star quarterback at E. M. Daggett Junior High, and many of his feats were chronicled in Fort Worth's daily newspapers.

The neighbors were a little surprised when the family packed up and moved away right before Bobby's junior year in high school. Even more unexpected was their destination. They moved into one of the most expensive neighborhoods in Texas, a suburb called Highland Park with its own school district.

Was it possible that the talented young quarterback had been recruited to play for the Scots? In the 1930s and '40s, such illegal recruiting was widespread in many Texas towns pining for a state championship. The oil and cattle industry had supplied plenty of fast cash for these misdeeds. It was not unusual in oil boomtowns like Breckenridge and Abilene for the head of the family to receive a hefty raise by uprooting his family and moving his blue-chip son to a place with a better football team. Highland Park possessed more than its share of wealth, so there was plenty of speculation that the Hamptons were chasing the money.

Layne and Walker would soon become the talk of an entire state. Russell ran a sophisticated offense, and the Scots almost overnight began to destroy the competition.

Because the Masonic Home could not find a replacement for

Russell in 1942, he volunteered to help with the Mighty Mites. He would spend a couple of afternoons each week coaching the Mighty Mites, then turn over the team to the captains. The rest of the time was spent at his paying job in Highland Park. Fortunately, Highland Park played its games on Friday nights, while the Mighty Mites suited up on Saturday nights. That season, Highland Park won the Dallas district, and the Masonic Home finished in a three-way tie for the Fort Worth district title. If the Mighty Mites had won the coin toss, both of Russell's teams would have met in the bi-district round.

"I would have been coaching both teams on the same night, and there is no telling how that would have turned out," he remembered. The Mighty Mites lost the flip, and he was left to coach only Highland Park.

Russell led the Scots to the state quarterfinals but lost to Dallas Sunset in 1942. A state championship seemed a lock the following year after the Scots beat their first twelve opponents by the combined score of 476–76. Against San Angelo Central High School in West Texas, the Scots led 20–7 to start the fourth quarter, but the Bobcats roared from behind to win 21–20.

Walker was distraught for missing an extra point. Bob St. John wrote in his book *Heart of a Lion* that Layne put his arm around his friend's shoulders and said, "They just beat the socks off us in that final quarter. Doaker, it's not your fault."

Layne took off for the University of Texas in the summer of 1944. A year later, Walker signed with the hometown team—SMU. His feats with the Ponies were mind-boggling considering the times. He rushed for 2,076 yards, passed for 1,786, intercepted 12 passes, and scored 303 points.

Former *Sports Illustrated* college football writer Dan Jenkins, one of the foremost authorities on the game, wrote in the foreword of Walker's biography, "Although he weighed only 166 pounds, and stood 5-10, he was quite simply the greatest all-round college football player who ever lived." Walker was the first player from the Southwest Conference to make All American for three straight years—1947, '48, and

Left to Right: Highland Park coach Rusty Russell with his three captains—Bobby Layne, Doak Walker, and Doug McDonald in 1944.

—*Texas Sports Hall of Fame*

Doak Walker carries the ball during his
Heisman Trophy season of 1948 at SMU.
                        —*Texas Sports Hall of Fame*

'49—and won the Heisman Trophy in '48. He made *Sports Illustrated*'s all-time team in 1969 during the centennial year celebration of college football. Grantland Rice once wrote, "Doak Walker is the most authentic player in the history of football."

The original pact made by Walker and Layne was to play college football together at the University of Texas. Walker, however, changed his mind after a brief stint in the Merchant Marine following high school.

"Doak went to SMU because Rusty Russell was coaching there," Layne said. "We had both played for Rusty in high school and liked him a lot."

The duo played against each other for the first time at SMU's Ownby Stadium in 1945. Early in the game, Walker scored the first touchdown of his college career on a carry around right end that he cut back against the grain. Splitting the Texas defense, he sprinted 45 yards to the end zone for a 7-6 lead. He also kicked the extra point.

Layne, however, would rally the Longhorns in the fourth quarter with his second touchdown pass of the day and a 12-7 victory. Walker and Layne walked off the field with their arms draped around each other's shoulders.

Walker's Merchant Marine duty did not preclude him from being drafted into the Army in 1946, and he did not play for the Mustangs that season. However, with SMU moving into the Cotton Bowl in the 1947 season, fans of both teams could not wait for the Walker-Layne rematch. A standing-room-only crowd of 50,000 witnessed a game even more electrifying than in '45.

SMU opened the game with a long kickoff return. Two plays later, Walker hooked up with Dick McKissack on a 10-yard completion to the 5-yard line. Running the reverse, Paul Page scored on the next play.

Layne passed the Longhorns straight down the field to the 11-yard line. Fullback Tom Landry, who would become a Dallas Cowboys coaching legend, blasted between the guard and tackle to score Texas's first touchdown.

On the next possession, Walker's passing, running, and receiving moved the Mustangs into scoring position. His 37-yard reception set up SMU's second touchdown with McKissack scoring from the 1-yard line. Walker kicked his second extra point of the day.

Layne's 67-yard touchdown pass to Byron Guillory made it 14-13. A missed extra point, though, left Texas trailing by one. Rallying for a late score, Landry would slip on a muddy field on fourth down at the 30-yard line, thus ending the Longhorns' final hopes.

Because Layne's college eligibility was up, the former high school teammates would not be playing each other again. Their head-to-head matches ended in a 1-1 tie. In 1947, Walker was named All-American and he also finished third in the Heisman Trophy balloting as the Mustangs finished with an undefeated record.

Few collegiate players could match Walker's 1948 season. Two minutes into the game against Texas, he zig-zagged his way through the entire Texas defense, leaving players strewn all over the field on a 67-yard touchdown run. In the second quarter, he scored on a 1-yard plunge, then passed 18 yards to Kyle Rote for SMU's final score in a 21-6 romp of the Longhorns. That day, he carried 9 times for 72 yards, completed both of his passes for 39 yards, caught 3 passes for 20 yards, punted 4 times for a 42-yard average, played a total of 55 minutes, and called the offensive plays flawlessly.

Walker won the Heisman Trophy and made All-American for the second straight year. Little wonder that the Cotton Bowl, which opened in 1947, was called "The House That Doak Built". Seats were being added each year to accommodate the onrush of fans.

In the late 1940s, the biggest American sports stars were Joe Louis, Ted Williams, Joe DiMaggio, Jackie Robinson, and Doak Walker. The only collegian in that group was Walker, a living portrayal of Jack Armstrong, whose face was gracing far more magazine covers than all of the others.

Walker would miss about half of the 1949 season with injuries and illness, but still finished third in the Heisman Trophy balloting. Selected in the first round of the 1950 draft by the Detroit Lions, he was soon on his way to the Motor City to be reunited with Layne.

Walker's six years in Detroit (1950–55) were hardly as impressive as his collegiate career, even though the Lions did win titles in 1952 and 1953. Upon his retirement at the age of twenty-eight, Walker said he felt he could accomplish no more. "At least I got out with all of my teeth and with both knees," he said.

Detroit fans just wished walker had stayed longer, and that he and Layne could have provided more championships.

In 1965, as Layne and Walker swaggered into the governor's office, the receptionist's eyes widened. She would not have been more impressed if President Lyndon Baines Johnson and John Wayne had just showed up at the same time.

Layne spoke first. "Ma'am, we're here to see the governor. I am—"

"I know who you are. You're Bobby Layne. I watched you play at UT. And you, sir, are the famous Doak Walker."

The men looked at each other and smiled.

"Just about sums it up," Layne said. "So can you imagine why we're here?"

"Not really," she said.

"Well, you see, we're the coaches of the Texas Big 33 team, and we've got another big game coming up against the high school boys from Pennsylvania. We lost the first game because the people up north cheated. That's why we need to talk to the governor."

"I assume you didn't make an appointment," she said.

"That's right," Layne said, "but—"

"I know. You didn't need one. You and the governor've been friends for twenty years. John saw every game you played at UT."

Like the governor, she had watched Layne play from 1944 to 1947 and would never forget the excitement. In the 1946 Cotton Bowl, he accounted for every point in a 40–27 victory over Missouri. He ran for 3 touchdowns, passed for 2 more, caught a 50-yarder for another, and kicked 4 extra points. That year, he finished eighth in the Heisman Trophy voting to Army's Glenn Davis, and sixth the next season to Notre Dame's Johnny Lujack.

The fans worshipped Layne. He played every down at full tilt, often sporting a bloody jersey and a cut lip. His passes wobbled, but the ball normally found the target. When Layne tucked the ball to run, he was like a jaw-rattling fullback rumbling into the open field. He once started against Arkansas with tonsilitis and a 103-degree fever. Braced by a couple of whiskey shots, he accounted for every point in a 19–0 victory.

Connally's receptionist knew the governor would be happy to see Layne and Walker. So she turned and hurried down a long, narrow hallway toward his office. In a couple of minutes, she returned, still smiling.

"Mr. Layne and Mr. Walker," she said, "the governor will gladly see you."

A couple of over-the-hill football lions smiled.

Connally stood as they strolled into his office. "Hello, Bobby. Hello, Doak," he said. "I read about your big loss up in Pennsylvania. Guess that's why you're here."

Layne snickered. "Most embarrassing dang thing that ever happened to me in my whole life, Governor. The Big 33 people in Pennsylvania scheduled the game on the same day as our North-South game. They knew we wouldn't be able to take our best players. Shoot, we couldn't find a quarterback who could throw on a straight line."

Layne's face reddened. "We've got an emergency here. The Pennsylvania bastards insist we play this year on August 14. And guess what? That happens to be the date of our North-South game. We're screwed *again*. That's why we gotta ask you to step in."

"I've got no pull with those Yankees," Connally replied.

"But you can tell our Texas coaches association to move the North-South game up a week."

The governor smiled. "Now you want me to piss off every high school coach in Texas. That'll cost me votes."

Layne knew the Texas High School Coaches Association was not about to yield to the Big 33 team, and why should they? The North-South game had been played every year since 1935. The THSCA would never give up a single blue-chipper to a team that had been embarrassed a year ago in Hershey.

That was why Layne and Walker needed the governor's intervention. That was why they were not giving up. It did not matter if the game was football or dice. Layne was obsessed with winning and rarely lost. Things could turn ugly when he did. After dropping ten grand at a backwater casino in Lubbock one night, he shut down the craps game by curling up on the table and falling asleep. When the manager asked him to jump down, Layne said, "Hell, mister, I bought this table. It's mine till I wake up tomorrow morning."

With a furrowed brow, Layne looked directly into Connally's eyes. "Let me tell you what those sorry Hershey fans did to our kids last year. They blamed 'em for the Kennedy assassination. Dang right. They said that Kennedy wouldn't have been killed nowhere else but Texas."

The assassination of John F. Kennedy was both a grave and a personal matter with Connally. He was riding in the jump seat of the midnight blue limousine when it made the wide turn from Houston onto Elm Street in downtown Dallas at 12:30 P.M. on November 22, 1963. The second bullet fired by Lee Harvey Oswald struck Kennedy in his upper back, tore through his neck, and exited his throat. The same bullet passed through Connally's upper back and exited his chest, about two inches below his right nipple. Just as the third bullet struck Kennedy in the head, Connally cried out, "Oh my God, they're going to kill us all!" The limousine sped three miles to Parkland Hospital, where the president was declared dead at 1:00 P.M. Connally spent almost two weeks in the hospital. Several months passed before he was back to decent health.

Connally was haunted by the president's death. Hearing about the terrible slurs from the Hershey fans served to reopen old wounds. The Texas kids should not have to suffer that indignity again, he thought.

"I'll talk to the coaches association and get them to move their game up a week so you can take the best players to Pennsylvania," Connally said.

"That's great, John," Layne said. "And I need your backing on one more thing. You see, I need some Negroes on my team. Those Yanks had a bevy of 'em last year. That team was big, fast, and tough. We need more speed."

"Sounds okay to me," Connally said. "Just make damn sure you win this time."

Six months later, Layne stood in the bright Pennsylvania sunlight and smiled. His eyes scanned a clipboard with the names of his star players. It was the first day of practice for the 1965 Big 33 all-star game, and the players were warming up around him. Connally had fulfilled his promise to Walker and Layne. The Texas North-South game, scheduled for the Cotton Bowl in Dallas, was moved up a week to August 7. On August 14, the Texans would line up against Pennsylvania with the best team the state could offer.

Layne could have not been happier. He winked at his best friend. "Doaker, we've got us one helluva football team here," he said. "We're going to kick some Yankee ass. These are the biggest, ballsiest ballplayers that Texas has ever produced."

Layne knew he could back up his boasts. The tireless work of Fred Cervelli in compiling the Texas team had been an overwhelming success. He had been assisted by two writers from his staff, George Pharr and Ken Estes.

Cervelli had told Estes and Pharr, "The simplest thing to do would be to pick all of our players from the all-state team, but we're not going to do that."

That would have been impossible since there were eight all-state teams that year numbering 234 players. The previous season, a total of 60,000 players had participated in 5,000 games for 1,200 different schools. Nine million fans had watched them play.

Canvassing the entire state for the best players seemed an impossible task for a trio of small-town sportswriters. Traveling by automobile from Orange to the vast territory of West Texas would have required a drive of at least fourteen hours. El Paso, on the western tip of the state, was almost a thousand miles away.

In those days, sportswriters had no access to the Internet or ESPN. The Sunday edition of the *Dallas Times Herald* took about a week to arrive by mail. The only sources for outside information were the AP and UPI wire service machines that clattered constantly in the corner of the newsroom. Neither provided much high school coverage.

Cervelli and his staff knew how to cover their local high school football territory like three overworked vacuum cleaners, but they rarely ventured past Beaumont, some thirty miles to the west. Still, they seemed undaunted. They worked overtime without overtime pay. They set up a 16 mm film projector in the middle of the newsroom and watched reel upon reel of game films. Cervelli often rose from bed in the wee hours of the morning to drive to the office before dawn.

One morning in the early darkness, he forgot his key to the office. So he hunted for an unlocked window and started climbing. Halfway through the window, someone grabbed his pants and started pulling. The man whipped him around and pointed a flashlight in his eyes.

"You're under arrest!" the cop shouted.

"Hold on, I'm Fred Cervelli."

"I don't care if you're Fred Astaire. You're going to jail."

After some fast talking Cervelli convinced the officer that he was, indeed, the newspaper's sports editor. The cop still made him go home and find his key.

Cervelli would soon realize that his best source for picking players was the *Dallas Times Herald* blue-chip list, compiled by Bob Galt. Each year, Galt conducted a secret vote of the eight Southwest Conference coaches, who ranked in numerical order the most highly coveted high school seniors in Texas. In the spring of 1965, that list included twenty-three players. Sixteen of those blue-chippers made the trip to Pennsylvania for the Big 33 game team.

At the top of the list was Norman Bulaich, a fast and hard-running halfback from La Marque, near Galveston. With Bulaich toting the football from the seventh to the twelfth grade, the La Marque teams lost a grand total of 3 games. Local sportswriters proudly named him "the Galloping Ghost of the Gulf Coast." Bulaich was the only unanimous selection to the blue-chip list.

Two players had tied for second with seven votes apiece—Bill Bradley of Palestine, in East Texas, and Chris Gilbert of Spring Branch High School, near Houston.

During the first Big 33 practice on August 9, 1965, Layne could not take his eyes off Bradley. The ambidextrous quarterback/safety was rated among the top 5 recruits in America. Bradley passed right-handed and punted left-footed. He could also pass left-handed and punt right-footed. He made the all-state teams in football, basketball, and baseball. The Detroit Tigers had offered a $25,000 signing bonus and a AA assignment in Birmingham—a flattering deal for an eighteen-year-old switch-hitting shortstop—but Bradley's heart was set on the University of Texas. After all, Darrell Royal had virtually moved into the Bradley home during the recruiting season.

Playing for the North squad in the 1965 Texas all-star game, Bradley proved why he was so admired. After the South took a 6–0 lead in the first quarter, he answered with a 3-yard quarterback sneak to tie the game. Playing both ways, he intercepted a pass in the third quarter. In the fourth quarter, Bradley led the North team on a long touchdown drive, then scored around end from 7 yards. The North won 12–6. Twenty-seven of the thirty-one sportswriters covering the game had voted him the game's outstanding back.

So it was no surprise that the Pennsylvania sportswriters were anxiously waiting for Bradley when the team arrived in Hershey the next morning. They congregated at a downtown hotel called the Cocoa Inn and surrounded him as he walked through the front door.

Bradley grinned and told the writers, "Yeah, I think we can handle these big ol' boys from Pennsylvania. I know they'll outweigh us by about thirty pounds a man, but believe me, we're faster and a lot more athletic. I know that our Big 33 team lost last year. But, gentlemen, we didn't come all the way up here to lose again."

Bradley knew what he was talking about. The Texas team boasted three of the best running backs in the country. Garland's Ronnie

Scoggins, Bulaich, and Gilbert had accounted for 3,375 yards and 52 touchdowns as high school seniors.

One of the most talked-about players in Hershey was Jerry LeVias of Beaumont Hebert. (The school's name is pronounced *Hee*-bert.) Three months earlier, on May 22, LeVias had attracted national headlines by becoming the first Negro athlete to sign a scholarship offer with a Southwest Conference school. SMU coach Hayden Fry shocked the elite white college football fraternity when he marched into Beaumont with flashbulbs popping. He openly made a mockery of a longtime "gentlemen's agreement" among SWC coaches not to sign Negro players.

"I don't care what they're saying in Austin or Houston or anywhere else in Texas," Fry said. "Jerry LeVias is one of the best football players in Texas, and he's playing for me. It won't be long before every roster in our conference has Negroes."

The Texas players were seated in the wooden bleachers of the Hershey practice field when Bobby Layne strolled across the emerald grass with his head held high and his eyes focused on the task. The players could not wait to hear what he had to say. The talk on the plane ride from Dallas to Hershey had been all about Layne.

"I hear he's crazier than a henhouse rat," Bradley told Bulaich. "My daddy said he drank all night and played his best games with horrendous hangovers."

"Hell, I heard he drank at halftime," Bulaich said.

"But, by God, he won," Bradley said. "I remember when I was a little kid watching him play on our little TV back in Palestine. Daddy had to keep adjusting the rabbit ears. The picture was snowy, but I could see him firing those wobbly ducks to Doak Walker. He won two championships and would've got another one if not for breaking his leg."

That summer of 1965, Layne still walked with a slight limp. He was a little overweight and carried a paunch beneath his golf shirt. Otherwise his boyish face and thick blond hair belonged to a man in his midtwenties. Layne pulled a Marlboro from the pack with his lips and struck a match. His eyes searched the rolling hills. He thought about Pittsburgh some two hundred miles to the west and wondered what the Steelers fans remembered the most about him. He had not even taken the team to the postseason, but what else was new?

"Okay, boys, you know why you're here," he began. "Hershey is a long way from home. Hope you don't get homesick. We're going to be here for a while."

Layne laughed at his own little joke, and his eyes brightened. "Look. We're going to have some fun here. We're going to practice a little. I'm going to give you some time to chase the girls around town, and I know they're aplenty. We were here a year ago, and they look almost as good as Texas girls."

A cheer went up in the stands.

"I don't care what you do with your free time," he went on. "I don't care if you drink or smoke. Just put the butts in the ashtray and the beer cans in the trash can. In my book, there's not much you can do wrong around here after dark. But if you lose this game to these Pennsylvania hillbillies, don't *ever* talk to me again."

Thirty-three players sat in stunned silence. Layne paused, turned away, then wheeled around to face the boys again. They were not moving or breathing.

Layne chuckled and said, "Okay, you knuckleheads. I believe you're going to win. So get up off your butts, because it's time to go to work."

Moments later, as footballs flew through the air. Layne and Walker watched LeVias run one fly pattern after another without breaking a sweat. Strong-armed Rusty Clark of Houston Westbury and Bradley heaved the ball as far as they could. Still, they could not overthrow LeVias, who was forced to slow down to catch most of their passes.

Layne grinned as he watched LeVias sprint down the field, easily outrunning anyone trying to cover him.

"Hell, that kid's got parakeet legs," he said, "but he's still the speediest doggone youngster I've ever seen. No baloney, Doaker. Right now, he'd be the fastest man in the National Football League."

LeVias stood 5'8" and weighed 148 pounds. Around the beefy Texas all-stars, he looked like a team manager. No one could explain how someone that small could start in the same backfield at Beaumont Hebert High School for four straight years with the likes of Mel and Miller Farr.

Known as Jerry "the Jet," LeVias was so fast that no player in the state could cover him one-on-one. He accounted for 43 touchdowns passing, running, receiving, and returning kicks his final two high school seasons, including 6 in one game against Houston Aldine.

College recruiters could barely believe LeVias's acceleration. He seemed to have an extra gear, or three. Clifton Ozen, his high school coach, said, "Jerry is so fast that sometimes his blockers can't get out of his way."

A long-standing tradition among high school football coaches was to pad the statistics of their star players to attract college interest. Ozen did just the opposite. Realizing no self-respecting recruiter would believe the sheer enormity of LeVias's numbers, Ozen took an eraser to his statistics and deflated them.

This seemed okay to LeVias because he never figured he would play football in the first place. Because he was so small, LeVias did not consider playing organized tackle football until the eighth grade. In order to be issued a practice uniform, players at Ford Middle School were required to weigh 120 pounds. LeVias could muster only 115 pounds when he first stepped on the scales. Coach Enous Minix recorded his weight and told the youngster to come back next year.

Instead, LeVias walked around the schoolyard and returned ten minutes later.

"Coach, I'd like to be weighed again," he said. "I think these scales are wrong."

The needle went straight to 120 pounds. Minix gladly jotted down the number on his clipboard, then watched as two piles of rocks came tumbling out of the boy's pockets.

"I'm really sorry, Coach," LeVias said. "I hope that you won't tell Coach Ozen."

Minix could not wait to tell Ozen.

That afternoon, Minix was smiling when he saw Ozen. "Clifton, Jerry LeVias weighs only 115 pounds. But that boy wants to play football so bad that I say we let him on the team."

"Hell, why not?" Ozen spat a stream of chewing tobacco that stained the grass a dark yellow. "That kid's got something we just can't measure. It's called guts. He's going to be a better player than Warren Wells."

Over the next five football seasons, LeVias would gain only twenty-five pounds, but his reputation in the stadiums of southeast Texas would grow with each passing game. Cervelli did not hesitate to include him on the Big 33 roster, even though he had been shunned by the North-South selection committee.

On the day he walked onto the practice field in Hershey, LeVias felt blessed that he had been included on such an elite team.

"When I got to Hershey, all I heard about was 'Bill Bradley, Bill Bradley, Bill Bradley,'" he remembered. "He was the greatest athlete to ever come down the pike in the state of Texas. Everybody was writing about him. Everybody was talking about him. But we also had some other great players. It was a great feeling just to be around those guys."

The coaches were thrilled to see Bradley throwing to LeVias that first day in Hershey, but there was a flip side to their joy. They knew that LeVias's mere presence created an uneasy stir among the players. After all, he was a Negro player who had already achieved star status. Granted, there were two other Negroes on the Texas team, but they came without headlines, hoopla, or great promise. Furthermore, James Harris and George Danford would be rooming together.

The coaches knew it would be difficult to find a roommate for LeVias. It was a simple fact of life in Texas that blacks and whites lived separately. The boys on the Big 33 team had been raised by parents who resisted integration. They were told that the mixing of the races was neither the Christian way nor the right way to live. Some of their parents were members of the Ku Klux Klan.

Layne and Walker asked around and found no takers for LeVias. The white boys just weren't used to being around Negroes. None of the white players on the Texas team had ever suited up with or even played against a Negro. Moreover, LeVias had never played with or against white players. Growing up in an all-black neighborhood in Beaumont, he rarely even saw white people. At age eighteen, he counted no white friends.

After watching LeVias and Bradley get along so well that first day, Layne and Walker decided to ask Bradley if he would room with the Negro. He was the best candidate. Bradley might have been deeply rooted in East Texas, but he seemed different from the racist stereotype. The reach of his personality included everyone in the room, and then some. Clearly, he had never met a stranger. Everyone liked him. Even as a kid, he had been considered the leader of every team he suited up for.

Even Bradley's music suggested that he was far more cool than the others. He listened to the Temptations, the Four Tops, and the Isley Brothers. At night, when WLS out of Chicago boosted its signal to 50,000 watts, Bradley turned up the car radio as he slowly motored along Mallard Street in downtown Palestine, past the Tastee-Freez and Heck's, another hamburger joint. On Mallard Street, boys in boots and jeans, and girls in skirts and saddle oxfords, gathered for a little beer drinking and a lot of backseat necking.

Bradley's loud singing could be heard through the open windows of his hot Camaro. He knew the words as well as Eddie Kendricks of the Temptations or Joe Stubbs from the Four Tops. Norm Bulaich once said of Bradley, "He invented the term 'free spirit.'"

Most of the kids listened to Elvis. Bradley was stuck on Bo Diddley and his hard-driving rhythm guitar. *Who do you love? . . . I say, who do you love?*

A few weeks after graduation, Bradley and his best friend, Curtis Fitzgerald, had driven fifty miles to Tyler for the Bo Diddley concert. They were the only white faces in the crowd.

So it was not surprising that first day in Hershey that Bradley was singing an Isley Brothers song as he strolled into the Cocoa Inn.

It's your thing, do what you wanna do.
I can't tell you who to sock it to.

As he approached the front desk, Bradley dropped his suitcase. It clattered on the floor. The man behind the counter was an assistant with the Texas traveling contingent. Plopping down a room key on the counter, the short, bald-headed man said, "Bill, I have a question for you."

"Shoot," Bradley said.

"Well, you see, hoss, we've got a small problem here. Have you ever heard of a boy named Jerry LeVias?"

"Doesn't ring a bell," Bradley said, "but that doesn't mean anything. I'm from Palestine, and news doesn't travel fast out in East Texas."

Bradley was not telling the whole truth. He had read the big, bold headlines about LeVias in the *Palestine Herald-Press*. That very morning, he had been throwing passes to LeVias on the practice field. He was impressed with the youngster's overall athletic skills.

"Are you sure, Bill, you've never heard of Jerry LeVias?" the man asked.

"Nah."

"Well, you see, Jerry LeVias is a little nigger. And I was just wondering if you would mind rooming with him."

Bradley grimaced. "Let me tell you one thing, sir. Around my house in Palestine, we aren't allowed to say that word. Now, I know that Palestine's back in the sticks. We've got more Ku Klux Klan than you can count. But my daddy works around the porters on the railroad. In fact, he's around colored folks a lot. So he won't let you say that word 'nigger' in his house."

The man grinned and said, "So you wouldn't mind rooming with him?"

"If Jerry LeVias is a football player, I'd be happy to do it," Bradley said.

Then he scooped up the key, smiled, and walked away. The Big 33 week was going to be even more fun than he'd thought.

3

The Comeback Kid

That Jerry LeVias was suiting up for the Big 33 game three weeks before his nineteenth birthday was a triumph over the devil's disease.

Back in 1953, Jerry's happy world turned upside down as he began the second grade. The mere task of rising from bed required a boost-up from a family member. Almost overnight, the seven-year-old changed from a feisty, vibrant, and unbridled child to a sickly kid. He no longer went outside to play. One morning, as he wrestled just to place his feet on the floor, he looked up to see his paternal grandmother, Ella LeVias, wiping tears from her face.

"Jerry, we've got to get you to the doctor today. I mean *today*."

The terrible aching began in his knees. Then came the numbness. Every day, he looked down at the bony legs and wondered what had gone wrong. With both hands, he would lift one leg, then release the limb and watch it fall back onto the mattress. This made no sense to a boy who months earlier had chased rabbits through the woods and caught a few. At full sprint, he would lean down and pat the jackrabbit's white tail. Then he would gleefully watch it bound away in full flight.

That was before the dreaded disease invaded his body and rendered his limbs virtually useless.

The trip to the doctor's office merely added to his confusion.

There were two doors at the entrance—one marked WHITES and the other COLORED. Jim Crow laws were still prevalent in Texas, especially in the southeast sector of the state, where the Ku Klux Klan often ruled the night. Blacks and whites rarely mixed in Beaumont, even in the workplace. Negroes drank from the "colored" fountains, lived in all-black neighborhoods, attended "Negro" schools, and rode in the back of the bus.

The civil rights movement in America was nothing more than a sketchy blueprint. In Montgomery, Alabama, Rosa Parks had yet to spark racial tensions by refusing to give a white passenger her seat on a city bus. Martin Luther King Jr. was still an assistant pastor of the Dexter Avenue Baptist Church.

The bad vibe of racial division never took a day off in Beaumont. When Ella and little Jerry walked into the doctor's office that day, they were barely acknowledged by the white nurse. With a casual wave of the hand, she directed them to the colored waiting room. After a long wait, Ella began to lose her patience.

She stormed over to the nurse and said, "It's been over an hour, and we are still the only colored folks in this waiting room. I bet you don't treat the white folks like this."

The nurse smiled weakly and said, "We don't have many colored doctors." Then the nurse pointed to little Jerry, who was sitting with a towel wrapped around his head.

"What exactly is wrong with that colored boy?" she said. "Why does he have that towel wrapped around his head?"

"He can barely walk," Ella said. "We don't know what is wrong. That's why we're here. Could we please see the doctor?"

"Be patient," the nurse said with a forced smile.

When Ella returned to her chair, Jerry said, "How much longer, Grandma? This thing on my head is getting itchy." Furthermore, the contents inside the towel were emitting a terrible smell.

"Grandma, how much longer?" he said pointing to the towel.

"Just a little longer," she said.

Ella LeVias was known for her home remedies. Packed tightly

inside the towel was one of her favorites—collard greens. A leafy green vegetable that belongs to the cabbage family, collards are loaded with antioxidants. Ella may not have known that, but she knew they had worked for children and grandchildren as long as she could remember.

After more than an hour's wait, the nurse finally waved Ella and Jerry into the examining room. Once Jerry was perched on the table, the physician slowly unwrapped the towel and said, "Looks to me like we got a mess of greens. Sure smells good," the doctor continued as he moved the stethoscope around Jerry's chest, listening to his heartbeat. "Got any more? I'm feeling hungry for collard greens."

Ella was in no mood for his wisecracking. "This boy can barely use his legs," she said. "Now you're making jokes."

The doctor gently lifted both feet and slowly returned them to the table.

"Let me see you try it," he said. "Lift up your legs."

"I can't," Jerry said. "Grandma knows I can barely move my legs."

Tears rolled down Ella's cheeks again. "It's polio," she said. "It's the devil's disease."

The word "polio" was rarely spoken in the early 1950s. Like cancer, it was a disease that adults did not care to discuss for fear they would curse everyone in the room. In the past year, more than sixty thousand cases had been reported, with three thousand deaths. Parents lived in dread that their child would be next to die.

Polio had struck fear into America for three long decades. No one was sure where it came from or how to get rid of it. Parents were instructed to keep their children away from crowds. When the polio epidemic arrived in the 1920s, movie theaters were shut down, schools were closed, and drinking fountains were abandoned. Some houses were quarantined. The most famous case of polio in American history belonged to Franklin D. Roosevelt, who contracted the disease in 1921. In spite of being paralyzed from the waist down, he was elected president of the United States an unprecedented four times. Due, in part, to complications of high blood pressure, he died of a massive stroke in April of 1945.

Roosevelt's long bout with polio created an urgency to find a cure. In 1947, Dr. Jonas Salk was recruited by the University of Pittsburgh to develop a virus research program. Salk was thought to be closing in on a vaccine in 1953, but no one could be sure when it would be made available. Ella LeVias knew it might take several more years to arrive in Beaumont, located in the far reaches of southeast Texas.

On the day she sought medical help, Ella looked warily at the young doctor and asked, "Will we ever have a cure for polio?"

"I'm not sure," he said, his eyes no longer connecting with hers.

"Hey, wait a minute here," she said. "Young man, you worry me. Are you really a doctor?"

"Well, I was in medical school for a while. I haven't graduated."

"What happened?"

"Ran out of money. Plus, Negroes aren't really welcome in Texas med schools."

"So what do you really know about polio?"

"I know it will put you in a wheelchair. I know it'll kill you."

Ella peered at the doctor with sad eyes.

"I hear the vaccine is coming," she said. "But what are the chances of a little colored boy from Beaumont getting it? I'm sure the white kids will get it first."

The "doctor" could only shake his head.

"In the meantime, we'll get Jerry fitted for some leg braces. Hopefully someday there will be a vaccine."

"I don't want to see my boy in a wheelchair," she said. "I guess the only thing I can do is keep praying."

Jerome LeVias was born on September 5, 1946, in Beaumont. Charlie and Leura LeVias already had two daughters, and the prospect of feeding and clothing a third child on their modest paychecks was going to be difficult. So, like many other kids in that era, he was sent to live with his maternal grandparents.

Gerald and Adel Wright lived nearby in Kirbyville, it planted deeply in the East Texas Piney Woods, where the towering trees blocked out much of the sunlight. The rickety and unpainted farmhouse where Jerry grew up provided few comforts. There was no electricity or running water, and the outhouse in the back raised a terrible stink. Even store-bought toilet paper seemed too expensive. Jerry ran to the mailbox every day with hope of retrieving one precious item—the Sears, Roebuck catalogue. When it arrived, he would come tearing back down the dirt road, yelling, "Look, Grandma! Toilet paper!"

Living on the farm near Kirbyville was a lonely existence. It was little wonder that Jerry knew virtually nothing about the white man's existence. Every few weeks, the family went into the nearby town of Magnolia Springs to purchase necessities. The trip could be a rude awakening. The sign on the edge of town read, NIGGER, DON'T LET THE SUN SET ON YOUR BLACK ASS. His grandfather made a point of reading the sign out loud every time the old truck rolled into Magnolia Springs.

"Adel," he would say, "you gotta remind me to get us out of this town before five o'clock."

"No problem, Gerald," Adel would say. "We don't need to hang around here too long anyway. I hate this town."

In Magnolia Springs, white folks openly flaunted their shotguns. Jerry was nervous walking the streets and much happier when the truck was headed home.

For the most part, the farm was a happy place. Jerry woke up to a wood-burning stove. He learned to milk cows and churn butter. One of his chores was taking corn to be ground at the mill. He bathed outside in a number three washtub. One of his favorite things was sitting with his grandmother on the front porch while she weaved quilts from the raw cotton.

"It was a great experience because I learned never to take anything for granted," he recalled. "But I sure was glad to get back to the city."

That was, until he contracted polio.

"There was a period of time when I couldn't walk at all," he remembered. "The doctor put me in leg braces, gave me the medicine he could give me, and sent me home. After a while, I could walk with the braces. I prayed one day that I could walk without the braces."

The braces came off about two years later, in 1956, and his doctor had no explanation as to why he regained strength in his legs. One explanation might have been his polio vaccine, but no one could be sure. Playing touch football with his cousins Mel and Miller Farr was taboo, according to his parents, but Jerry could not resist. Jerry admired Mel and Miller. They babysat him and never left him behind, even with braces on his legs. The Farr brothers lived just down the street. Their mother was Jerry's dad's sister. The entire family went to the same church. They all ate Sunday dinner together.

Most important, when Jerry struggled in postpolio, Mel and Miller still made sure to pick him for their touch football team.

"In touch football, you always had to pick sides," Jerry remembered. "The only reason I got to play football was because Mel and Miller were my cousins."

Still, the games on the street could turn physical. One afternoon, he returned home with a bloodied face and his shirt in tatters.

"Jerry, how did you get your clothes torn?" his mother asked.

"Well, I was playing football with my two cousins, and I thought it'd be all right with you. Besides, my sisters said it was okay."

She scowled. "Next time, you ask me before you decide to go out in the streets and play football. It's just too rough. The only places you are allowed to go are school and church."

Leura LeVias was merely trying to protect a son whose physical condition was not the best. His growth had been stunted by the polio. Jerry was still about a head shorter than everyone else in his fourth-grade class, including the girls. In spite of his skinny legs, though, he was still gaining speed.

One day at John P. Odom Elementary School, Jerry was playing with the boys when the football bounded into a group of girls jumping rope. As he tried to retrieve the ball, he bumped into a girl named Velma Hicks.

"I caused Velma to miss her turn on the jump rope," LeVias remembered. "She said she was going to get me. She hit me in the back of the head. Every day from then on, she was chasing me. When another girl beats you up, all of the other guys think you are a sissy."

For the entirety of the hour-long recess, Velma Hicks chased Jerry from one school playground to the other. Then the boys started bullying little Jerry and stealing his bicycle.

Being Jerry LeVias was not easy. It seemed he was always a target. In elementary school, he could write with either hand but chose to be left-handed because it felt more natural. This led to a scolding from his teacher in the fourth grade, who said, "When you go to the chalkboard to write, Jerry, you have to do it right-handed."

One of his aunts chided him, "Jerry, if you write left-handed, then you are the child of the devil."

Yet Jerry would not stop writing left-handed, even when the kids yelled harsh things at him. "Jerry, you are dumb. You are *retarded*. You are affected."

In the fifth grade, Jerry was fortunate enough to change schools and get away from Velma Hicks. Thanks to her, though, he had managed to develop some footspeed that was noticed on the playground by one of his teachers, David Green.

"Jerry, you sure are fast," Green said. "In fact, you are so fast that I want you to come out for our flag football team."

After a few games, the light went on. He was much faster than the other kids and loved the idea of zooming past them to catch touchdown passes.

With football in his life, Jerry could begin to dream.

4

"As Rough as the Guff"

Clifton Ozen was a big, blustery man whose boisterous laughter seemed to rattle the walls at Hebert High School. Standing 6'2" and pushing 300 pounds, Ozen (pronounced *Oh*-zan) was the most-feared man on the north side of Beaumont.

The Hebert football practice field was situated directly across Glenwood Street from the LeVias home. Jerry could hear the thundering voice of the big man as he sent the team through drills on weekday afternoons in the fall. He could see the Hebert coach swinging a paddle the size of a Louisville Slugger and connecting with the boys' backsides. *Whop!* Jerry was too frightened to go outside. Regardless, he could not take his eyes off the wild scene unfolding just across the street. It was a kind of beautiful chaos with footballs flying and leather popping. His eyes searched the field for his two cousins.

"There they are," he would yell. "I love you, Miller and Mel."

Inevitably, his sister Charlena would interrupt her studies, crack the bedroom door, and yell, "Cut it out, Jerry."

At three o'clock sharp each afternoon, the team bus pulled up to the curb adjacent to the practice field. He could hear the players singing a line from the school song over and over:

Lift your head and hold it high!
The Hebert Panthers are passing by . . .

One day, as he returned home from elementary school, he walked slowly along the sidewalk, pausing to watch the players warm up before practice. Normally, he would have scooted through the front door before anyone noticed. This day, though, he lingered in the front yard, hoping to get a better view of the bigger-than-life Panthers. That was when he heard the voice.

"Hey boy, get your butt over here. *Hey boy!*"

Suddenly, it occurred to Jerry that the coach was yelling at him. He ducked his head and hustled toward the front door, but he could still hear *Hey boy!*

Summoning all of his courage, he turned and set his gaze on the man, who smiled. Then it happened. His little legs began to carry him across the street against his own will.

Ozen looked like a mountain standing before him. As he spoke, Jerry thought of the Wizard of Oz.

"I've been watching you peeking through the blinds," Ozen said. "I thought you were a little mouse."

"No, sir, I'm not a mouse. I'm just a little kid who hasn't grown much. You see—"

"I see. You are way too small to play football."

"Well, sir, I had polio when I was a kid, and it stopped me from growing."

"But you're plenty big to be my water boy."

Jerry paused to consider what the big man had just said.

"I've never been a water boy. Guess I could try."

"Then take off across that street and pour me some water into the biggest container you got. Make it cold. And hurry, boy. I'm thirsty."

Ozen figured the kid would come stumbling back across the street, sloshing the water everywhere. Instead, Jerry located a quart jar in the pantry, filled it up with water, added some ice, and screwed the lid on tight. Then he delivered it.

"Youngster," the coach said, "you might be little, but you've got some brains."

Ozen guzzled the contents and burped loudly. Then he said, "Now, boy, go get me some more water. I'm still thirsty."

On his third trip across the street, Jerry noticed that some of the players were glaring at him. One of the linemen yelled, "Hey, boy, what about my water?"

Ozen raised his hand and said, "Shut up unless you want me to paddle your butt. He ain't your water boy. He's *mine*."

With Ozen's thirst quenched, he blew his whistle. It was time for the Panthers to start the daily scrimmage. "First offense versus first defense," he bellowed.

As the helmet rattling began, Ozen started to brandish his paddle. He would yell, "Don't make me use my paddle on you boys. I'm as rough as the guff!" Ozen repeated it three times. *"I'm as rough as the guff."*

"What does that mean?" Jerry asked.

"It means I'm the baddest man in the valley," Ozen said.

Actually, it meant loud flatulence in street slang, but Ozen never revealed that translation to anyone.

In the community of black football, Clifton Ozen was one of the biggest names. He was considered one of the three best Negro coaches in Texas, along with Willie Ray Smith of Beaumont Charlton-Pollard and Joe Washington of Port Arthur Lincoln. He had played every position on the field at Texas State in the late 1940s. He was fast in spite of his size and was a terror running the football. More than anything, he wanted to become a successful high school football coach.

Ozen made his mark on the all-black Prairie View Interscholastic League (PVIL) in 1959 by throttling Dallas Lincoln High School 37–0 to win the league's state title. He knew that Hebert wide receiver Warren Wells was the best high school player in the state, white or black, but that he would never be allowed to play for an all-white Southwest

Conference team. He would go off to all-black Texas Southern in Houston and pray that the pro scouts somehow found him.

Ozen often dreamed of breaking down the Texas color barrier with one of his black players, but he knew all of the doors were padlocked. Texas Negroes played a terrific brand of football but had few options for college beyond Texas Southern and Prairie View A&M in their home state and Southern University and Grambling in Louisiana. Negro football players were so overlooked that most of the white-owned newspapers refused to cover the all-black games, or to run their photos. (To their credit, the *Beaumont Enterprise* and the *Port Arthur News* did staff most of the all-black games.) The North-South high school all-star game each year in Texas was a tightly knit all-white affair. In fact, Negro high school coaches of the era were not allowed to be full members of the Texas High School Coaches Association.

For the record, "African American" and "black" were not the politically correct terms in that era. White people often thought it was polite to call Negroes "colored people."

"We felt good when white people called us 'the colored,'" LeVias remembered. "Because a whole lot of them called us niggers."

Men like Ozen could only hope and pray for racial equality. If someone had told him that the Big 33 Football Classic would come along in a few years and Negroes would lot be allowed on the Texas team, he might have swallowed his whistle.

In the meantime, Ozen was just trying not to swallow his chewing tobacco. His players often gave him a wide berth because, without warning, he might unleash a long stream of Bull of the Woods. Ozen's favorite brand was advertised on television with four bulls singing in perfect harmony, "Bull of the Woods can't be beat . . . Bull of the Woods, smooth and tasty chewing treat."

As Ozen's personal water boy, one of Jerry's chores was to make sure he had plenty of chewing tobacco. It frustrated the players to no end that LeVias brought water to the coach but not to them. They struggled with dehydration and "cotton mouth" all through practice.

The Hebert players were always trying to get Jerry's attention.

One sidled up to him and whispered, "Next time, boy, you bring *me* some water."

Another said, "Don't worry about Ozen. Just bring *me* some damn water."

Each time they spoke, Jerry inched closer to the coach. He knew he might need protection.

At the end of the practice, Ozen gathered the team in a circle around him.

"We got the biggest game of the year coming up Thanksgiving against Charlton-Pollard," he said. "I'm giving you a six o'clock curfew. If I see you driving your cars around town after dark, or necking in the park, I'm going to bust your asses. You hear me?"

The laughter rumbled up from his large belly. Then his face turned as serious as a Baptist preacher's.

"Listen up, now. Jerry here is going to shine your shoes after practice. A nickel a shoe."

"Yessir, Coach," one said. Then they all nodded in agreement.

"And if I hear you're shorting Jerry, I'll smoke your butts."

"Yes, sir," they said in unison.

A few days later, Charlie LeVias was surprised to find his supply of shoe polish shrinking fast. He always went to work with a spit shine on his shoes. Furthermore, he was a highly organized man who kept up with his stuff. That night, he approached his son. "Jerry, have you been shining your shoes with my polish?"

"Well, kind of."

"Kind of what?"

"I've been shining the Panthers' shoes over on the football field."

Charlie was baffled. He knew virtually nothing about football, much less Panthers across the street.

"It's the Hebert football team, Dad," Jerry said. "They're the Panthers. They practice football every day. I get a nickel a shoe."

Jerry reached into his pocket and the nickels came spilling out.

With his head down, Jerry said, "Dad, I'm going to start buying to

buy my own polish. And I'll pay you back for what I already borrowed."

Charlie smiled. "That's good, son. Working for your money is the
right thing to do. Just don't let it interfere with your studies."

Growing up near Kirbyville in deep East Texas, Charlie LeVias
was forced to quit school at the height of the Great Depression in the
early 1930s. At age fourteen, he went to work in the lumber mills. He
married Leura Wright, and the couple moved to Beaumont in 1940 and
began a family. Charlie took a job at Dresser Industries as a janitor
and worked his way up to foreman in the paint department. Leura
became the housekeeper for a wealthy family that had moved to
southeast Texas from Michigan.

"My dad was a very proud man," Jerry LeVias recalled. "He went
to work clean and he came home clean. That was very admirable for
a man who worked in the paint department."

Charlie LeVias was proud of his son for taking a job at age twelve
shining shoes. Each day, Jerry polished the shoes and neatly arranged
them on the floor outside of each locker. That was before some of the
players stopped paying.

"If you tell Ozen, I'll whip your butt," one said.

Jerry told no one. Word, however, circulated back to the coach.
One by one, the freeloaders were called into his office. He grabbed
each one by the back of the neck and hollered, "Look at me, deadbeat.
You're a hero to that kid. Why do you stiff him on a good shine? What's
he supposed to think?"

The next day, Jerry was happy to be paid in full. The money was
not the reason he was along for this ride, though. As the days passed,
the kid with the skinny legs had come to love the Hebert Panthers.
They were like a team of big brothers. He never missed a practice. The
kid was always the first to arrive and the last to leave.

No one loved football nights better than little Jerry. Around five
o'clock, the team bus would wind through the neighborhoods with the
players hanging out of the windows, singing "Lift your head and hold

it high! The Hebert Panthers are passing by!" Hundreds of fans lined the streets, cheering them on. Jerry was right in the thick of it, waving to his new buddies.

"One of these days, I'm going to be on that bus," he yelled.

At night, he would march through the LeVias house, singing, "Lift your head and hold it high!"

With a puzzled expression, his father said, "Hope you're not thinking about joining the football team, Jerry. You're never going to be big enough. You know that."

His mother spoke up, "Oh, Charlie, he's just a water boy. Little Jerry knows he's too small to ever play football."

They were aware that little Jerry was getting his first taste of football on the sixth-grade flag football team. Ozen, along with David Green, had persuaded him to try the game.

The coach said, "You might be little now, but who knows? You might eat a mess of collard greens and a bucket of fried chicken and grow up to be a big man like me. Shoot, I was skinny as a yard rake once. I started eating and the next thing I knew I was the greatest player in the history of the Texas State. Did I ever tell you—"

"I know, I know, coach. Ozen 31, Texas Southern *nothing*. Ozen 31, Prairie View College *nothing*."

"Hold on, little fella," Ozen said. "Now, I did beat both of those teams by myself—but I only scored 21 points against Prairie View A&M."

Before long, Ozen started coming to Jerry's flag football games. This surprised the teachers and the principal at the elementary school because he had never come to "scout" one of their football players. When Jerry spotted the big man on the sideline, he did his best to break a long run for a touchdown.

"Look at that little boy run," Ozen would crow. "One of these days he'll be starring for the Hebert Panthers. And you know who his coach will be? Ol' Clifton Ozen his own self. We're going straight to state with Jerry LeVias!"

Ozen smiled as little Jerry scored touchdown after touchdown.

"Jesus, boy, you are fast," Ozen said. "I had no idea you could motor on baby sticks like that."

Jerry split time between playing flag football and working for Ozen. The coach was so impressed that he gave him a promotion.

"You're now my student trainer," Ozen said.

"What does that mean?"

"It means that you keep fetching water and do everything else I ask you to do."

LeVias turned thirteen on September 5, 1959. As a birthday present, the Hebert Panthers won their first state championship in the highest classification of the Prairie View Interscholastic League.

Jerry wanted to be the next Warren Wells, or perhaps the next Willie Ray "Beaver" Smith Jr. of Charlton-Pollard. He could not believe his eyes when he sat in the stands and watched the Beaumont Soul Bowl on Thanksgiving of 1959. Wells and Smith tore up the field with long runs as the game rocked back and forth. He could have never imagined the kind of excitement those two players created. Hebert finally won the game on a last-minute touchdown by Wells, but Smith was the player Jerry would never forget.

"To me, Willie Ray Smith Jr. was the best player to ever come out of Beaumont," he said. "I just could never take my eyes off of him when he carried the ball."

Like other black stars of the time, Smith could not even think about playing football at the all-white Texas institutions. However, his coach and father, Willie Ray Smith Sr., was a friend of legendary Iowa Hawkeyes coach Forest Evashevski, who was coming off a 1958 Big Ten title and a victory over the California Bears in the Rose Bowl.

Iowa's first black player had been Frank Kinney Holbrook in 1895. When he scored a touchdown against Missouri in '96 to give Iowa a 12–0 lead, the Tigers players walked off the field and did not come back.

The first black All American at Iowa was Duke Slater, in 1921, who also made All Big Ten from 1919 to 1921. George Jewett was the first black player in the Big Ten, playing with Michigan from 1890 to

1892. Jewett was studying medicine at Michigan and had a run-in with the dean of medicine. So in 1893, he transferred to Northwestern, where he finished his football career.

The Big Ten football teams could brag about being among the first to integrate racially, but the conference began to back off from its liberal stance in the 1930s and '40s. Fewer and fewer black players were recruited. The blacks who did participate in that era were benched when their teams played southern teams like Tulane or Georgia Tech.

By the late 1950s, when Beaver Smith came along, black players were prevalent again in the conference. That was why Willie Ray Smith Sr. made friends with Big Ten coaches like Michigan State's Duffy Daugherty and Evashevski whenever he attended coaching schools in Dallas, Houston, or San Antonio. He knew he would need other options when his sons grew up. Beaver would be the first of the Smith family to travel almost a thousand miles from his native state to Iowa City to play big-time football.

Jerry often wondered if he would be as good as either Wells or Beaver Smith. He was not even sure he was big enough to make the eighth-grade team. He chose not to try out for the tackle football team until he received some bad news. His girlfriend had decided to break up with him and to go with one of the football players.

Jerry decided to take action. The next day, he put the rocks in his pockets, jacked up his weight to 120 pounds, and started catching passes like the next Warren Wells.

"I was heartbroken about my girlfriend," LeVias recalled. "But when she saw me scoring touchdowns, she came right back to me."

His parents were still against him playing football, so Jerry kept it a secret around the house. They thought he was still the student manager. When friends around the neighborhood said, "I saw Jerry at the game last night, and he was looking good," Leura and Charlie LeVias just laughed.

"Oh, yeah, Jerry is a fine student manager," Leura would say. "And as far as looking good, he's also a fine dresser."

Jerry knew that his parents would soon become suspicious. He was rapidly becoming an outstanding receiver for the middle school team, and folks around town were talking about him. The smallest player in the lineup jetted past defenders and scored virtually every time he touched the ball.

The local newspaper was covering all of Jerry's games, and that was developing into yet another problem. So Ozen bribed a sportswriter from the *Beaumont Enterprise* not to spell LeVias correctly.

"Here's five bucks," he told the reporter. "I don't want to spell Jerry's name right one time. I want it to be L-E-Z-N-I-A-Z. Lezniaz, got it?"

"Coach, I will do my best," the reporter said. "But if I screw up on spelling Lezniaz, don't get mad at me."

Jerry needed all of the cover he could muster. Charlena turned out to be a great ally. When the parents started asking about the whereabouts of her brother, she usually had an excuse handy.

"He's the water boy," she would say. "No, he's the team trainer. No, he's the shoeshine boy. Jerry just has a lot of things going, you know."

On a night when Jerry was supposed to be trying out for the school play, he came home with a bad limp. He had run out of excuses. Charlie LeVias wanted some honest answers.

"Son, are you playing tackle football?"

"Yes, sir."

"Jerry, you're too small. Just look at yourself. The other kids are a head taller than you. If you're going to disobey me, you must want to play football really bad."

"I do, Dad. I'm really good. We've won all of our games this season, and we've got one more to go."

Charlie LeVias looked at the floor and shook his head. He had managed to finish only the sixth grade because of work and could barely read and write. Still, he knew how to read a bedtime story, and his kids never knew of his educational deficiencies.

"Jerry, we've never had a single LeVias go to college," he said. "It has been my dream that you be the first."

The father then looked upward, as if searching the heavens for answers. He found one.

"Here's the deal, Jerry," he said. "I can tell that football is important to you, and that's okay. You just keep studying and you keep making straight A's, and I will allow you to keep playing."

Jerry LeVias jumped so high that he almost banged his head on the ceiling.

Being black in Beaumont in the early 1960s was not easy. Everything was separate and quite unequal. Three orders of the Ku Klux Klan thrived in Beaumont. The town of Vidor, located just to the northeast, boasted eleven orders of the Klan, along with the Grand Dragon and Queen Kliegel of Texas. The burning of crosses occurred on a regular basis up and down the Gulf Coast region of the state.

Charles Aaron "Bubba" Smith, a highly acclaimed professional football player turned movie actor, lived as a teenager in Beaumont and played for his father, Willie Ray Smith, at Beaumont Charlton-Pollard High School. He once said, "I am six foot eight. But when I drive through Vidor, I am four foot eight. I am sitting so low in my Cadillac that I can barely see over the wheel."

As an eight-year-old growing up in nearby Orange, Bubba was riding his bicycle through the woods one day when he happened upon a horrific sight. As the memoir *Kill, Bubba, Kill* tells it, Smith "hid behind a bush in North Orange and listened to the screams, smelled the hot flesh, and saw five white men burn the letters KKK in a [Negro's] chest."

According to his book, Bubba Smith knew only one white person during his time in southeast Texas. That was Butch Hoffer, a chubby, balding man who owned a clothing store downtown. Hoffer treated the young black man with respect whenever he walked into the store. Bubba, however, soon came to realize that Hoffer was being so friendly because his mother, Georgia Smith, was paying the family's clothing bill on time.

Buying clothes as a Negro in Beaumont in the 1960s could turn into one big headache. Neither clothes nor shoes could be returned or exchanged by Negroes.

"If you bought a pair of pants, and they turned out to be too small or too large, they were yours," Jerry LeVias recalled. "If you bought a pair of shoes and they didn't fit, you were not taking them back."

All of Jerry's pants were cuffed, sometimes halfway up his leg. His shoes were usually too big and stuffed with cotton in the back.

The hostility toward black people on trips downtown was palpable. The signs were everywhere—COLORED and WHITE. A black man did not dare to drink from a white fountain, or to use a white-only restroom.

"We were never taught to hate," Jerry LeVias recalled, "but the idea that you had the colored and the white fountains was a bit unsettling. My father never did let us drink out of those fountains. Before we left for town, you drank water and you used the restroom at home. Our father would not let us ride a city bus because you had to sit in the back. My dad never let us become second-class citizens."

Back in the early 1940s, as World War II raged in Europe and the South Pacific, Beaumont had been a thriving town. The population grew by more than 18,000 during the war because of the abundance of work in the refineries, the shipyards, and the munitions factories.

Black and white people managed to coexist in the workplace until 1943, when a white woman working in the shipyard accused a Negro of raping her. A riot ensued as more than four thousand people marched toward city hall. Black people were assaulted, black neighborhoods were ransacked, and black-owned restaurants burned down. On June 15–16, more than two hundred people were arrested and at least fifty were badly injured. The black man accused of raping the white woman was shot and killed by police as he "resisted arrest."

In 1960, seventeen years after the Beaumont race riots, Jerry LeVias was studying at the family's home on Glenwood when his dad came home from work early. He could never remember seeing his father around the house during a workday afternoon. Charlie's expression told Jerry that something had gone terribly wrong.

Charlie LeVias went to the closet and pulled out his .45 and a shotgun. He then said, "Jerry, I need your help. We're going to barricade the front porch." The two began carrying furniture and firewood onto the front porch, and Jerry realized that all of the neighbors on Glenwood Street were doing the same thing.

Charlie looked at his son sternly and said, "The Klan is going to be coming down this street tonight. This afternoon, a white woman accused a colored man of raping her. It's the same thing that triggered the race riot long ago. We're going to be ready this time. When they show up with their hoods on, we'll catch them in our crossfire. Son, we are ready to go to war."

As darkness settled over Beaumont, Jerry sat with his dad on the front porch. Through the streetlights, he could see the neighbors brandishing their guns. It was the longest night that Jerry could remember. When the sun finally rose over Beaumont the next morning, he had never felt such relief. Not a single gunshot had been fired. The Klan uprising had turned out to be just a scare—this time. There would be other nights when the firewood would be stacked high on the front porch and the guns came out of the closet.

Jerry's father allowed him to go out for the junior high team as a ninth grader. Little did Charlie LeVias know that Clifton Ozen had bigger plans for his son.

On the first day of August workouts, Jerry found himself lining up with the high school team. It was the first time in the history of Hebert that a ninth grader would play with the varsity. But there was more. Weighing in at 128 pounds, he would be a starter in the same backfield with Mel and Miller Farr, his cousins. Don Bean, one of the fastest sprinters in the state, was the fourth member of the backfield.

Ozen's offensive plan for the season was to confuse, confuse, confuse. One play, Mel Farr would line up at quarterback, with LeVias taking the snap on the ensuing down. The first time he carried the ball as a freshman halfback, he rocketed 65 yards to the end zone.

"We ran nothing but sweeps," LeVias recalled. "We were the fastest kids on the field, and Clifton turned us loose. In the fall, we were the offensive backfield, and in the spring, we were the 4×100 relay team."

In 1961, Mel Farr was already being scouted by UCLA, and his older brother, Miller, was receiving attention from smaller schools in Texas and a few big ones beyond the state's borders. It was LeVias, however, stealing the show because of his speed. He finished his freshman year as the leading receiver and the No. 2 rusher behind Mel Farr.

The students at Hebert and Charlton-Pollard could not wait each year for the biggest football game of the season. It was called the Soul Bowl and played on Thanksgiving in alternating Stadiums. Each year, Hebert versus Charlton-Pollard decided the district championship, with the winner advancing into the Prairie View Interscholastic League playoffs. Every year, it was standing room only with about 25,000 in attendance.

"When Hebert played Charlton-Pollard, no one would work, die, or get married," LeVias remembered. "If you were married to someone who went to Hebert or Charlton-Pollard, you got divorced that week. People came over from Houston for the game. No weddings were scheduled. Guys who worked at the refineries bet their paychecks."

Hebert versus Charlton-Pollard was one of the classic rivalries in the history of Texas high school football, comparable to Houston Yates versus Wheatley, Odessa Permian versus Midland Lee, and Abilene High versus Amarillo. The greatest Soul Bowl of all was staged in 1962 during LeVias's sophomore season.

During the regular season, Beaumont's all-black teams had to play their games on Tuesday and Thursday nights because on Friday nights the city stadiums were reserved for the all-white teams. On Thanksgiving, though, there was not a high school stadium in Texas that could accommodate the 25,000 fans for the Soul Bowl.

Lining up on both sides of the ball for Charlton-Pollard were Bubba and Tody Smith. Bubba, a senior, had been scouted by Iowa, Kansas, Michigan State, and UCLA since his freshman year when he stood 6'7" and weighed 270 pounds. Weighing over 300 pounds as a senior, he was considered the greatest player in the history of Texas high school football. Tody, his younger brother, was known as "El Toro" because he was as strong as a bull.

Fans of the Soul Bowl were accustomed to the loudness of the Thanksgiving game, but nothing could compare to the energy and electricity of the place in 1962. As many as five players suiting up that day would someday play big-time college ball, albeit for out-of-state teams. Willie Ray Smith Sr. and Clifton Ozen were considered the two greatest Negro coaches in the state. Smith had won 215 games while coaching at Lufkin Dunbar, Orange Wallace, and Charlton-Pollard. His two championships came in 1949 and '54 at Wallace. Ozen had won the 1959 state championship and compiled 121 wins.

Everyone knew that in a different era, Smith and Ozen would have been coaching at an integrated high school with the highest classification in the state. Former Oilers and Saints coach Bum Phillips coached Texas high school football for more than twenty years before ascending to the pro ranks. He told Ty Cashion, author of *Pigskin Pulpit*, "The coaches I liked I liked because they were good football men. Willie Ray Smith and Joe Washington were good football men. It never occurred to me that they were black and I was white. Hell, they were friends of mine and they were good coaches."

Growing up in Denton, about thirty miles north of Dallas, Smith had been tagged with the nickname "Doll" because of his good looks, but he was better known for his famous limp. In 1934, Smith was standing on the Denton Square when he heard gunshots. A couple of notorious outlaws named Bonnie Parker and Clyde Barrow were trying to spring two men from the Denton County jail. Doll Smith, an innocent bystander, took a stray bullet from a machine gun in the right thigh. He spent the better part of the next five years in a Dallas hospital with a wound that would not heal. It was not unusual for a black man in Texas to receive poor medical attention. Furthermore, penicillin was not yet available. A doctor recommended amputation, but Smith said, "I came in here with two legs and I'm leaving with two legs." The leg slowly healed, but the coach would walk with a defined limp throughout his career.

No one loved Hebert versus Charlton-Pollard more than Ozen and Smith. A handful of white fans tried to get tickets to the game, but it was almost a lost cause. Most had been swept up by the black fans. Looking into the stands before the game, Ozen and Smith knew who the dozen or so white faces belonged to. They were the coaches and scouts of the Big Ten and Pacific-8 (AAWU) conferences. Both sections of the country had been recruiting black players for decades. They began to invade Texas in the late 1950s when Willie Ray Smith Jr. was tearing up the competition for the Charlton-Pollard Cougars. The out-of-state coaches in 1962 would spend most of the afternoon with their binoculars trained on Bubba Smith, but they also planned to take some notes on Hebert's sophomore scatback Jerry LeVias.

Fans of Hebert were already enamored of LeVias. Each time he touched the ball, they would chant, "Jerry the Jet!" or "Bring it home, Jerome!"

The opening kickoff traveled to the Hebert 10-yard line, where LeVias stuck it beneath his left arm and took off like a rocket. He blasted through a large opening at the 30-yard line and was suddenly past the entire coverage team. No one was going to catch the fastest player on the field that day as LeVias returned the kickoff 90 yards for a touchdown. The extra point gave Hebert a 7–0 lead.

Lining up at quarterback, Mel Farr scored the second touchdown on a 51-yard run around right end. In the second quarter, Farr passed 31 yards to LeVias for another touchdown. The Panthers had sprinted to a shocking 20–0 lead at halftime.

The uphill battle that Charlton-Pollard faced in the second half seemed unwinnable. In the locker room, Willie Ray Smith went straight to the chalkboard and yelled, "Hey, Bubba, listen up!"

On offense, Bubba would be moved from center to fullback. Bubba had rarely carried the ball during his high school career. Based on his performance in the second half, though, no one would have ever guessed it. Powering through the center of the line, he gained huge chunks of yards as the Cougars cut the lead to 20–7.

Bubba remained at middle linebacker on defense, but to contain the speed of LeVias and the Farr brothers, he started lining up 3 yards deeper. Roaming the field from sideline to sideline, Smith almost single-handedly shut the Hebert defense down. The boisterous Hebert crowd was reduced to a whisper as Charlton-Pollard started to roll. A 12-yard reception by Smith and a good kick cut the lead to 20–14. Smith then kicked a 33-yard field goal to make it 20–17.

When Smith scored the winning touchdown on a 7-yard run with two minutes to play, the Charlton-Pollard fans almost lost their minds. Nothing in the history of the rivalry could compare to the 24–20 comeback victory that is still remembered and talked about all over southeast Texas.

"We lost," LeVias said, "but it was still one of the greatest games I've ever played in."

Beaumont Hebert was a terrific place for a young man like Jerry LeVias to grow up. He believed in the school motto, "Whatever Hebert does, it must be the best." Hebert could compete academically with any other high school in the state and sent its share of graduates to places like Harvard, Yale, Stanford, and Rice. As important, it provided an unmatched sense of community.

Hebert was built within the Pear Orchard section of Beaumont in 1922 on land donated by two ex-slave brothers, Usan Hebert and Ozan Blanchette. A two-story redbrick building was erected on Lela Street, and a stucco vocational center was constructed nearby. An entire athletic complex was built in the early 1940s.

Clifton Ozen ruled both the football field and the hallways of Hebert High. Not only were the Panthers one of the fastest teams in the state, they were also one of the most disciplined. Ozen took no "guff" off of anyone.

"We would be in the locker room at halftime and Clifton would say, 'Son, don't make me take out my paddle,'" LeVias remembered. "On the practice field, the big man was always running behind somebody, hitting them with that doggone paddle."

Inside the high school, all of the male teachers carried wooden paddles in their back pockets for discipline. Little wonder that in the Kingdom of Ozen, halls and classrooms were always quiet.

No one was a bigger hero on the north side of Beaumont than Jerry LeVias. It seemed his status grew with each game. During his junior season, he gained more than 1,000 yards in all three major categories—running, passing, and receiving. He also scored 22 touchdowns.

One of the traditions at Hebert was for the girls to hand the football players apples as they walked down the hall to class. Most days, Jerry needed a large basket to haul them around.

"Jerry was the best football player that I ever coached," Ozen recalled. "He was also the sweetest kid I'd ever been around. I wanted to do everything I could for him."

5

Everywhere Else but Texas

With each passing day in the fall of 1964, Clifton Ozen grew more frustrated with the lack of interest from Texas recruiters in his star player. The Southwest Conference coaches were not attending the Hebert High School games, or asking for Jerry LeVias's films or his statistics.

For three years, Ozen had tried to downplay LeVias's statistics for fear the recruiters would think they were trumped up. When he started to release LeVias's real statistics, the numbers were off the charts. During his career at Hebert, LeVias was averaging 40 yards per kick return and 10.8 yards from the line of scrimmage. Even more impressive, he had averaged 4.3 touchdowns per game the previous two seasons and had scored on TD runs of 73, 71, and 68 yards in *one game*.

One person Ozen did not need to convince was *Orange Leader* sports editor Fred Cervelli, who had covered his games and knew LeVias's tremendous value. Most important, Cervelli was the head of the Big 33 selection committee.

"Bobby Layne is going to love Jerry LeVias," Cervelli told Ozen. "I don't care what the college coaches around the state are saying. We're going to need him next August in Hershey, Pennsylvania, because we're planning to beat the socks off those people. Jerry's going to do just great."

In spite of the lack of interest from the SWC coaches, major college recruiters from Oregon to Oklahoma lined the Hebert High practice field each afternoon to watch number 23 do his thing. Jerry LeVias did not disappoint. Clifton Ozen made a point of calling long pass plays for LeVias so the recruiters could "ooh" and "ahh" as he zoomed past defenders and caught the ball.

"That's my boy!" Ozen crowed as he roamed the practice field. "Gentlemen, Jerry LeVias is the king of Texas high school football."

The recruiters came from places like Oregon, Oregon State, California-Berkeley, UCLA, USC, Michigan State, Oklahoma, and Arizona State. The most famous of the group was John McKay, who had won his first national championship two years earlier at USC while going 11-0. The top-ranked Trojans had defeated No. 2 Wisconsin 42–37 in the Rose Bowl.

Recruiters from the Midwest and West Coast flocked around LeVias like ducks on a June bug, but Ozen could look around his Hebert practice field and not see Darrell Royal from Texas, nor little Jess Neely of Rice, nor Abe Martin from TCU. It was clear from their absences that the Southwest Conference was taking a pass on LeVias, just as it had on other great players from the Beaumont area in recent years, including Bubba Smith, Warren Wells, Willie Ray Smith Jr., and the brother tandem of Mel and Miller Farr.

One reason that SWC coaches ignored LeVias was an overall resistance by many white Texans to accept black people. There was the age-old problem of Negroes eating at white restaurants and staying at white-only hotels. It was still taboo in Texas to accept Negroes into businesses run by white people.

Gil Steinke of Texas A&I, a small NAIA (National Association of Intercollegiate Athletics) college in Kingsville, had already figured out a way to overcome that problem. In 1960, Steinke had signed the second black football player to attend a predominantly white college in Texas. The first had been Abner Haynes at North Texas State in 1956.

Steinke's first black player was halfback Sid Blanks, who would become a team captain in 1963. Steinke had to figure out a way to feed his star player and to find him a place to stay when the Javelinas played on the road. He was not about to allow Blanks to eat in the kitchen or to stay in some seedy hotel away from his teammates. Steinke had a way of using unorthodox tactics to get what he wanted.

Steinke and Blanks were prepared for that first road trip when the team bus pulled up to the all-white restaurant. Steinke turned to Blanks and said, "Sid, do you know you know all of your lines?"

"*Sí, señor*," Blanks said.

As the team filed into the restaurant, the manager stopped Blanks at the door. Steinke went to work.

"Why are you stopping this man from entering your restaurant?" he asked.

"Because we don't serve niggers—I mean the colored," the manager said.

Steinke grinned and said, "What if I told you this man is not a Negro, that he's actually a Mexican. Would you serve him then?"

"Well, I guess so," the man said. "We do serve Mexicans."

Steinke turned to Blanks and said, "Show this man that you're a Mexican."

Blanks proceeded to reel off several lines of fluent Spanish that had been taught to him by his coach.

Steinke then said, "So you see, sir, this man is of Mexican descent. And you will let a Mexican eat in your diner."

The restaurant manager smiled, shook his head, and said, "Well, okay, I guess."

It was not the last time that Steinke used this strategy with Blanks, or any of his future black players. Steinke went on to win six NAIA national championships with teams composed largely of black players, as well as compiling a thirty-nine-game winning streak. One of those Negroes was Robstown guard Gene Upshaw, who in the years ahead helped the Oakland Raiders win two Super Bowls. Upshaw remains the only NFL player to participate in Super Bowls in three different decades (1968, 1977, and 1981) for the same team. He made the Pro Bowl six times and was inducted into the Pro Football Hall of Fame in 1987. He made his biggest contribution to pro sports in his twenty-five years as the executive director of the NFL Players Association, from 1983 until his death in 2008.

Upshaw could thank Steinke for knocking down that first door.

More than anything else, Steinke helped the black Texas athlete overcome anonymity. Simply, the white stars of Texas in the mid-1960s received tenfold the exposure of the blacks. The big-city newspapers barely covered the Negro teams. Full-blown segregation in Texas football was not about to change. Lasting more than a half century, and driven by widespread public approval, the separation of the races across Texas high school sports seemed as common as fiddle-playing bands and Fleetwood Cadillacs. The University Interscholastic League erected a color barrier that stood tall and strong. The message was clear: Black and white kids all over the state would play on separate fields. Only a handful of Texas school districts had chosen to integrate by the fall of 1964.

This seemed odd since an American president from Texas had pushed harder than anyone else for social integration across the country. Lyndon B. Johnson had fought tooth and nail for a civil rights bill that had initially been proposed by John F. Kennedy on June 11, 1963, five months before his assassination in Dallas. Johnson signed the Civil Rights bill into law July 2, 1964, outlawing major forms of discrimination against racial, ethnic, national, and religious minorities and women. The bill also enabled the U.S. attorney general to join lawsuits against state governments that operated segregated school systems.

As Jerry LeVias and the Hebert Panthers continued to play a full schedule against all-black teams, the WHITES ONLY signs were coming down all across Texas. Jim Crow laws were vanishing. In less than two years, Barbara Jordan of Houston would be elected to the Texas Legislature, becoming its first black female member.

However, the Civil Rights Act was having little impact on Negro high school students in Texas. Segregation among the Texas high school football teams was older than the Model T Ford. The high school football boom began around 1910. The most celebrated teams were

Amarillo, Abilene, Wichita Falls, Waco, Breckenridge, and Dallas Highland Park. They were as white as classroom chalk. These players were the darlings of the state and played before huge crowds. The Texas oil boom drove the economy and built huge stadiums that were filled to the brim every Friday night. The all-white University Inter-scholastic League thrived on money, manpower, and prestige. It main-tained a large office in Austin with several employees.

Meanwhile, the Negro teams were relegated to the Prairie View Interscholastic League (PVIL) that employed one person and lacked a bank account. The black teams wore ragtag uniforms and played in rickety stadiums, normally on the wrong side of the tracks.

This did not, however, stop the all-black schools from playing a brand of football that often exceeded the all-white teams. The most famous of the all-black squads were Beaumont Hebert, Beaumont Charlton-Pollard, Lufkin Dunbar, Houston Yates, Dallas Lincoln, Fort Worth Terrell, and Austin L. C. Anderson.

In 1963, a black player named Warren McVea from San Antonio had burst onto the scene. Playing for Brackenridge, one of the state's few integrated high schools, he was moved from halfback to quarter-back and gained more than 200 yards and scored 6 touchdowns in a bi-district game against crosstown rival Robert E. Lee. At the time, it was considered the greatest high school game ever played in Texas. Linus Baer of Lee answered McVea's remarkable feats by scoring 5 touchdowns as the Rebels came from behind to win the game 55–48.

Months later, McVea would forsake his other seventy-two scholar-ship offers and sign with the University of Houston, still not a major player in Texas college football. McVea was also the first Negro high school player in Texas to intercept headlines from the white stars like Steve Worster of Bridge City, Bill Bradley of Palestine, and Tommy Nobis of San Antonio Jefferson. At the end of the sixties, a poll was taken in Dave Campbell's *Texas Football* regarding the best players of the decade. McVea was selected as the No. 1 player in the state.

In spite of the long reach of segregation, the black players outperformed the white ones in the 1960s. In that decade, five players from the PVIL would make it all the way to the Pro Football Hall of Fame, while none of the whites reached Canton. Dick "Night Train" Lane, who played at Austin L. C. Anderson High School in the 1940s, was the first black player from the state to reach the Hall of Fame. Here is the list of the six enshrinees from the PVIL and their high school years of graduation.

Dick "Night Train" Lane (1946) He was born to a prostitute, who abandoned him as an infant. He was lying on the ground, swathed in old newspapers, when Ella Lane heard a baby crying. She adopted and raised the child. After high school, he traveled eight hundred miles to play one season of junior college football in Nebraska, then enlisted in the army. Lane fought briefly in Korea. Returning to the States, and living in Los Angeles, he still dreamed of playing pro football. Each morning, the military bus that carried him to work passed the Los Angeles Rams practice field. One day, he told the bus driver to stop. He walked into the Rams offices and asked for a tryout. Remarkably, he was signed the next day. In 1952, this twenty-five-year-old rookie playing a 12-game schedule shattered the NFL record with 14 interceptions. The record still stands in spite of the NFL switching to a 14-game schedule in 1961 and to 16 games in 1978. Lane was named All-Pro six times, played in seven Pro Bowls, and in 1969 was elected the greatest cornerback in the first fifty years of the NFL. Still fourth on the all-time NFL interception list with 68, Lane was enshrined in 1974.

Charley Taylor, Grand Prairie Dalworth High (1961) A star running back, Taylor received no scholarship offers from the major Texas universities. So he left the state to play at Arizona State, where he was twice named an All-American receiver. He would be the third player drafted in 1964, by the Washington Redskins. The Redskins, owned by well-known racist George Preston Marshall, had ironically integrated just two years ahead of Taylor's arrival. To the glee of Redskins fans, Taylor held every NFL receiving record, including receptions (649), receiving yards (9,110), and touchdowns (79), when he retired in 1977. He also played on Washington's Super Bowl VII team that lost 14–7 to the undefeated Miami Dolphins. He was enshrined in 1984.

Gene Upshaw, Robstown High (1963) With the Southwest Conference schools ignoring him because of his race, Upshaw opted for Texas A&I College. During a fifteen-year career with the Oakland Raiders, Upshaw played left guard on three Super Bowl teams. He was enshrined in 1987.

Kenny Houston, Lufkin Dunbar High (1963) Coming out of this small PVIL school in the Piney Woods of East Texas, Houston received only one football scholarship. He accepted the offer from Prairie View A&M, where he played center and linebacker. He was not selected until the ninth round in the 1967 AFL Draft by the Houston Oilers. Moving from linebacker to safety, he made all-league twelve straight years, six with the Oilers and six more with the Washington Redskins. He intercepted 49 passes and recovered 21 fumbles. He was enshrined in 1986.

Emmitt Thomas, Angleton Marshall High (1963) One of the best high school players coming out of Texas in the early 1960s, Emmitt Thomas was almost forced to walk on collegiately. He finally received a scholarship offer from Bishop College in Dallas. Thomas went undrafted in 1966 and signed as a free agent with the Kansas City Chiefs. He led the AFL in interceptions in 1969 with 9 and starred in Super Bowl IV as the Chiefs defeated Minnesota 23–7. He still ranks eleventh on the all-time NFL interception list with 58. Thomas was enshrined in 2008.

"Mean Joe" Greene, Temple Dunbar High (1965) Green still remembers the indignity of not being allowed to dress in the Temple

High School Stadium locker rooms. He was informed that the locker rooms were reserved for the all-white teams. Even more humiliating was learning that the Southwest Conference would ignore him because of his race. He was forced to settle for North Texas State in Denton. Still, the Pittsburgh Steelers made him the fourth overall selection of the 1969 draft. All he accomplished in Pittsburgh was playing on four Super Bowl champions and making All-Pro nine times. He was enshrined in 1987, his first year of eligibility.

Like the talented black stars before him, Jerry LeVias's greatness was concealed by the clouds of segregation. Still, there was no denying that he was one of the five most talented players in the state in the fall of 1964.

When Ozen did not hear from Darrell Royal by October of 1964, he picked up the phone and placed a long distance call to Austin.

"Coach Royal," Ozen began. "I just wanted to let you know that I have an exceptional Negro here at Hebert High School, and his name is Jerry LeVias. He is a player who would qualify both athletically and academically for the Southwest Conference."

When Royal asked about LeVias's weight, Ozen informed him that he tipped the scales at 153 pounds.

"Well, he's just not big enough for our program, or the Southwest Conference for that matter," the coach said. This seemed odd coming from Royal. After all, his first star player at Texas was Palestine's 148-pound halfback James Saxton, who played for the Longhorns from 1959 to 1961. Saxton led the team in rushing, receiving, and all-purpose yards in 1960 and became Royal's first consensus All American in 1961.

Before Royal could hang up the phone, Ozen said, "Coach, is there any chance you could come down here to Beaumont to see Jerry play before the season is over?"

"No, Clifton, we're chasing another national championship, and we've got Arkansas coming up this Saturday. Just don't have the time."

What really stood between Royal and LeVias was the "gentlemen's agreement" among the Southwest Conference coaches not to sign Negro players. As a result, the out-of-state recruiters would continue to swoop into Texas and to grab the best black players that any state had to offer. Oregon State coach Tommy Prothro did not mind traveling twenty-five hundred miles to Beaumont to scout LeVias. For years, Prothro had remained open-minded about recruiting Negroes. This approach helped him turn around a languid Oregon State program. The Beavers had finished with a 1-8 record the year before he was hired in 1955. On January 1, 1957, Prothro led them to the Rose Bowl with ten Negroes on a forty-seven-man squad. They made it again on January 1, 1965.

In an era when most college coaches were cut from the same blue-collar cloth, Prothro took a cerebral approach to the game. He wore horn-rimmed glasses and a fedora and carried a briefcase. He played competitive bridge. As a football coach, he believed that speed was the fastest road to victory. In the late 1950s, Prothro would send Negro running backs Paul Lowe and Amos Marsh into professional football. In fact, Prothro had traveled more than three thousand miles to recruit Lowe out of Homer, Louisiana, during a time when black players in the Deep South held little or no hope of playing major college football.

In the fall of 1964, Prothro was dead set on signing LeVias. He spent so much time at the Hebert practice field that Ozen approached him one day and said, "Tommy, I wonder if they still know you back at Oregon State."

Prothro laughed. "If I could get LeVias to sign a letter of intent, I would never need to come back to Texas."

Two years earlier, Ozen had noticed the same glint in the eye of Michigan State coach Duffy Daugherty when he flew into Beaumont and recruited the socks off Bubba Smith of Charlton-Pollard. Bubba's dream had been to play at the University of Texas, but Darrell Royal had totally confused him when he said, "I can sign you to a scholarship, but I'm not so sure I can put you on my football roster."

Bubba's older brother, Willie Ray Jr., had been passed over by every major college in Texas because of his race, but that did not stop the likes of Michigan State and Iowa from making scholarship offers. In spite of suffering a knee injury his senior year, Willie Ray Jr. signed with Iowa. After two years of unhappiness, he transferred to Kansas, where he crossed career paths with Gale Sayers, later to become known as "the Kansas Comet."

Willie Ray brought Sayers back to Beaumont during Christmas break. During a touch football game in Beaumont's Iberia Park, Willie Ray showed up Sayers with his speed and dazzling moves.

"My brother was a much better player than Gale," Bubba Smith said. "When Gale came to Beaumont, we just weren't that impressed with him."

Willie Ray's career ended with another knee injury at Kansas. In the meantime, Sayers won All-American honors for two straight years en route to a Hall of Fame career with the Chicago Bears.

In his memoirs, published in 1983, Bubba Smith wrote, "There is no telling how far Willie Ray would have gone if he hadn't gotten hurt."

In the fall of 1963, Bubba Smith was coveted by the Big Ten schools. His native state wanted no part of him. Signing with Daugherty meant he would travel thirteen hundred miles to East Lansing, Michigan, where the frozen wind and the blizzards cut down with a keen blade.

The year 1963 had been a confusing one in America. A white supremacist toting an army rifle had ambushed and killed civil rights activist Medgar Evers in Mississippi. On the flip side, more than a half-million people had marched into Washington, D.C., in support of civil rights. The highlight of the demonstration was an address by the Reverend Dr. Martin Luther King. He was wildly cheered when he said, "I have a dream that one day on the red hills of Georgia, the sons of former slaves and the sons of former slave owners will be able to sit down at the table of brotherhood."

When Bubba Smith left for Michigan State, it was a day of cele- bration, but a bittersweet one for Willie Ray Smith Sr. It was too bad that Dr. King's dream had not become a reality a few years sooner. The father was happy that his son would play for a respected and tradition-rich football program like Michigan State, but the prospect of rarely seeing him play was a sad one. Then, too, Willie Ray Sr. felt certain that his third son, Tody, would also be forced to play college football out of state following his high school graduation in 1967.

Bubba Smith would dominate Big Ten football for three straight years and make consensus All American twice. At 6'8" and 310 pounds, he ransacked opposing lines and averaged 11 quarterback sacks a season. He inspired the Michigan State student body to chant, "Kill, Bubba, kill!"

In the infamous 10–10 tie against Notre Dame in 1966, a total of seventeen black players started for Michigan State. One of the stars was wide receiver Gene Washington of La Porte, Texas, just seventy miles from Beaumont.

"All of the southern players were outcasts from our own states," Washington said. "All of the states we were from, they would not take black athletes. We bonded at Michigan State because we all had similar stories. We could make a contribution. That was very important to us. We didn't talk about it all of the time, but we knew we had something to prove."

Notre Dame–Michigan State became an instant Classic because it was a late-afternoon game on national TV. With Notre Dame going for the NCAA championship, an entire nation was watching.

"That was the game that started the coaches in the South thinking about recruiting the black athlete," Smith later recalled. "They couldn't ignore us anymore."

Smith thrived as a football player at Michigan State and loved the entire experience. Even so, he was homesick for Beaumont. Asked by a group of teammates to make a spring break trip to Florida, Bubba replied, "I'm going home to eat my mama's cooking."

After Smith left for MSU, the next great black athlete to leave Texas was Mel Farr, who was a three-year all-state player for Hebert High School. He signed with UCLA in the spring of '64 and would become a consensus All American. Farr and Smith would meet in the January 1, 1966, Rose Bowl. Thanks to Smith, the Spartans had not lost a game all season. But with Farr gaining 87 rushing yards, that streak ended. UCLA jumped to a 2-touchdown lead and won 14–12.

The question on everyone's mind back in Beaumont was this: Would LeVias follow Mel Farr to UCLA or Bubba Smith to Michigan State? It seemed certain that he would be rejected by the Southwest Conference.

That was before a tall man wearing aviator sunglasses walked onto the Hebert practice field in November of 1964.

Upon seeing the man approach, Ozen extended his hand and said, "Hello, Coach, damn glad to see you. I hope that you are serious about signing Jerry LeVias. This young man could really make a difference."

The wheels of progress were finally starting to roll.

6

Wunderkind

More than 150 miles north of Beaumont, Bill Bradley was making headlines across the entire state as a three-sport all-state player in Palestine. He threw right-handed, punted left-footed, and was a switch-hitting shortstop for the baseball team. The debate raged each day as to whether he should sign a football scholarship with the University of Texas or a baseball contract with the Detroit Tigers.

All of this chatter was nothing new. Bradley had been the focus of conversation in the barbershops and feed stores since he was in the fourth grade.

It all began when his elementary school principal picked up the phone and called the basketball coach at the middle school. Charles Ham had been watching the fourth grader dribble behind his back, between his legs, then spin and nail the 15-foot jumper. During recess, even Ham liked to play basketball with the talented kid.

Ham called Bob Knight at the middle school and said, "I'm sending this kid to practice with your team. He will be starting point in the first game he plays in. Hell, Bob, he's got All American written all over him."

At age ten, Bradley stood 4'8" and weighed 80 pounds. He was a head shorter than all of the players on the middle school team. Nevertheless, at one o'clock every afternoon, he was let out of the elementary school to walk to the middle school and practice with the seventh and eighth graders, a team of twelve- and thirteen-year-olds.

Just as Ham had predicted, Bradley starred at point guard on the middle school team as a fourth grader. He averaged 10 points a game. Knight was considered the roughest, toughest coach in Palestine. He reminded fans of the other. Bob Knight who would become famous coaching the Indiana basketball team beginning in 1971, Bob Knight of Palestine disciplined his players with a long, wooden paddle and loved to watch them play dodgeball. Seeing a boy take a ball to his face made him laugh. If two boys ever started to fight, he did not scold or punish them. He simply handed over the boxing gloves.

"He was a great coach for a kid like me," Bradley recalled. "Boy, he made you tough."

That Bradley was ready to play with the older boys at the age of ten was no surprise to his father, Joe Hill Bradley. From the day that William Calvin Bradley was born, on January 24, 1947, his dad worked overtime to make his son the best all-round athlete he could be. The elder Bradley had once dreamed of becoming a major leaguer, but it never worked out. Because his family needed another paycheck, Joe went to work for the railroad at age twelve. His father was a "horse-trader," a term for a wide-ranging deal-maker, in the tiny town of Dodge, Texas. He did not make enough money to support a family of ten children. Joe Hill Bradley spent as much time as he could on the baseball diamond, but it was not enough to impress the pro scouts. He was offered a few contracts, but the money was nominal and the assignment was Class A or lower.

At the age of eighteen, Joe Bradley decided to marry Mildred Pauline Rainey. They moved to Palestine, where Bill would be their second child. Every toy in Bill's crib was a ball. He would roll around the baseball and softball all day with both hands. Posing for his first infant photo, he bounced a basketball. The happy kid never stopped smiling.

Not long after Bill Bradley was delivered, the family noticed he was using both hands equally well. Joe and Mildred Bradley soon sought a specialist to determine if their son was ambidextrous. The doctor told the parents that if your brain is set left of center of the skull, you are right-handed. The opposite setting makes you left-handed. Bill Bradley's brain was perfectly centered. According to the doctor, the kid was ambidextrous, and that would come in handy for a kid with a love for the games.

When their son was two years old, Joe and Mildred Bradley would sit him down on the grass behind the baseball backstop and leave him there for the entirety of the game.

"They said I would sit there and watch every pitch," Bill said. "I wasn't jerking around or crying. I was loving every minute of it."

His older sister, May Bradley, recalled watching her brother through the picture window in the backyard playing baseball by himself. He would swat a wadded-up ball of aluminum foil with a plastic bat. Then he would carry his "ball" inside and dunk it over a curtain rod.

Like Bill Bradley, David Dickey was a sports star with great promise growing up in Palestine. Like all of the others, he played all sports year-round. He was a year older and a grade ahead of Bradley and was amazed at how quickly the kid learned the game of baseball.

"I was stealing home once when I was in Little League on a wild pitch from Bradley," Dickey recalled. "He took the throw from the catcher and put his glove right above the plate. He didn't reach out to tag me. He just left the glove there. And I remember thinking, 'Who taught him to do that?'"

The answer was Joe Bradley. When Joe returned home from his job during the summer months, father and son would roll up their sleeves and really go to work. In the family's backyard, the father was practically obsessed with teaching his son the nuances of the game: bunting, fielding grounders, and hitting the cutoff man. Until well past dark, they played pepper, a fast-paced game that involves a batter hitting short grounders to one or more fielders. The young boy grew up

Bill Bradley playing shortstop for the Palestine
Wildcats.

—Texas Sports Hall of Fame

throwing right-handed and hitting left-handed. By the time he reached Little League, he was a natural switch-hitter. Joe Bradley coached every baseball and softball team his son played on.

On his days off, Joe Bradley also coached baseball camps. Naturally, his able assistant was his young son.

"I was kind of like my dad's guinea pig," Bill recalled. "I already knew everything he was coaching other kids. So I was a natural for the job."

A kid growing up in Palestine in the 1950s and early 1960s had virtually no chance of seeing Major League Baseball in person. The closest team was the St. Louis Cardinals, 725 miles to the northeast. So the Bradleys listened to Harry Caray and Jack Buck broadcasting the Cardinals games on the radio. Occasionally, they watched the *Game of the Week* on Sundays, which usually involved the New York Yankees. Their games were aired about 80 percent of the time. It seemed that everyone in America was familiar with Mickey Mantle, Yogi Berra, Roger Maris, Whitey Ford, and Billy Martin.

Listening to the games on the radio or watching them on TV was not the same as being at the ballpark. Joe Bradley was so determined to expose his son to the Major Leagues that he purchased a train ticket for the twelve-year-old boy and sent him to St. Louis by himself to see the Cardinals play at Sportsman's Park.

"Most parents wouldn't have sent a kid my age that far on a train," Bill said, "but I knew the conductors, and it was a helluva lot of fun. In fact, it was the happiest day of my life."

Everyone in the small town was impressed with Joe Bradley's athletic gift. They knew he could still play the game. One summer, a traveling four-man fast-pitch softball team called "the King and His Court" came to town. The "King" was Eddie Feigner (pronounced *Fay*-ner) who threw a smoking underhanded fastball that was about the same speed as Nolan Ryan's during his heyday. Feigner's fastball came in so fast that he usually pitched from second base. He needed only three fielders because it was rare when the batter made contact. This miniteam was often featured on ABC's *Wide World of Sports*.

During a celebrity game, the "king" struck out Willie Mays, Willie Mc-Covey, Brooks Robinson, Roberto Clemente, and Harmon Killebrew, all in a row.

When he came to Palestine, he could not strike out Joe Bradley.

"Every grown man in Palestine wanted a crack at Eddie, and he gave them all a chance," Bill remembered. "My dad was the only one to get a hit."

Joe Bradley stroked a double into the left-field gap.

At age fifteen, Bill Bradley was introduced to semipro baseball by his father. But because of his amateur status, he was one of two players who did not get paid. The other was one of his best friends from Palestine High School, Danny Westmoreland. The team was composed of a wide mixture of talent. The college players returning home for the summer were trying to keep sharp. Many of the older guys in their thirties and forties were washed-up players from a Major League past. The level of play was close to AA quality. The Palestine Pals played every Saturday against all-black teams from Tyler, some fifty miles away.

"It was called the Watermelon League," Bill said. "We walked across a corn patch and through a farmer's gate to get to the baseball diamond. Let me tell you, it was straight out of *Field of Dreams*."

The Watermelon League was so named because the players ate watermelon and fried chicken between games. Remarkably, young Bradley was the best player on the Pals, and it did not go unnoticed by the baseball scouts. He could hit and field as well as anyone who suited up. The scouts were already starting to take notice.

By the time that Curtis Fitzgerald met Bradley in the seventh grade, he was already familiar with the legend. He had watched the fourth grader beat the middle school kids in every event the Palestine Rotary Track and Field Meet had to offer.

"When I met Bill, I just knew that he was running on a different fuel than the rest of us," Fitzgerald said. "I mean, he was an old pro when he was a little kid."

Fitzgerald and Bradley shared a seventh-grade home room. Each year, the winner of seventh-grade basketball intramurals played the champion eighth-grade team. The eighth graders were bigger and stronger than the younger boys. As coach of the seventh-grade team, Bradley needed to come up with a creative strategy.

On the morning of the big game, Bradley gathered the kids around him.

"Okay, fellas, this is what we're going to do. We're going to stall. That's right, hold the ball. If they can't get ahold of the ball, they can't score."

Bradley was copying the "Four Corners" offense that had been made famous by North Carolina coach Dean Smith. Because college basketball did not have a shot clock in that era, Smith was known to stall in the second half with a lead. Bradley, like many other kids, had seen it work on TV.

"One of the junior high coaches watched us play the game, and he laughed his ass off," Fitzgerald recalled. "We never took a shot unless it was a lay-up. Meanwhile, the eighth graders were so tired they had their tongues hanging out. And we beat them 8–7."

The townsfolk of Palestine often argued which sport was Bradley's best. The talk was that Joe Bradley was going to push his son toward Major League Baseball, but by the ninth grade, football was also becoming his game.

That was before Mildred Bradley stepped in. She decided that the football team could do without her son. He weighed barely a hundred pounds, and his mother believed he would need to grow a lot more to handle a physical game against boys that were fifty pounds heavier.

Fitzgerald knew that some arm-twisting would be required to get Bill back on the team. Mildred Bradley was a spirited woman who knew how to dig in her heels.

"When Mrs. Bradley decided to tell you what she thought, she *really* told you what she thought," Fitzgerald said. "It was pretty hard to change her mind when her mind was made up."

Fitzgerald rounded up the entire ninth-grade team, and together they walked several blocks to the Bradley home on Inwood Drive. When the twenty boys filed through the door, Mildred Bradley was standing in the middle of the living room with her arms crossed.

"You boys might as well go back to school," she said. "Bill is not playing any more football until he gets bigger. Given the fact he's not growing very fast, I doubt he will ever play football again."

Fitzgerald almost got down on his knees. "Mrs. Bradley, will you at least hear us out?" he asked.

"You've got fifteen minutes," she said.

Four hours later, she finally relented. The mother of the best little athlete in Palestine could not believe the testimonials.

"With Bill on our team, we've got a chance to make it all the way to state, Fitzgerald said Without him, we've got no chance. Mrs. Bradley, we've never made it past the first round of the playoffs. Shoot, we haven't won district in football since 1948."

Bradley's teammates loved him. They were so in awe that they often found themselves watching him instead of carrying out their own assignments. He stood only 5'6", but was dunking a basketball in the ninth grade.

"Bill Bradley was the most complete athlete that I ever saw," David Dickey said. "He was the field general in baseball, football, and basketball. Bill Bradley was everything."

If high school track had offered the decathlon in that era, Bradley might have been the best in America. He pole-vaulted, high-jumped, and ran the sprints and the hurdles. Bradley loved to "psych" the competition in the high jump. For the first several rounds, he would not even take off his warm-up suit, choosing instead to pass as the bar went up and up. He would wait until one or two competitors remained before he jumped. There were a few meets when he did not even remove his warm-ups and still cleared the bar with ease. This was several years before the "Fosbury Flop" backward over the bar was popularized, and high jumpers were still using the "straddle technique," going over the bar facing downward. Bradley cleared 6'4" to win the state AAA events for two straight years.

By his tenth-grade season in football, Bradley had moved into the starting lineup and went both ways. Fans were suddenly hopeful that the Wildcats would win the District 7-AAA title for the first time since 1958. They had failed to win a state championship in '58 in spite of having perhaps the best athlete in Texas playing halfback. His name was James Saxton, and in 1959 he would become the No. 1 recruit of coach Darrell Royal at Texas, where he would win All-American honors in 1961 and vie for the Heisman Trophy.

As a sophomore, Bradley was the second coming of Saxton. He played offense and defense, punted, kicked off, and booted extra points and field goals. He also returned kickoffs and punts. He teamed with David Dickey to form the best backfield in District 7-AAA. Unfortunately, Dickey broke his wrist in the second game of the 1962 season, and the Wildcats again missed the playoffs.

In Bradley's junior year of '63, the Wildcats lost their opening game to Lufkin from the AAAA ranks, one higher than Palestine. Then they lost to Corsicana, led by all-state running back Jim Hagle, by the score of 27–7.

In the third game, against Nacogdoches, the Dragons assigned three defensive players to Dickey. Bradley carried the load of the offense, accounting fot 4 touchdowns, 2 passing and 2 running. Palestine won 28–14 to start a seven-game winning streak. The Wildcats had plenty of fun along the way. Against Henderson, Dickey was going in for a touchdown and had one foot already across the goal line when Bradley snatched the ball from behind and carried it into the end zone. For good measure, Bradley kicked the extra point.

"That was just Bradley being Bradley," Dickey said.

The district title game would come down to Palestine versus Jacksonville. The archrivals met every year in the season finale and this time they would play at Jacksonville's home stadium, known as the Tomato Bowl.

Jacksonville grabbed a 6–0 lead, but Dickey returned a punt 75 yards for a touchdown, and Bradley kicked the extra point for the 7–6 victory. For the first time in fifteen years, the Wildcats had won the

District 7-AAA championship. They would meet Corsicana in the bi-district round.

Corsicana won the coin toss. Hagle, who haunted the Wildcats in the second game of the season, returned the kickoff 90 yards for a touchdown. After the ensuing kickoff, a fumble at the 20-yard line by Jerry Reeder led to another Corsicana touchdown and a 14–0 lead.

Bradley then intercepted a pass and sprinted 26 yards into the end zone, but he was flagged for pass interference and the touchdown was voided. "It was a clean interception all the way," Dickey remembered. "Besides, how could there be pass interference when you intercept the ball?"

Both Bradley and Dickey scored touchdowns, but Corsicana won the game 21–14.

"I swear that if we had not lost the coin toss, we would have won the state championship that year," Dickey said. "Hagle beat us with that kickoff return to start the game."

As fate would have it, Corsicana rolled all the way to the state title game and defeated Pharr–San Juan–Alamo 7–0.

With Dickey graduating and accepting a football scholarship to the University of Arkansas, Palestine fans wondered if the Wildcats would ever win a state title. They would have one more crack at it with Bradley.

7

"Hard Drinking Railroad Man"

Growing up in Palestine was a rough-and-tumble experience for Bill Bradley. His father was a good provider, role model, and great coach for a sports-obsessed kid. However, working as a dispatcher for the Missouri Pacific Railroad, Joe Bradley was suspended three times because of train wrecks with casualties. Each time, the Bradley family was forced to move into a smaller house with a lower monthly rent.

"My dad always covered for the engineers," his son said. "If there was a major wreck, especially on a passenger train, my dad would take the blame. That's just the way he was. He didn't want the engineers getting in trouble."

It was no coincidence that Joe Bradley's three brothers were engineers. The Bradleys were a tight-knight family. They had stuck together since childhood, growing up poor in East Texas. They all took railroad jobs as baggage handlers about the same time.

Palestine might have been a small town, but there was nothing undersized about the railroad work. Palestine was a hub for the Missouri Pacific line, linking Houston to St. Louis. Night and day, the locomotives rumbled and the whistles blew. The switching stations were often crisscrossing madhouses. Fast-moving trains required split-second decisions. The railroad dispatcher was the equivalent of an air traffic controller. Stress could be overbearing. In the early 1950s, Joe Bradley communicated with the engineers through Morse code. The job got a little easier years later when they began to work with two-way radios. Still, unlike a traffic cop, Joe Bradley could not see the traffic he was directing. He operated in constant turbulence. The smallest error could lead to disaster.

Railroad people in that day were known for their binge drinking, and, away from work, Joe Bradley was no exception.

"My dad was a hard-drinking railroad man," Bradley said. "But, hell, all the railroad people drank because of stress."

When the workday was over, it seemed, every grown man who lived within walking distance of the Bradley home liked to drink.

The Baptists still ruled Palestine in an era when the county was dry. The locals leaned on two bootleggers. Sug Gaines, who weighed close to 400 pounds, worked the downtown area. He kept pint bottles hidden in a long coat, even during the hot summer months. Pat Morris's territory covered rural Palestine. Because the two men never infringed on each other's turf, peace existed among the bootleggers.

"We all lived within about two blocks of the other side of the tracks," Fitzgerald said. "People didn't mind spending their paychecks on whiskey."

Bradley recalled, "Our parents were good, hard-working people. They just liked to drink."

This did not mean that Joe Bradley did not love his family and his community.

"My daddy liked everybody, and everybody liked him," said Bill's sister, May. "He also loved us all. There was not a night when he did not come up in my bedroom to kiss his daughter good night."

Growing up in Palestine was not always easy. Curtis Fitzgerald barely knew his dad. Otis Ray Fitzgerald was in prison on the day Curtis was born. He was rarely a free man. Otis Ray robbed a store in nearby Athens and went straight to the Big House. During his appeal, he was locked up in the county jail. The sheriff happened to be Otis Ray's cousin. As it turned out, Otis possessed a sense of humor. He managed to break out of jail while locking the sheriff behind bars. His final act was to steal the key.

"He did a lot of time for that one because he was convicted of stealing government property," Curtis said.

Otis Ray once stole more than $100,000 from a high-end poker game in Galveston. After playing in the game around the clock for two days, he stood up and brandished a pistol. Otis Ray took off for Beaumont with the bag of money. Along the way, he opened the bag and, to his dismay, discovered that more than $80,000 of his loot was in IOUs.

A few years later, Otis Ray finally saw the light and took a job on an oil rig off the Galveston coast. He regularly brought home large sums of money.

"His boss told me that my dad was the best derrick man he'd ever had," Curtis said, "but the workers were playing craps during the breaks, and my dad was winning all of their paychecks. So his boss had to fire him."

When Otis Ray went back to prison for a long stretch, Valley Lee Fitzgerald divorced her husband and decided to remarry. Sadly, she wed yet another alcoholic, who turned out to be violent.

"He beat my mother," Curtis said. "It seemed that every day I was either trying to kill my stepdaddy or he was trying to kill me."

Little wonder that Curtis spent most of his time at the Bradley home.

"Bill was much more than a friend to me," Fitzgerald said. "He was my brother. Plus, I loved Joe Bradley like a father."

Everyone knew, though, there were times to stay out of Joe Bradley's way. The neighborhood boys were playing in the Bradley backyard one afternoon as Joe Bradley watched the 1964 World Series between the New York Yankees and the St. Louis Cardinals on the family's brand-new television. The boys could hear Joe ranting and raving and cursing the TV. Joe was a lifelong fan of the St. Louis Cardinals, having listened to their games on radio since childhood. It was a rare treat to see the Cardinals on TV, but with the World Series tied 3–3 and headed into Game Seven, Joe was feeling an inordinate amount of stress. On top of that, his new Sylvania TV was on the blink.

"There was a horizontal line in the picture," Curtis recalled. "Mr. Bradley was drinking beer and getting madder by the minute. He would get up to adjust the TV, then go back to drinking his beer. Then all of the sudden we heard a loud *Ka-bloom*! Mr. Bradley shot out the TV."

He had pulled out a .410 shotgun from the closet and blown the picture tube to pieces.

Joe Bradley was not the only hard-drinking man in the neighborhood. Some people thought that hard-running fullback Jerry Reeder developed a stutter because his dad was an alcoholic.

Fitzgerald said, "I hung around with Bill and Eddie Bentley and Jerry Reeder. All of our fathers drank. We became a support group for each other."

The boys in the Bradley neighborhood developed a tough hide for many reasons. They all started competing in organized sports in the first grade and by the sixth grade were working various jobs.

"I started paying Social Security when I was twelve years old working a farm," Bradley said. "I got only twenty-five dollars a week, and they still withheld Social Security. I hauled hay and dug ditches, just like a lot of the kids."

Upon reaching high school, they were hardened and ready to compete. Coach Luke Thornton told the *Palestine Herald-Press*, "My Palestine boys are tough. I really don't believe there is a tougher group of players pound-for-pound any place else in Texas."

Ethel Reed, a secretary in the school district's administration offices, came up with a sign to prove it. Placed above the locker room door, it read, THROUGH THIS DOOR PASS THE TOUGHEST BOYS IN THE STATE OF TEXAS.

To understand the toughness of the Palestine boys was to know the steely resolve of Curtis Wayne Fitzgerald. In the years ahead, Fitzgerald would enlist in army aviation. In 1968, young men across America were dodging Vietnam in every way imaginable. The stories of atrocities in the war zones were widely told. American casualties peaked at 16,589 in '68. To avoid being drafted into the army, a college friend of Fitzgerald's had blown off his right big toe with a shotgun blast.

Unlike some of the others, Fitzgerald did not hesitate to answer the call of duty. After his football career was cut short as a wingback for Arlington State College, he went off to helicopter school and was soloing after his ninth flight. With the war escalating, pilots were forced to learn fast.

"I enlisted because a couple of my buddies had been killed over there," Fitzgerald recalled. "I still don't know why I chose to go to helicopter school. Hell, I'd never flown anything bigger than a model airplane in my whole life."

After a few weeks of training, Fitzgerald was headed into a hell like no other.

"War is a lot like football," Fitzgerald recalled. "In football, you get hit in the head and you loosen up and you're fine. In war, you get shot at and all of the adrenaline is flowing and you feel better. My attitude in combat came a lot from my football-playing days. The night before a big football game, you were nervous and you can't sleep. The night before a dangerous mission, I could not sleep at all. War, of course, is far more serious. But the night before a big game, I was nervous as hell, too."

In February of 1969, Fitzgerald's aircraft set down in the Central Highlands of South Vietnam. He was prepared to transport supplies and to fly rescue missions in an area where the heaviest action was going down. He had chosen one of the most dangerous assignments the war had to offer. He was ready to fight and die for his country.

Fitzgerald was stationed in Pleiku, situated in the rugged mountains of the so-called tri-country area, close to the borders of Laos and Cambodia. He and the other pilots of the 189th Army Assault Helicopter Company, "the Ghost Riders," were mostly responsible for transporting the Special Forces known as Green Berets into battle and back. Most were camped in nearby Dak To.

His first few weeks in Vietnam were spent in menial tasks. Fitzgerald found time to help out at a nearby orphanage run by a couple of French nuns. The nuns needed money to vaccinate the kids against smallpox and polio. So Fitzgerald pilfered a few bucks from the poker pots and asked for donations from his fellow pilots. The kids were vaccinated, and everything was running smoothly at the orphanage.

One afternoon, his radio blared, "Fitzgerald, you need to get over to the orphanage fast." Then came sobbing sounds from the radio.

Vietcong soldiers had learned that the orphanage was receiving American assistance. As revenge, they stormed the school and amputated both arms of each orphan. When Fitzgerald arrived, most of the kids were impaled on bamboo sticks. A young girl was sticking straight up from an iron spike jutting from the top of the front gate.

Fitzgerald sobbed uncontrollably. Then he began the somber task of burying the dead.

The American pilot knew he would never be the same. He had once been an outspoken opponent of water torture for enemy soldiers. A type of "waterboarding" took place every day at his camp for the purpose of forcing the Vietcong to reveal secret information. Soldiers were dunked in a 55-gallon drum, then held beneath the water until they felt a drowning sensation. It was enough to make anyone say anything.

Fitzgerald quickly changed his stance on water torture after witnessing the atrocities at the orphanage. The next day, he was helping to push "Charlie," a nickname for the Vietcong soldiers, beneath the water and holding them there.

Fitzgerald was so angry that he awoke each morning ready to fight. He would roar off into battle hoping to kill all of the VC in his sights. He carried a hatred in his heart that he had never experienced before.

Every spring, more than twenty thousand Vietcong streamed along the Ho Chi Minh Trail and crossed the border from Cambodia into South Vietnam. The plan was to cut the country in half. These battlas would inspire Hollywood to produce movies like *We Were Soldiers* and *Hamburger Hill*.

Fitzgerald's introduction to this gruesome chaos came in the middle of May of 1969. Staged in the jungle-shrouded area known as the "mountain of the crouching beast," the battle at "Hamburger Hill" would emerge as one of the most famous in the war.

From dawn until nightfall, Fitzgerald and his crew shuttled soldiers—dead or alive—back to the base at Dak To. Some of the bodies from the napalm-scorched hill had been lying around for days. Little wonder that the featured song of the movie *Hamburger Hill* was "We Gotta Get Out of This Place." The first sight of the bullet-riddled bodies with maggots crawling from the blackened skin caused Fitzgerald to vomit on his lap.

"These were the first dead Americans I'd ever seen," he remembered. "They'd been exposed to the heat for two or three days, and they were bursting from the sun. They smelled like dead animals. It was a horrible odor that I carried with me for the rest of my life."

So steep was "the Hill" that Fitzgerald actually flew sideways, keeping the skids so close to the hill that they were scraping the embankment. From below, U.S. Army soldiers tossed the dead bodies into the belly of the helicopter. The aircraft was so weighted down that Fitzgerald was forced to slow, then hover before flying away. Each day, the cockpit was riddled with bullets, and the pilot knew how lucky he was to be alive.

On the ninth day of Hamburger Hill, his luck ran out. That morning, the Vietcong fired into the engine compressor. The aircraft began to spin. Fitzgerald radioed for help.

"We're going to need somebody to pick us up pretty quick," he said. "No. Check that. We're going to need a chopper *now*."

As they rose into the smoky sky, a barrage of bullets pierced the fuel tank and gasoline spewed in all directions.

"As we lost fuel, the helicopter actually flew better because it was lighter," Fitzgerald recalled. "But we eventually crashed and needed a ride from another helicopter."

It was the first time he had been shot down. As the young pilot would say, "I lost my cherry that day at Hamburger Hill."

Due to the scarcity of experienced pilots, Fitzgerald got all of the action he wanted, and then some. One of the major obstacles of rescuing soldiers was the mind-boggling height of the trees. Fitzgerald was one of the first pilots to discover that the blades of the helicopter could be transformed into a weed-eater. After setting the helicopter down in the tops of the trees, the pilot would chop away until he was within 100 to 150 feet of the ground. Then the crew would drop the ropes to the ground and hook the American infantrymen trying to escape the Vietcong.

In some cases, no more than six or seven Green Berets were sent into the jungle to battle five hundred Vietcong soldiers. Most of the time, they came away with ten times more casualties.

"It was the craziest bunch of guys I'd ever seen," he said. "They'd ambush the Cong and then come running. I'd hear them over the radio yelling, 'We're in a shitload of trouble, Curtis! Come get us!'"

Landing Zones barely existed, so the only option would be to chop away at the tall timber. With his hands firmly on the cyclic and the collective sticks, and his feet on the rudder, Fitzgerald's task was to lock his eyes on a single object to keep the aircraft from moving even one inch. During one mission, his right hamstring began to cramp, so he asked the rookie copilot named Mike Renfro to take over.

"Things were getting pretty hairy," Fitzgerald said. "So I looked over at Mike and he was throwing up in his helmet."

Suddenly, they were under heavy fire. Fitzgerald heard a scream behind him and turned to see his door gunner naked in a state of horror.

The crew chief yelled, "Hell, he's all right. All they did was blow his f—— clothes off."

Upon arriving back at the base in Dak To, Fitzgerald was tagged with a new nickname, "Woodchopper Six." His company commander, George Morgan, said, "You have managed to turn a perfectly good machine into a wood chopper." His punishment that day was to replace the rotors, that happened to weigh 6,000 pounds apiece. The task took all night, and Fitzgerald was up and flying the next morning on no sleep.

Shot down four times, Fitzgerald found himself at a crossroads when his Vietnam tour of duty ended after twelve months. Most sane men would have happily hopped a C-130 out of Vietnam, but Fitzgerald looked around at the dwindling number of talented and experienced pilots in his platoon and felt a sense of duty. The average age of the twenty-two airmen in his camp was nineteen.

Instead of abandoning so many novices, he decided to sign on for six more months. Most of the pilots possessed fewer than a hundred in-country flying hours, meaning they would be doomed to disaster. It was widely accepted that you needed three hundred hours of in-country flying to shift into the pilot's seat. If Fitzgerald shipped out, there would be two rookies flying together. Moreover, the company commander and executive officer had been relieved of duty, leaving the group with no leadership. Fitzgerald was promoted to captain and company commander. He knew the burden resting on his shoulders those final six months in Vietnam would be heavier than the Kon Plong Plateau.

The morning of April 3 came catastrophically close to removing that burden. That day, Fitzgerald led a brigade of choppers into one of the bloodiest battles of the war. His crew was attempting to resupply a Special Forces camp called Dak Seang, not far from his home base of Pleiku. For the second straight year, the North Vietnamese at twenty thousand strong were pouring into the Central Highlands. He had been shot down a year earlier trying to resupply the same camp. The odds would not be in his favor.

The North Vietnamese soldiers he faced were the real bad guys. Dressed in olive drab uniforms, they were not the usual amateurs in their black pajamas. This mission would require the guts that only Fitzgerald could muster. He flew through smoke and fire as hundreds of bullets penetrated his windshield and pinged about the cockpit. Suddenly, one of his best friends in another helicopter was shot down, and his mission escalated into an emergency rescue.

Fitzgerald's chopper was under such heavy fire from the NVA machine guns that he called for more air strikes. As he slid along the ridge of hill, his UH-1 "Huey" was catching enemy fire from above and below. He considered aborting, but said out loud, "F—— it, those are my friends down there." He made a low pass as the bullets broke through the windshield. He caught brass shrapnel in both sides of his neck. A bullet ripped through his right shoulder. As the turbo engine began leaking fuel, he heard the voice of fellow pilot Mike Renfro over the radio. "Fitz, you are on fire!"

He shifted his .38 revolver into his lap to protect his testicles from shrapnel. Every red light on the dashboard was lit. It was all he could do to keep the bird in the air. He headed for a bomb crater with grass growing high around it. One of the rotors tore loose as the chopper spun sideways and landed squarely in the crater. The *ping-ping-ping* stopped, but only for a few seconds.

"Mayday! Mayday! We are down in some heavy shit. We need a ride. Fast!"

Job one for Fitzgerald was to get his fellow pilot to safety. He and the two crew members dragged him into the high grass of the bomb crater. Again Fitzgerald called for backup, and a helicopter soon arrived. Instead of running for the rescue aircraft, he stayed behind and provided cover for his three men. He had set up M-60 machine guns at both ends of the bunker. He was also armed with an M-16 and an M-79 grenade launcher.

Fitzgerald spent most of his time running from one end of the bunker to the other, firing off the machine guns, hoping to slow the enemy. He was sorely outmanned and regretted not boarding the rescue chopper. He radioed for more help and received no response. He knew that the choppers thropping above were loaded with men and supplies. They were not coming to help him anytime soon.

This is the biggest mistake I've ever made in my life . . .

Then he heard a friendly voice over the radio. It was one of his best friends, fellow pilot William Day.

"Fitz, we are loaded, but I will be there in a minute. We won't be there long. I'm going to touch the skids, so you'd better be there."

Fitzgerald could hear the chattering of a Vietnamese colonel in the copilot's seat. He was protesting the rescue effort. May responded, "F—— you and shut up. I'm going in to get my friend."

Fitzgerald also heard the voice of an American colonel demanding that May not attempt the rescue. He said to himself, "I will get even with that sonofabitching colonel someday."

In the blink of an eye, Fitzgerald turned just in time to see one of the bad guys swing an SKS rifle at his head. He hurdled the soldier as the rifle caught him on the ankle. Both fell and began to wrestle in the high grass. The American pulled his survival knife from his belt and swung it into the belly of the enemy. He ripped him all the way up into his sternum and heard the man take his last breath. He yanked hard, but the knife was stuck in the gristle and would not come loose. He pulled again and again until he finally said to himself, "They will give you another knife, dummy."

He rose to his feet, and the race was on. The rescue helicopter was 5 feet above the ground and dropping fast. With several Vietcong soldiers chasing him, and bullets flying over his head, the wingback from East Texas tore out for the goal line as the clock wound down. He was running so fast when he reached the helicopter that he forgot to stop. Both of his thighs slammed into the bottom edge of the door. He was suddenly racked with a burning pain.

"I'm shot, I'm shot," he yelled. He turned over to check for blood. "Wait a second. I'm not, I'm not. I just hit the damn side of the helicopter."

Three crew members scrambled to pull him on board. He rose to his feet as the helicopter ascended rapidly into the smoke-filled sky. He turned to see the dozens of soldiers who had been firing at him moments earlier. For good measure, he grabbed an M-16 and fired downward at the green-clad men, hitting absolutely nothing.

One of the perks of being a captain and company commander was that he could catch a flare ship to happy hour at the naval air base about two miles away. The officers' bar was stocked with premium Scotch, bourbond and vodka, along with an assortment of what he called "round-eye nurses."

The clock had just struck ten and Fitzgerald was about two steps from the bedroom door of one of the American women when his radio blared, "Captain Fitzgerald! Captain Fitzgerald, we need you back at the base immediately. They are *here*."

Minutes later, after a quick flight home, he stumbled into a room filled with army generals wearing from one to three stars. His eyes could barely comprehend what he was seeing. Not a single general had ever visited his post. It did not help that he was drunk and steadying himself on one of the walls.

"Just like the movies, they pulled out the tripod with the maps of Cambodia," he said. "They instantly told me that this mission was top secret and that I would be the liaison from the Army Assault Helicopter Company. Yes, I was drunk. And what they were telling me seemed impossible."

Days earlier, President Richard M. Nixon had ordered the invasion of Cambodia. On April 30, as Nixon publicly announced his controversial decision, Captain Fitzgerald filled some huge shoes. He became the air mission commander who led hundreds of helicopters across the border. Millions of Americans watched on live TV. Over three days, Fitzgerald's air brigade delivered fifteen thousand troops into action.

It would the crowning achievement of a great career. With his head held high, "Captain Fitz" boarded a plane back to the States. He would become one of the most-decorated soldiers in the history of the war. For his bravery at Dak Seang on April 3, 1970, he won a Silver Star and a Purple Heart. He also picked up three Distinguished Flying Crosses, three Bronze Stars, and nineteen Air Medals. In 2008, he was honored at the Texas Capitol in Austin with a proclamation from U.S. Congressman Jeb Hensarling, a Republican from Dallas.

In part, Hensarling's proclamation read, "One of the greatest perks I receive as a congressman is to give honor and recognition to people like Curtis Fitzgerald. I don't do this just because it feels good. If I don't do it, I am derelict in my duties."

8

In Search of a State Title

On December 12, 1964, Curtis Fitzgerald was visibly frustrated as he paced the sideline in the most disappointing game of his life. His right arm was broken below the shoulder and already fitted for an Aircast. Palestine trailed Wichita Falls Hirschi High School 23–0 in the state semifinals with ten minutes to play. The Hirschi fans were already celebrating, and why not. The great Bill Bradley was having trouble throwing completions with either hand, thanks to 4 dropped balls.

Making matters worse was the early departure of Texas coach Darrell Royal from the stadium. Two hours earlier, the Palestine fans were thrilled to see Royal walking into the press box with kickoff approaching. They knew he had come to scout "their boy." Watching the legendary coach descending the aluminum stairs early in the fourth quarter was as deflating as his arrival had been exciting. With Palestine losing by more than 3 touchdowns, Royal had seen enough. He had chosen to beat the traffic out of Arlington for the two-hundred-mile drive back to Austin.

As the Longhorns coach headed toward the exit, Bradley saw the Hirschi fans clapping him on the back and offering scraps of paper. Royal was a deity in Texas, having won the national championship the previous season, along with 39 of his last 41 games. The Longhorns would travel to Miami in three weeks to play Alabama, coached by

As a high school quarterback in 1964 with the state champion Palestine Wildcats.

—*Texas Sports Hall of Fame*

Paul "Bear" Bryant and quarterbacked by Joe Willie Namath, in the Orange Bowl.

Bradley felt heartbroken as he watched Royal leave. He stepped into the huddle and said, "Coach Royal is gone and our fans are booking next. Five thousand of 'em traveled all the way from Palestine just to see us punch our ticket to the state championship game. Hell, boys, we need a touchdown."

Bradley knew it would be virtually impossible to pull off a comeback without his favorite receiver, Curtis Fitzgerald. On the final play of the first half, Fitzgerald had broken his arm while trying to intercept a pass. The helmet of teammate Mike Meyer had torpedoed into his upper arm, and Fitzgerald heard the bone pop.

En route to the locker room at halftime, the team was forced to walk along the edge of the stands of the Hirschi rooting section. An inebriated woman spotted Fitzgerald and began battering him about the head with her umbrella.

"You little sonofabitch, serves you right that you broke your damn arm," she said. "Serves you right to suffer, boy."

If not for the fast work of team manager Jim Flanagan, she might have broken the other arm. Flanagan grabbed Fitzgerald and pushed him toward the locker room.

Fitzgerald was examined by Palestine's team physician Dr. Bob Burns, who quickly determined that the humerus bone was fractured. From the elbow to the shoulder, his upper arm had already turned deep purple and was swollen.

"You need to go straight to the hospital," Burns said. "Your arm looks like a gut-shot deer."

"Ah, Doc, I want to hang around and the watch the game."

The doctor paused, then said, "Well, okay—but you go straight to the hospital when you get back to Palestine."

Fitzgerald stood on the sideline in the third quarter, watching Hirschi run all over the Wildcats. He noticed another doctor walking toward him. This time, it was Dr. Leroy Mathis wondering why Fitzgerald had not left for the hospital. Observing his agitated body language from the stands, Dr. Mathis knew that the hard-nosed player was about to bolt onto the field without asking his coach. Dr. Mathis could attest to Curtis's toughness, having known him since childhood.

"Come on, Curtis, let's go to the locker room and look at that arm again," he said.

As Mathis rolled up the jersey, he looked through the clear plastic and shook his head. "You need to go straight to the hospital," he said.

"Ah, Doc, I want to stay and watch the game," Fitzgerald said.

"I'm against that," the doctor said, "but we're going into the fourth quarter. Curtis, dammit, don't try to go back into the game. I'm leaving right now so I can meet you at Palestine Methodist. When the bus gets back, go straight to the hospital."

"Yes, sir, I will."

Returning to the sideline, Fitzgerald was approached by coach Luke Thornton.

"What did the doctor say?"

With a straight face, Fitzgerald replied, "Coach, the doc said I *don't* have a broken arm. He said I can go right back in the game."

The coach smiled, squeezed the Aircast, and said, "Hell, boy, get your butt back in there."

There was no time to waste. Curtis sprinted toward the huddle, popping and then shredding the Aircast as he ran. Pieces of plastic littered the ground, leaving a trail of tidbits. The Palestine crowd cheered wildly.

Bradley put up his right hand like a stop sign as Fitzgerald approached the huddle. "Fitz, get the hell out of here."

"It's okay, Bradley," he said. "The doc cleared me to play."

"Bullshit."

"Well, he really didn't—but Coach thinks he did."

The best friends shared a hearty laugh. Then Bradley stepped back into the huddle and said, "Okay, fellas, we've got to figure a way to win this game. We're down 23–zip. The call is X-right, V-slant. Curtis, look for the ball quick. It's coming to you."

·   ·   ·

The top-ranked Palestine Wildcats had started the season with a shocking loss to Athens High by an even more shocking score of 28–7. In the preseason polls, they had been the unanimous selection as the No. 1 AAA team in the state. Against Athens, Bradley had completed only 2 passes for 12 yards as the offense bumbled and stumbled all over the field. The next week, the Wildcats tumbled all the way to seventh in the statewide polls.

Palestine then clicked off wins of 26–8 over Terrell and 34–6 against Ennis but fell behind 7–0 early in the 7-AAA district opener against Henderson. With the Wildcats trailing 7–6 in the fourth quarter and continuing to struggle on offense, Fitzgerald halted one Henderson drive with an interception at the Palestine 5-yard line, then returned another for the winning touchdown. The Wildcats won 14–7.

As the season progressed, and the offense struggled, Bradley decided to start changing a few of the plays called by his coach. Between downs, an angry Thornton would walk several yards onto the field and yell, "Dammit, Bradley, stop changing my plays."

In the huddle Fitzgerald would grin and say, "Pay no attention to him. Your plays are working. His aren't."

Against the Center High Roughriders, Bradley passed for 2 touchdowns and ran for another as the Wildcats rolled to a 34–0 victory. The senior quarterback continued to find his passing rhythm against Kilgore, and the Wildcats won 28–16. Bradley mixed in running plays for the thick-legged Jerry Reeder. In spite of his bulk, Reeder ran the 100-yard dash in 9.9 seconds and was the anchor leg on the 440-yard relay team.

Late in the season, Bradley was developing into the one-man show that everyone had hoped he would become. When it came to passing, running, and punting, he was in the top 5 statistically statewide in all three categories. Fans were beginning to sense that this would finally be their championship year.

Bradley's feats were being written about on a regular basis in the newspapers of Dallas, located about a hundred miles to the northwest. Legendary sportswriter Blackie Sherrod had written columns about two of Bradley's games for the *Dallas Times Herald*. Sherrod also happened to be one of the closest friends of Darrell Royal, and let it be known that Bradley's best collegiate choice would be the University of Texas.

When a player like Bradley gains such notoriety so early in life, problems often develop within the team structure. The cutest girls in school followed Bradley around on the streets of Palestine. His photo was on the cover of the *Palestine Herald-Press* sports section practically every day. Even so, his teammates said the attention never went to his head.

Palestine tackle and fellow senior Bob Stephenson recalled, "I watched Bill every second of the day from the time we hit Little League baseball. We played football and basketball together through our senior years. Usually, when one guy gets all the attention, like Bill, you get jealous. I was never jealous of Bill Bradley. To us, he was the ultimate team man."

After Kilgore, the Palestine defense registered its second shutout in three weeks, defeating Pine Tree 8–0. Bradley scored the game's only touchdown on a 10-yard sprint-out. Next was the biggest game of the year against archrival Jacksonville in the annual Tomato Bowl. Fueling the hate between the teams was the distance of only thirty-five miles between the schools.

Thornton asked Bradley to give the pregame pep talk.

"Look," Bradley began. "There's nobody we hate more than the damn Jacksonville Indians. We're going to whip their asses, then steal their girlfriends."

The offense faltered in the first half, and Jacksonville led 7–0 at the intermission. Then the Palestine offense started to motor on the stout legs of Reeder. Behind 7–0 with four minutes to play, the do-or-die drive began at the Wildcats 29-yard line. Bradley patiently milked the clock with short bursts by Reeder and quick hits to Fitzgerald. With less than a minute to play, Reeder powered his way into the end zone and the Wildcats trailed 7–6.

From the start of the season, the Wildcats had chosen to forego the extra point kick, opting instead for the 2-point conversion. They had been successful about 90 percent of the time. Bradley's favorite call on the 2-pointer was the high alley-oop pass to tight end Bob Stephenson, who, at 6'2", was a giant for the times. Stephenson could barely jump more than two or three inches, but his outstretched hands were usually too high for the shorter defenders.

Bradley stepped into the huddle and said, "Bob, I'm going to you." Stephenson calmly drawled, "No, Bill, give the ball to the man who got us here."

So Bradley handed off once more to Reeder at right tackle, and he powered his way into the end zone for the 2-pointer. Palestine had managed to defeat Jacksonville 8–7.

That night, Wildcats captured their second straight district title and finished the regular season with an 8-1 record. It was their fourth district title in the history of the school, dating to its opening in 1915. The first championship came in 1922. Not once, however, had the Wildcats ever advanced past the first round of the playoffs.

What they faced next was the game of the year—a rematch with Athens in the bi-district game. Once again it became evident that Bradley was the best all-round player in Texas. He ran and passed the ball, punted, returned kickoffs, handled the kickoffs, and was the best safety in Texas. He played every minute and second of every game. Against Athens in a scoreless tie, Bradley fielded a punt at the Palestine 37 and began snaking his way through the tacklers. He burst into the open field at the Athens 40 and would have reached the end zone if he had not briefly stumbled and been pushed out of bounds at the 3-yard line by Athens's Dwain Kirksey. Three plays later, Bradley pitched to Ronnie Jones around end for the touchdown, then passed to Stephenson for the 2-pointer for the 8–0 lead.

At that point, Thornton decided to forsake the pass, and Palestine's running game began to chew up the clock. It was the fourth shutout by the Palestine defense.

In the state quarterfinals, more than 3,000 fans traveled a hundred miles to Mesquite for the game. They saw the Wildcats breeze past Bonham 22–0 as Bradley passed 6 yards for a touchdown and set up another with a 35-yard interception return to the 5. He alley-ooped the 2-point conversion pass to Stephenson. Jerry Reeder returned an interception 72 yards for the final score.

Palestine was electric following the Bonham victory. An editorial in the *Palestine Herald-Press* read, "This issue of the Herald-Press is an illustration of a spontaneous surge of community backing of the very fine youth of Palestine High School."

The following Saturday would be the most historic day in the small East Texas town. Palestine would meet undefeated Wichita Falls Hirschi at Arlington State College, situated in the midcities between Dallas and Fort Worth.

With 10:46 showing on the scoreboard clock and Palestine trailing Wichita Falls Hirschi 23–0, Bradley hit a quick-slanting Fitzgerald and the wingback broke three tackles, sprinting to the Hirschi 13-yard line. He pumped both arms wildly along the way, showing total disregard for his fractured arm. His miraculous recovery had provided the Wildcats with a fresh shot of adrenaline. The 43-yard gain triggered a blast of energy through the stadium that was palpable. The Palestine fans were on their feet and shouting at the top of their lungs once more.

On the next play, fullback Jerry Reeder carried twice to the 4-yard line, and Bradley sprinted around right end for the touchdown. His looping pass to the outstretched fingertips of Stephenson cut the lead to 23–8.

Fitzgerald continued to play like a youngster with two good arms.

"When you are seventeen years old, you believe that you are bulletproof," he later said. "Hell, you think you can jump tall buildings."

The Wildcats needed to cover 81 yards on the next drive. Bradley fired over the middle to Fitzgerald, who caught the ball at midfield and broke three tackles, going all the way to the 29 for a gain of 52 yards. Bradley sent John Ballard McDonald down the sideline and heaved a tall, arcing pass into the end zone. Bradley knew overshot the receiver, but McDonald hauled it in at the back line. Bradley to Stephenson for the 2-point conversion cut the lead to 23–16.

The defense held on three downs, and Bradley returned the punt 25 yards to the Wildcats 35-yard line. The Hirschi fans had grown silent. On the next play, Reeder bolted straight up the middle as McDonald knocked down two defenders with one block, clearing a wide path at midfield. The sound from the Palestine side of the field was like the roar of a train. The Wildcats had missed only three 2-point conversions all season, and this one would provide a 1-point lead. This time, Bradley's pass toward Stephenson was batted down.

Hope began to fade with four minutes to play as the onside kick was recovered by the Huskies at the Hirschi 45-yard line. With the clock ticking down, Hirschi moved into Palestine territory and faced a fourth and 1 at the 46. The Huskies were on the brink of advancing to the state finals, a remarkable feat since Hirschi High had opened its doors only two years earlier. Even more impressive, coach Jess Stiles had compiled a record of 23-10-1 in three seasons with a start-up program that began with a team of sophomores and juniors. Most start-up programs require at least five seasons to find success.

In 1964, Stiles and the Hirschi Huskies were competing in the long shadow of one of Texas's most revered football programs. The Wichita Falls Coyotes had started playing football in 1911, and from 1930 to 1964 they had captured five state titles.

With a little more than two minutes to play, the Hirschi Huskies were sitting in the catbird seat. Their fans were standing and swaying to the music of the band. Hirschi could punt the ball to the Palestine 20 and know that the odds were against the Wildcats driving 80 yards in the final two minutes. However, Stiles also knew that Bradley held the hot hand. So Stiles chose to roll the dice in hopes of ensuring that Bradley would not touch the ball again that day.

An uneasy stir began on the Hirschi side of the stadium as the offense trotted to the line of scrimmage. Stiles had chosen to go for it.

"We were shocked," Bradley said. "I made the call for the defensive backs and linebackers to walk up to the line of scrimmage. If they'd thrown a pass, the receiver would have been behind us and the game would have been over."

Fullback John Bates was met at the line by practically the entire defense. He actually lost ground as the ball was turned over to Palestine with 2:09 to play.

Bradley broke the huddle quickly and looped a pass over the middle beyond the grasp of wide receiver Bill Heidelberg. The quarterback scuffed the ground with his cleats and looked down. Then he heard the roar of the crowd. Heidelberg had dived for the ball. With his body fully extended, he reached out with his right hand and the ball stuck in his palm. First down at the 19-yard line.

Then Bradley saw something that made his heart sing. Standing at the back of the end zone was Darrell Royal. After leaving the stadium early in the fourth quarter, he and recruiting coordinator Russell Coffee had listened to the game on the radio. They had driven about twenty miles when the Wildcats started coming back. Then they turned around and drove back. They stood on the end line as Royal pumped his arms, clapped his hands, and cheered for the Wildcats. A normally composed man, Royal was way out of character.

On the next play, Reeder gained 3 yards. Bradley passed over the middle to Fitzgerald and suddenly realized his mistake. Fitzgerald caught the ball and went down at the left hash mark with 12 seconds and counting. The Wildcats were out of time-outs, so Bradley rushed the players to the line of scrimmage.

With nobody open in the end zone, Bradley found Fitzgerald standing open at the sideline. He whipped the pass to Fitzgerald as two defenders converged. *Get out of bounds, Curtis.*

With four arms wrapped around him, Fitzgerald fought his way over the boundary line. Suddenly, Fitzgerald's world was spinning out of control. He went down on one knee and thought he would faint. He was exhausted and dehydrated and in great pain. He looked up at the clock and thought he saw 1:02. Instead, it was 00:02. He stumbled back to the huddle.

The Palestine boys huddled, they breathed like spent racehorses.

"I've got to the throw the ball in the end zone," Bradley yelled over the crowd noise. "Curtis, get open. One more time, baby."

It seemed as if the entire Hirschi defense tracked Fitzgerald into the end zone. Defenders surrounded him. Bradley knew he would have to buy time, so he rolled left, retreated, and rolled left again. The Huskies were reaching and grasping for his jersey. As the clock ticked to 00:00. Bradley fell backward. His right arm came forward weakly, and the ball wobbled into the air. Fitzgerald leaped as the ball suddenly disappeared. Six bodies were on top of Fitzgerald, and no one could tell who had come down with the ball. Officials began to peel off the scarlet-clad players and could hear Fitzgerald moaning at the bottom of the pile. He was holding the ball. Two Huskies were trying to wrestle it away from him. One official got a glimpse of the ball in Fitzgerald's arm and threw two arms straight up. Touchdown.

Darrell Royal jumped for the sky. In the east stands, Joe and Mildred Bradley cried. Fitzgerald was still on the ground when McDonald jumped on him and began to punch him in the stomach.

"Get off me, John Ballard!" Curtis yelled. "Dammit, I've got a broke arm."

Still lying prone, but with his head turned sideways, Bradley saw his best friend catch the pass of a lifetime. He had released the ball about two seconds after time had run out. His pass was the ultimate "Hail Mary."

As the Hirschi players were pulled off Fitzgerald, several Wildcats piled on top of him in celebration. From the sideline, the other Wildcats and all of the coaches ran onto the field like men whose hair was on fire. They hoisted Bradley onto their shoulders. More than 4,000 wide-eyed fans streamed behind the players as the cops turned their backs.

Atop the press box, ninth-grade coach Billy Smith stared at the ground some 40 feet below where the broken remains of his 16mm camera lay. He had become so excited just before the final play that he knocked the camera over the rail. It hopelessly fell beyond his outstretched fingers. The film would be recovered in near-perfect

Halfback David Dickey, teammate of Bill Bradley at Palestine High, suited up with the Arkansas Razorbacks in 1967. His number 44 inspired author Jim Dent to wear the same one during his football playing days.

—*David Dickey*

condition, but Dale never pulled the trigger on the final play, so the most historic moment in the history of Palestine football was never recorded.

At the end of the game, newspaper reporters rushed toward Darrell Royal. His quotes would be like gold for the morning editions.

"It was the greatest effort I've ever seen in my life, high school, college, or pro," he said. "We are really looking forward to Bill Bradley playing football for us in Austin."

Down in Orange, sportswriter Fred Cervelli read the Associated Press account of the game and circled Bill Bradley's name in black ink.

"We've got to get this Bradley kid for the Big 33 game next August," he said to himself. "This is the kid who will bring us a victory against Pennsylvania!"

The Palestine fans quickly left the stadium, heading home to start the biggest celebration in the history of the little town. Meanwhile, the Hirschi fans sat slumped over in their seats for several minutes, too stunned to move. As they finally began to file out, the scream of an ambulance siren pierced the silence. One of the Hirschi fans had suffered a heart attack on the final play of the game.

Three hours later, the yellow school bus carrying the Wildcats home stopped almost a mile away from Palestine High.

The bus driver turned to Thornton and said, "I can't get any closer. Every man, woman, and child in this town is standing outside of the schoolhouse. I heard over my radio that some of them are a little drunk."

The fans had formed a gauntlet in the darkness that stretched from the top of the hill on Crockett Street all the way down to Mallard. It seemed the entire cheerleading squad and drill team was waiting to blitz Bradley as he stepped off the bus. Some of them tore at his clothes until his girlfriend, Jan Cheatam, arrived and shooed them away. Several of the girls then grabbed Fitzgerald, whose right arm was in a sling. "Hold on, ladies," he said. "I got a broke arm. But I'm still up for a little cold beer and a whole lotta parking later on."

The 4,000 fans had no gifts to bear. So they started stuffing money in the players' pockets—fives, tens, and twenties.

A wide-eyed man with whiskey on his breath ran up to Curtis and yelled in his ear, "Curtis, you've got to tell me about the game—"

"Hold on, Uncle Floyd," Curtis said. "Slow down a little."

Floyd McNeil proceeded to tell his nephew that he'd stayed behind to work his regular job that day. He was loading asphalt into a truck and then driving it to a parking lot under construction. When he arrived at the parking lot, he would turn the truck over to the foreman, who scattered the asphalt. Then McNeil would jump into a second truck and drive back to the asphalt plant.

One of the dump trucks had a working radio, so he drove it slowly. The other did not, so he revved the engine and drove at top speed.

In the final minute of the game, McNeil was hurtling toward the parking lot in the truck with no radio when a cloud of smoke gushed from the engine.

"I blew the damn engine," he told Curtis. "I was stuck out on the highway when the game ended. You've got to tell me what happened."

Curtis cleared his throat, grinned, and said, "Well, Uncle Floyd, you're just not going to believe it . . ."

The Palestine High football team celebrating after the miraculous 28–23 comeback against Wichita Falls Hirschi in the state semifinals of 1964. Bill Bradley is standing in the back, leaning against the wall.

—Bill Bradley

9

Bradleyville

In the state championship game against San Marcos, Bill Bradley left no doubt that he was the best high school football player in Texas. Two touchdown passes, a rushing TD, and 3 interceptions propelled Palestine to a 24–15 victory over the Rattlers on a day when a freezing north wind ripped through Texas A&M's Kyle Field.

Afterward, Bradley met a mob of reporters in the corner of the locker room and showed his typical humility.

"I don't think it was my best effort," he said. "I really thought it was more of a team game."

One of the more interesting developments was that Dr. Bob Burns cleared Curtis Fitzgerald to play in spite of breaking his arm the previous week against Wichita Falls Hirschi.

"Dr. Burns worked all of those chiropractor tricks on my arm," Fitzgerald said. "Or maybe it was the voodoo."

The Bradley-to-Fitzgerald combination had provided the winning touchdown with no time remaining in the Wichita Falls Hirschi game a week earlier. In the first quarter of the AAA title game against San Marcos, the combo clicked again. After Bradley intercepted a pass and returned it 25 yards to the 9-yard line, he fired to Fitzgerald in the middle of the end zone for a 6–0 lead. The 2-point conversion failed as Bradley's pass was batted down at the line of scrimmage.

San Marcos answered and converted the extra point to make it 7–6. That lead, however, would evaporate within three minutes. Jerry Reeder intercepted a pass at the Palestine 46-yard line and returned it 26 yards. Three plays later, Bradley passed 8 yards for the touchdown to Bob Stephenson, regaining the lead 12–7. Palestine's next touchdown in the third quarter was a 1-yard sneak by Bradley. After Jerry Reeder scored from the 2-yard line for a 24–7 advantage in the fourth quarter, coach Luke Thornton emptied the Palestine bench. That was when the celebration began on the Palestine side of the field.

That night, thousands of Palestine fans again mobbed the players when the team bus returned to the high school. This time, they came bearing real gifts.

As the bus crawled down the hill on Crockett Street, Fitzgerald eyed the large crowd and said to Bradley, "This time, I hope they give us some whiskey." Indeed, Sug Gaines and Pat Smith provided the pint bottles that were purchased at a discount rate and handed out like Christmas candy.

Remembering that right, District Judge and town historian Bascom Bentley said, "until Bill Bredley brought us a state title, nothing had ever happened in Palestine."

In the weeks ahead, Bradley's life would take off like a fast train to St. Louis. Each day, his mailbox was filled with letters. The first came from Fred Cervelli, who invited him to play in the Big 33 game.

"Bill, our coach Bobby Layne is going to love you," the letter began. "We lost to Pennsylvania last year and we've got to win in 1965. You will have a great time. We really need you."

The other letters were from coaches across America. Ara Parseghian of Notre Dame, Paul "Bear" Bryant of Alabama, and USC's John McKay wrote long personal letters, promising to make Bradley the starting quarterback by his sophomore year. Every coach in the Southwest Conference knocked on his door. More than a hundred offers had been extended nationally.

Darrell Royal of Texas had already made the biggest play for

Bradley, but there was no guarantee he would not opt for Texas A&M. Newly signed coach Gene Stallings was a member of the legendary "Junction Boys," the courageous band of players who had survived Bear Bryant's hellish training camp in 1954, when seventy-three players quit in ten days. Working on Bryant's staff at Alabama in 1964, Stallings had helped coach the Crimson Tide to a share of the national title. Stallings's return to his alma mater had spurred a wave of headlines that worried Royal, who beat a path to Palestine at least once a week to see Bradley. If Royal was not in Palestine on a particular day, Texas recruiting coordinator Russell Coffee could always be found in "Bradleyville," a name given the town by the college recruiters.

No high school football star in the history of the state would receive more honors than Bradley. Virtually every newspaper, wire service, touchdown club, and chamber of commerce in Texas recognized him as the High School Player of the Year.

Each day, Bradley was compared to one of the hottest sports names to ever hit East Texas, "Dandy" Don Meredith. Like Bradley, Meredith was a multisport star with an emphasis on football and a certain path to greatness.

Ten years earlier, Meredith had earned all-state honors in football and basketball in Mount Vernon, a small town situated in the tall pine trees of East Texas. Fans flocked from miles away to see Meredith perform at Tiger Stadium in the fall. When basketball season started in Mount Vernon, fans drove for miles to pack the little gymnasium. In the winter, rural Texas became rural Indiana.

Just before Christmas of Meredith's senior year, the Tigers traveled a hundred miles to Dallas for the prestigious Dr Pepper Tournament. He tossed in 52 points in one game to break the tournament record, then led his team past much larger Crozier Tech and Dallas Woodrow to bring home the first-place trophy.

Meredith continued to star on the basketball court, but football was still his best sport. As a senior, he became the top blue-chip recruit in the state and one of the most recognized in America. Bear Bryant practically begged Joe Don to sign at Texas A&M, where he was then head coach. Meredith cried and said, "Coach Bryant, there's no place I'd rather be than A&M, but you got no *girls*." So he took off for SMU and the bright lights of Dallas.

Meredith became the first neon light of the Dallas Cowboys from 1960 to 1968. His light glowed even brighter during a twenty-one-year broadcasting career. Meredith played the comic foil to Howard Cosell on ABC's *Monday Night Football*.

Turn out the lights, the party's over . . .

Bradley had Meredith written all over him. He was considered one of the best basketball players in the state. David Dickey called him "a white Meadowlark Lemon." In the mid-1960s, Lemon played with the Harlem Globetrotters, a fabulously talented all-black team that combined athleticism with comedy and performed in exhibition games all over the world. Their signature song was a whistled version of "Sweet Georgia Brown." The song made it all the way to Palestine for the home basketball games. As the players warmed up to "Sweet Georgia Brown," Bradley whipped behind-the-back passes to his teammates, who rattled the rim with slam dunks. Then the 5'10" Bradley would save the best dunk for last as the fans rejoiced. It was nothing new, though. They had been watching him dunk the basketball since he was a 5'6" freshman.

"Bradley was just a fabulous all-round basketball player," Dickey said. "The first thing you learned was to keep your head on a swivel because his passes came out of nowhere and they might just smack you in the face."

As a high school senior, Bradley turned down a basketball scholarship to Lon Morris College, coached by Leon Black, whose career took off in 1967 when he was hired by the University of Texas. That year, Bradley was the star quarterback for the Longhorns. During Black's first season, the coach was asked by a reporter to name the best player on the UT team.

"The best basketball player on this campus no doubt is Bill Bradley," Black said. "He would easily be the best player on this team."

●   ●   ●

Bill Bradley running the ball at the
University of Texas in 1966.
　　　　　—Texas Sports Hall of Fame

Near the end of the spring in 1965, Bradley let it be known that his future would either be with the University of Texas or professional baseball. Darrell Royal admitted that he was getting nervous.

"Bill Bradley might just become the best player to ever suit up for the Longhorns," Royal said. "Waiting for him to sign is making me as nervous as a pig in a packing plant."

Bradley signed with the Longhorns in February, but said he would consider Major League Baseball if he were drafted in one of the low rounds. Scouts had been following his career since he participated in semipro baseball at the age of fifteen. The switch-hitting shortstop with both power and speed was considered one of the top prospects at his position. When the baseball draft rolled around in May, Royal held his breath, then found no reason to exhale. Bradley was drafted in the first round by the Detroit Tigers, a team with many holes to fill. They had finished fourth in the American League in 1964 with shortstop Dick McAuliffe hitting .241.

Everyone knew that the lifelong dream of Joe Hill Bradley was for his son to play in the Major Leagues. Baseball was young Bill's first love. As a two-year-old, he was smacking a rolled-up piece of aluminum foil around the backyard with a plastic bat. Before long, everyone in Palestine knew that Bill possessed the talent to make the Big Show. However, Joe Bradley also recognized the value of education. Joe and his brothers had gone straight to work for the railroad, but older sister May had followed a different route. By going off to college, May Bradley had developed the ambition to be a doctor. She would become one of the first female gynecologists in the country.

"Just look at your Aunt May," Joe told his son. "I want you to go to college and have that kind of opportunity."

The Tigers offered a $25,000 signing bonus with plans to send him to AA Birmingham his first year. Team officials told him he would be in the Major Leagues in two to four years. The offer was tempting, but Bill was close to his father, and Joe Bradley stood firm on him seeking a college degree.

Bill called Darrell Royal in Austin and committed to the

Left to Right: Bill Bradley, Texas coach Darrell Royal, Joe Hill Bradley, and Mildred Bradley. Bill Bradley had just signed his letter-of-intent with Royal.

—*Bill Bradley*

Longhorns. Royal could not have been happier. The first three words out of his mouth did not make Bradley happy, though.

"No more baseball," he said. "I want you to commit to football. You will not be playing for the Texas baseball team when you get here."

Bradley's heart sank. Still, he stuck with his commitment.

Some four decades later, Bradley recalled, "I should have never agreed to *not* play baseball. I should have kept my baseball options open. That was a big mistake."

Preparing himself for the Big 33 game and the coming football season meant Bradley would go to work—baling hay. In the summer of 1965, he would have plenty of work to do on the 2,700-acre ranch owned by John Prothro, a wealthy Texas alumnus. Every summer, the Prothro Ranch produced fifteen thousand bales of Coastal Bermuda. Bradley would also be fixing and painting fences with the work lasting from dawn until dusk.

Bradley moved into a bunkhouse on the ranch along with two current Longhorns and one other recruit, his good friend Barry Stone, a tight end from Kilgore. The Prothro Ranch was located forty-nine miles from Bradley's front door on the outskirts of Tyler. A red dirt road led into an wrought iron entrance, and that opened into an 80-acre lake. The Guadalupe River rolled along the east side of the ranch. The boys baled hay by day and drank cold beer at night.

One afternoon, Bradley was driving a hay truck through a hundred acres of rose country on the edge of Tyler when he spotted a woman and her young children working the rose fields.

"I sure would like to have some of these roses for my girlfriend back in Palestine," Bradley said. "Her name is Jan Cheatham, and she's as pretty as they come."

The woman smiled and said, "A nickel a rose. That's a good deal."

Bradley gathered all of the roses he could handle and paid the woman. Then he said, "Who is this big youngster you've got working with you?"

"That is my son," Ann Campbell responded. "His name is Earl

Campbell, and he's nine years old. And someday he will be playing for the University of Texas, just like you."

Bradley grinned and said, "Ma'am, he's big enough to play for the University of Texas right now."

Each day, life on the ranch provided yet another adventure. John Prothro enjoyed all of the gratifications of being the richest man in East Texas. Parked on the ranch near his sprawling home was a twin-engine Beechcraft. One day, Prothro taxied the plane up to the small bunkhouse and told the college boys to "hop in."

"Where are we going, Mr. Prothro?" Bradley asked.

"We are going over to New Orleans, to a restaurant known as Brennan's," he said. "Best Eggs Benedict in the world. We'll have a little dinner, eat some Bananas Foster for dessert, then fly back in a couple of hours."

It would not be their last trip to New Orleans that summer. They also made a couple of short trips down to Houston for dinner in the Arts District.

In July, before Bradley left for Hershey, Prothro took an oil exploration trip to South Arkansas with his most respected geologist. The duo worked their maps and listened to some of the most experienced and respected wildcatters in the region, but Prothro's decision on where to drill was based strictly on gut instinct.

"Right here," Prothro said.

"Why here?" the geologist said.

"Because we are smack dab in the middle of Bradley County," Prothro said, "and there is no luckier man on the face of this earth than Bill Bradley."

The southern edge of Bradley County was located twenty miles from the Arkansas-Louisiana border. Within weeks, the drillers hit a mother lode of black crude that would pay $7 million. It seemed that everything Bill Bradley touched turned to (black) gold.

10

The Courtship of Jerry LeVias

Leura LeVias had grown tired of the college recruiters, especially the ones who came knocking on Sunday mornings.

She would swing open the door and say, "He's in church, and that's where *you* should be!" As she watched the man take off down Glenwood Street, she would shake her head and say, "I just know he'll be back."

The number of scholarship offers for Jerry LeVias had reached the century mark by mid-January of 1965. He would soon be catching flights to places like UCLA, Oregon State, California-Berkeley, and Arizona State. UCLA coach Tommy Prothro either called or came to the LeVias home each day.

In the mid-1960s, the NCAA placed few restrictions on the number of recruiting visits. Grown men were known to tail Texas's best players all day long—down the high school hallways, up the street, and all the way home.

The prayers of Hebert High School coach Clifton Ozen had yet to be answered. Not a single major college in Texas had offered LeVias a scholarship. Once again, the Southwest Conference was passing on a great Negro player because of the archaic "gentlemen's agreement." Ozen often wondered if a Negro would ever play in the backward league.

Not in two months had Ozen set eyes on the tall, lean man with aviator-style sunglasses. He prayed the man would return to Beaumont and show his cards.

One Sunday afternoon, that man removed his sunglasses at the front door of the LeVias home and walked in. The living room was filled with people watching TV. Every head turned to see the white man with the wide smile. He stopped briefly, extended his hand to Charlie LeVias, then moved on. He strolled straight into the kitchen.

With a furrowed brow, Charlie LeVias turned to his son and said, "Who's that white man in my house? Why did he just shake my hand and keep walking?"

"I'm not sure, Dad," Jerry said. "Maybe he's a football coach we haven't met yet."

Jerry turned back toward the television but noticed that his dad was still looking in the direction of the kitchen. After a few minutes, Jerry stood and walked slowly across the living room. He stuck his head into the kitchen and tried to listen. The white man was talking to his grandmother, Ella LeVias. They were standing next to a steaming pot on the stove.

"Now let me tell you one thing, Mrs. LeVias," he drawled. "I've been cooking pinto beans all of my life. Mine won't give you gas That's not easy to do. Let me give you my recipe."

Ella LeVias howled with laughter, then said, "Show me how to do it, Coach."

Jerry stepped into the kitchen, and his grandmother said, "Come on over here, Jerry, and meet coach Hayden Fry of SMU. He came all the way down here from Dallas just to talk to you. He seems to know a lot about cooking pinto beans."

Fry also knew that recruiting began in the Kitchen. Over the years, he had heard the stories about coach Paul "Bear" Bryant and his down-home style.

This was Bryant's modus operandi: "Go straight into the kitchen. Roll up your sleeves and plop your elbows down in the chicken batter. Help Mama cook her fried chicken. Then she'll tell her son where he's going to college—at the University of Alabama, for sure."

As the stranger walked across the kitchen and extended his hand, Jerry noticed that his sleeves were rolled up.

"Hayden Fry from SMU," the man said. "Mighty glad to meet you."

Jerry's eyes widened. "Coach Ozen said you might be coming by. But to tell you the truth, Coach, I've never heard of SMU."

"Well, it's a small private university up in Dallas with a football team that's going places. I got there a couple of years ago. We're going to win a Southwest Conference championship just as soon as I sign you to a letter of intent."

Jerry blinked twice and said, "Coach, are you offering me a scholarship?"

"Doggone right I am," Fry said, his smile wider than a Texas prairie. "As a matter of fact, this is a historic moment right here in your grandma's kitchen. But let's keep it quiet for a while. We might stir up all of those other schools trying to sign you."

Hayden Fry had been planning this day for more than two years, but few people knew it. When SMU president Willis Tate had offered him the head coaching job in December of 1961, Fry made one demand that seemed outrageous. "I would like to recruit black players," he said.

"Honestly, I don't think that's possible, Coach," Tate responded. "There is an agreement between the coaches in our conference not to recruit Negro athletes. So I guess I will have to rescind my offer."

Fry paused, then said, "No, Mr. Tate, I guess I will have to pass on your offer. And that is final."

At the time, Fry was happy with his job as quarterbacks coach at the University of Arkansas. The last two years, the Razorbacks had played in the Cotton Bowl and the Sugar Bowl. Fry knew he would be happy working as an assistant for coach Frank Broyles for many years to come. Broyles was one of the new bright minds in college football, and a man not lacking for ambition.

Fry never expected another phone call from Willis Tate, but the SMU president did reach out again a few days later. Fry did not know

Tate had been trying to find a way to integrate the football program for several years. He just did not know where to start. In truth, he was about as open-minded concerning race as anyone in Texas outside of President Lyndon Baines Johnson. He was a "liberal" before the term became popular. Recently, he had been excoriated as a "Communist dupe" in the *American Mercury*. He had been labeled a "pinko" by *Dallas Morning News* columnist Lynn Landrum. Tate knew that the Ku Klux Klan might burn crosses on his beautiful campus if he chose to break the SWC football color barrier. Nevertheless, he was willing to consider it. After all, SMU had been ahead of its time in 1952 when the university admitted its first Negro student, James V. Lyles, into the Perkins School of Theology.

During his tenure at SMU, Tate was known more as an academician than a rah-rah guy. In truth, though, he loved Mustangs football. In 1935, he had made All–Southwest Conference as a tackle in the historic season when SMU reached the January 1, 1936, Rose Bowl against Stanford. It had distressed him to watch the Mustangs limp along the last ten years with only two winning seasons.

Tate truly wanted a freethinking, ambitious coach like Fry. He also liked the idea of shaking up the conference by signing its first black player. So for the past few days, Tate had counseled with athletic director Matty Bell, along with faculty representatives Harold Jeskey and Ed Mouzon. He listened to their thoughts about integrating the football team. Everyone agreed that it was time to break the "gentlemen's agreement."

When Tate called Fry back, he offered him the job again. Then he laid down SMU's rules for integration. "First, the Negro you sign must possess the talent to be a starter. We don't need our first Negro to be sitting on the bench. His record in academics and citizenship must be impeccable. He will need 1000 on his SAT score, and that's 250 higher than the other athletes. Most of all, Coach Fry, I want you to make sure that this Negro football player be fully apprised of the possible backlash before he sets foot on our campus."

Fry was so overjoyed that he accepted Tate's demands and took the job on the spot. Then he said, "How soon can I get started finding this player?"

"Let me make something crystal clear," Tate said. "This will not happen overnight. You must search for the perfect player. This will take at least two years. Do you understand?"

"Yessir, I do," Fry said. "You will not be disappointed with the first colored player in the history of our league."

It had been Fry's dream for several years to coach Negro athletes. He had grown up in the West Texas boomtown of Odessa during the Great Depression of the 1930s, when Negroes were treated like third-class citizens. Unlike his white friends, Fry played with the black kids. When Negroes were forced to sit in the back of the bus or in the balcony of the movie theater, he often sat with them.

Upon entering the seventh grade, Fry could not understand why the whites and blacks went to separate schools. Fry often angered his coaches and teammates by saying the all-Negro teams might be better than the all-white teams—this in spite of the fact that he quarter-backed all-white Odessa High School to fourteen straight victories and a state championship in 1946.

In 1962, he was still confounded as to why the best Texas Negro athletes were forced to leave the state. So from his first day on the job, Fry started looking for the perfect Negro. The SMU staff did not mess around. Within a few months, they targeted a player who fit all of Tate's criteria. In mid-fall of 1962, assistant coach Charlie Driver walked into Fry's office and said, "I think I've found our man. His name is Jerry LeVias. He plays halfback at Beaumont Hebert. He's one of the best athletes I've ever seen. I've done a little checking. He goes to church every time the doors open. He's got great parents and a won-derful grandmother living right next door. He makes straight A's. He's never going to get into trouble."

Indeed, LeVias carried a little Bible in his pocket every day. He wore the number 23 because the Twenty-third Psalm was Ella's favor-ite Bible scripture. *The Lord is my Shepherd; I shall not want. He*

maketh me to lie down in green pastures. He leadeth me beside the
still waters. He restoreth my soul . . .

For almost two years, Fry and his staff had kept it a secret that they were interested in signing a Negro player. If the news had leaked to the press, Fry would have been in hot water with his university president. The coach managed to maintain his cover by showing up at Beaumont Hebert late in the day when opposing college coaches were gone. By December of 1964, though, Fry knew that it was time to put the full-court press on LeVias. He had done his research on Ella LeVias. That was why he had recruited her first.

"Mrs. LeVias," Fry said one day.

"Call me Ella."

"Ella, may I ask you a few questions?"

"Of course, Hayden. Go right ahead."

"I need to know what would make Jerry happy. I need to know what would make the LeVias family happy."

Ella smiled and said, "I want that boy to be the first in our family to go to college. This has also been the wish of his father since the day that little Jerry was born."

Fry listened and learned. Each time he came to Beaumont, he preached the need for education.

"Jerry, I truly believe that you will be a superstar for the SMU Mustangs," he said. "Down the road, you might play a little pro football. But what you will do for the rest of your life depends on your education. I can assure you that you will get a great education at SMU."

That day, Ella, Charlie, and Leura LeVias were standing beside Jerry. All were nodding in agreement. They were happy that Jerry was about to graduate with honors. He was ranked No. 6 out of the 240 students in Hebert High's graduating class of 1965. Everyone in the room would be overjoyed when Jerry graduated from college.

Fry also made one more pledge to Ella.

"Mrs. LeVias," he said, "I promise you that Jerry will call you at home right before every game we play. That way, you'll know he's doing okay."

That Fry had recruited the grandmother first was a stroke of genius. After all, it was her genes, along with those of her late husband, Charlie LeVias Sr., that had spawned the football talent around them. Grandson Miller Farr was already a star running back and kick returner at Wichita State, and Mel Farr had just signed as a halfback with UCLA. College football coaches across America were trying to get their hands on Jerry LeVias. There was a fourth football-playing grandson few people in Texas knew about because his family had moved to Seattle when he was a child. Clancy Williams, born in Beaumont in 1942, played college football at Washington State and eight more seasons as a defensive back with the Los Angeles Rams.

The four grandsons of Ella and Charlie Sr. would play a total of thirty-six seasons of pro football—Mel Farr twelve, Miller Farr ten, Clancy Williams eight, and Jerry Levias six.

In the view of Jerry LeVias, it was more the genetics of Ella than Charlie Sr. that had created so much football talent. "Charlie Sr. was a little guy," LeVias said. "From what I remember, my grandmother used to bounce him off the walls pretty good."

Charlie LeVias was the son of a former slave. His father had moved the family from Missouri to East Texas around 1900. Jerry's great-grandfather had worked for French slaveholders named LeVias. Later in life, Jerry would change the spelling of his last name to include a capital V because the slaveholders had spelled their last name that way.

As it turned out, Ella LeVias would have plenty of say on where her grandson Jerry would play college football. She had liked Hayden Fry from the moment she met him.

"There is something godly about that man," she told Jerry.

Fry knew the importance of spreading the gospel around the LeVias home. In his absence, he often dispatched assistant coach Chuck Curtis to shepherd the LeVias family. Curtis was raised the son of a Baptist minister in Gainesville, Texas. He knew the Bible from cover to cover and could talk religion to anyone.

Curtis happened to be one of the most interesting football men to suit up or coach the previous two decades in Texas. When he was a high school senior, his father moved to another church 225 miles away in Taylor. Chuck, however, stayed in Gainesville to keep his eligibility. The seventeen-year-old lived in a garage apartment by himself. He became an all-state quarterback as a senior. Still, all of the SWC coaches except TCU's Abe Martin had ignored him. He paid back the favor to Martin by leading the Horned Frogs to a league title in 1955 and a 28–27 victory in the 1957 Cotton Bowl over Syracuse and All-American running back Jim Brown. Curtis passed for 2 touchdowns and ran for another.

After a brief stint in pro football, Curtis took over a Jacksboro High School football program that had been in the dumper for ten years. In one season, he turned the Jackrabbits around and led them to the 1962 state title. The next year, he moved to Garland and replaced legendary coach Homer Johnson. Curtis led the Owls to back-to-back titles in 1963 and 1964. Only three other coaches in Texas history had won three straight state titles. No one had done it at two schools.

With his career taking off at a young age, Curtis jumped at the chance to join Fry's staff. He was a big, friendly man. The LeViases were always happy to see him. One day he was spotted walking up to their front door wearing his large white Stetson cowboy hat. Before Leura LeVias could let him in, several neighbors came tearing down the street. When Leura opened the door, a dozen people were standing on the front sidewalk behind Curtis.

"Leura, Leura," they said, "why is the county sheriff here? Is Jerry in some kind of trouble?"

Leura laughed and said, "No, this is Chuck Curtis of SMU. He's just here to visit with Jerry."

Fry and Curtis were determined to steer LeVias to SMU. First, they needed to educate him on the university. Kids growing up in the all-black Pear Orchard section of Beaumont did not watch the all-white SWC teams play on television. Instead, they huddled around the TV to check out Ernie Davis of Syracuse, Charley Taylor of Arizona State, and Prentice Gautt of Oklahoma. Davis would become the first Negro player to win the Heisman Trophy in 1961.

LeVias recalled, "I'd never watched the white teams of the Southwest Conference teams because I had no chance of going there. Shoot, I never even knew what an Aggie was."

Fry's sales pitch included one important message that he delivered every time he came to Beaumont.

"You are going to become the next Jackie Robinson," Fry would say. "Jackie was the first Negro player in the history of Major League Baseball in 1947. Jerry, by signing with SMU you are going to make a difference for your race. You are going to be a credit to your race."

LeVias listened to Fry but still took his recruiting trips to UCLA, Oregon, Oregon State, Washington State, Cal, Colorado, and Michigan State. Fry worried each time LeVias boarded another flight. He was especially concerned when LeVias went to UCLA. He knew that Jerry was extremely close to his cousin Mel Farr, the Bruins running back. Furthermore, UCLA coach Tommy Prothro was recruiting his socks off. Unbeknown to Fry, Jerry was staying longer in Los Angeles than the NCAA-sanctioned two-day visit. He was actually practicing with the team. Lining up in the same backfield as Mel Farr and Gary Beban (soon to win the Heisman) was a thrill.

On the SWC signing date in February, LeVias was not ready to commit. On that day, he was visiting Washington State in Pullman. He planned to visit several more schools from February to April on the West Coast before making his decision.

Ozen was getting nervous. He desperately wanted his player to become the first Negro athlete in the history of the Southwest Conference. LeVias felt obligated to Ozen because, without him, he would have never played football.

Charlie LeVias, however, was still on the fence about Fry and SMU. He admired Fry's strong Christian views, along with his promise to push his son toward a diploma, but the idea of young Jerry traveling almost three hundred miles to a city with a history like Dallas worried him. He called Fry one day in Dallas to express these concerns.

"Coach Fry, I'm a little worried that my son won't fit in with the

Dallas crowd," he said. "They killed our president in Dallas, and I hear that it is a racist town. Are you sure that Jerry's going to be okay in Dallas?"

In his best down-home drawal, Fry said, "Your son will be fine. He will have plenty of protection on the SMU campus. We will take care of him. I promise."

By the end of the conversation, Fry knew that he had not won over Charlie LeVias. By the middle of May, Fry and Curtis were getting more worried by the day. There were reports out of Seattle that he was leaning toward Washington State. Jerry's sister Angelena had married a running back named George Reed, who played for Washington State from 1959 to 1963. Reed was pushing WSU.

Then, on May 18, Ozen called a reporter from the *Dallas Morning News* and invited him to Beaumont for the signing of Jerry LeVias. The Hebert halfback had listened to the advice of his coach and had chosen to stay in Texas.

"You can be a pioneer," Ozen told LeVias. "There is no telling when we will get another chance to get a Negro in the Southwest Conference."

On May 22, 1965, LeVias penned his name to the conference letter of intent with SMU. Photographers from Beaumont, Houston, and Dallas came to the LeVias home to take photos of Jerry, Hayden Fry, Clifton Ozen, and the entire LeVias family.

Ozen told the *Beaumont Enterprise*, "He's an all-around good boy, just what the doctor ordered. He's the ideal type for the first colored player in the Southwest Conference. I've sent a lot of boys off to the big-time colleges and the pros. But as far as ability, grades, and intelligence, he's the best."

The coach had dreamed of this day. The color line in the SWC had finally been broken by his favorite pupil of all time. Ozen could boast of three ex-Hebert stars already suiting up in pro football—Warren Wells with Detroit, Anthony Guillory with the Los Angeles Rams, and Miller Farr of the Denver Broncos. Also in the pro ranks from the

Jerry LeVias signs with SMU in 1965. Left to right, front, Charlie LeVias, Leura LeVias, Jerry, and sister Charlena. Back, SMU asst. coach Chuck Curtis, Fred LeVias, and head coach Hayden Fry.

—*Texas Sports Hall of Fame*

"Golden Triangle" (Beaumont–Port Arthur–Orange) area was mammoth defensive tackle Ernie Ladd playing with the San Diego Chargers.

The ex-Beaumonters playing big-time college football at faraway places were Bubba Smith at Michigan State, Willie Ray Smith Jr. at Kansas, and Hebert's Mel Farr at UCLA. Also from the Golden Triangle was Aaron Brown of nearby Port Arthur Lincoln, an All–Big Ten selection at linebacker for the Minnesota Golden Gophers.

Ozen knew that by signing with SMU and breaking down the Texas racial walls, LeVias would follow a more direct route to pro football. Plus, for the first time, one of the great Negro players in the history of Texas would be playing big-time football in his own state. That was one reason the celebration was on . . . until Jerry picked up the *Beaumont Enterprise* the next morning and read the big, bold headline:

LEVIAS TO BECOME THE FIRST
NEGRO ATHLETE IN SWC HISTORY

Jerry said, "Holy crap!" It seemed that everyone except him knew he would be making racial history. This in spite of his long talks with Fry.

"I had no idea I was going to be the first," he recalled four decades later. "They had told me I would be a pioneer. But I didn't know I was going to be the 'first this' and the 'first that.' I am not a brave man. In the 1960s, I had read the stories and saw the TV news about black people being shot and hanged and the dogs biting on them. I did not knowingly plan to put myself into that position to be that person."

A sign of the harsh things to come was this statement by new Texas A&M coach Gene Stallings: "I don't think the Aggie football program would be any better by having a Negro on our team." Most of the other league coaches reserved comment.

A few days later, LeVias traveled to Dallas to meet the press. He stood before a legion of newspaper reporters with notebooks and pens poised.

"Do you think the Southwest Conference is ready for its first Negro ballplayer?" a reporter asked.

Jerry played it cool. "I don't know," he said, "but I guess we are about to find out."

Then he turned and walked away.

11

Arrival Day in Hershey

Late in the day, Bobby Layne clapped his hands and shouted encouragement to the Texas players on the Hershey practice field. The team had arrived in Pennsylvania from Texas earlier that day, and the first practice was rocking. Bill Bradley heaved a high spiral that found Jerry LeVias in perfect stride. A cheer went up as Layne signaled for the boys to circle around him.

"That's it, fellas," Layne said. "Pretty damn good practice for our first day in Hershey. I've gotta say that you boys look a lot better than the crew we brought up here last year. That still doesn't mean that we'll beat these fat bastards from Pennsylvania."

Layne chuckled and winked. "I want you to get yourselves a good night's sleep."

The players roundly booed their coach. Then Bill Bradley spoke up. "Before practice, you said something about cold beer and hot girls. When does that start?"

Pointing in the direction of the farmhouse, Layne smiled and said, "There are some good things waiting for you. Of course, you are responsible for finding the girls. But believe me, they are all over the place. Our players last year had a pretty good time."

The players hustled to hit the showers and to suit up in blue jeans

The Texas coaching staff: Left to Right clockwise, Mal
Kunter, Harley Sewell, Doak Walker, and Bobby Layne.
—*Fred Cervelli*

and T-shirts. They could not wait for the "good things that Layne promised." Sprinting all the way to the farmhouse, they found cases of Budweiser iced down in three large aluminum tubs.

"My favorite beer," Bradley said, laughing. "I wonder if Bobby knew my brand when he ordered this stuff."

Bradley grabbed a cold one and punctured the top twice with the kind of opener known as a "church key." Then he opened a second one and handed it to LeVias.

"Here you go, roomie," he said.

They tapped beer cans. LeVias took a couple of swallows. As Bradley threw his head back and chug-a-lugged, LeVias turned and spit his beer out. His new friend did not notice.

"Jerry, this is damn good cold beer," Bradley said. "You know, I wondered if a religious youngster like you would drink."

LeVias smiled. "Nothing wrong with a few cold ones from time to time. As long as you can handle your alcohol." He wanted to throw back his head and laugh at his own Johnny Carson joke, but he knew it was not the right time.

The boys were laughing and cutting up and enjoying their first night in central Pennsylvania. Danny Abbott, a 220-pound guard from Amarillo, walked up to Bradley and bear-hugged him, then lifted him above his head.

"Put me down, you big Indian," Bradley yelled. Abbott was of Native American descent, and most of the players called him "Chief."

The previous night in Dallas, Bradley and Abbott had played together in the North-South All-Star Game. Bradley had been named the most valuable back and Abbott the most valuable lineman. It was a good night for Darrell Royal, as both players were headed to the University of Texas in September.

Playing for the North team, Bradley had dazzled the crowd at the Cotton Bowl with his running, passing, punting, and kick returns. The North was a heavy underdog, according to the state's. Sporting press Bradley could not be stopped. He scored touchdowns on runs of 3 and 7 yards in a 12–6 victory. One of the highlights of the night was a

Texas quarterback Bill Bradley punting
during practice at the Big 33 game in
1965.

—*Fred Cervelli*

fourth-down completion to Chris Key in the second quarter that kept the first scoring drive alive.

"Bradley has more confidence than any kid I've ever seen," Texas assistant coach Russell Coffee said after the game. "He will always find some way to beat you."

Bradley rushed for 35 yards on 10 carries, but his overall statistics were more impressive. On defense, he made 4 unassisted tackles, broke up 3 passes, and intercepted 1, returning it 35 yards. He returned a punt 76 yards to set up a touchdown. He also punted for a 44.7-yard average.

Abbott was just as productive. He dominated both sides of the line just as he had done at Tascosa High School in Amarillo. He made 4 solo tackles, assisted on 4 more, and recovered 2 fumbles. He opened huge holes for the running game.

LeVias was snubbed by the North-South selection committee, comprised of high school coaches around the state. The game had been integrated a year earlier by halfback Warren McVea of San Antonio Brackenridge, but the committee wanted to keep a quota of one black player for the game. They chose James Harris of Brownwood. They must have figured that LeVias's 43 touchdowns his final two seasons at Beaumont Hebert was just not good enough.

Texas sportswriter Fred Cervelli, the one-man Big 33 selection committee for the Big 33, made LeVias one of his first choices. "You could be doggone sure I was going to pick LeVias," he said. "I considered him one of the very best players in the state."

As the Texans were getting to know each other on the back porch of the old farmhouse, Corby Robertson approached LeVias and extended his right hand. Robertson, the best linebacker in the state, had grown up wealthy in the Houston suburb of River Oaks as the grandson of oil tycoon Hugh "Roy" Cullen. However, he chose to attend a public high school with black players that afforded tougher competition than a private prep academy. Robertson excelled at Houston Lamar as a two-way starter and became one of Royal's first signees the previous February.

"I just want to tell you how happy I am that you're on the team," Robertson said. "I heard about all of the great things that you did in Beaumont. I'm also looking forward to playing in the same conference with you."

LeVias could not fathom what he was hearing. Oh, he had been treated well by the white men who had recruited him, but growing up on the black side of Beaumont, he had never been spoken to so cordially by a couple of white youngsters like Bradley and Robertson.

He smiled at Robertson and said, "That makes me feel good. I can't tell you how happy I am to be here."

As darkness settled over Hershey, the players could see the lights of an amusement park and a giant roller coaster about a half mile away. Layne had placed no restrictions or curfew on the team, so they were free to roam. Hershey would be their own amusement park for the next week.

Bradley finished his beer and pointed in the direction of the roller coaster. "Come on, roomie," he said. "We need to go check out the girls."

In the summer of 1965, Hershey was a sleepy little town with a population of 12,000 that banked on one product—chocolate. If not for Milton S. Hershey's decision to build a chocolate factory in his hometown in 1903, the Big 33 game might have never been lured to Hershey. Located close to the center of the state, Hershey was also a tourist attraction in the summer.

By the turn of the century, Milton S. Hershey was flush with $1 million in liquid assets (the equivalent of $29.9 million today) after selling his caramel company back in Lancaster. Little wonder that they changed the name of the place from Derry Township to Hershey when the chocolate tycoon moved in. Before long, the town revolved around the Hershey Bar and Hershey Kisses.

Hershey was known as "Chocolate Town, U.S.A." and "the Sweetest Place on Earth." So quaint was the little town that the streetlights were shaped like chocolate kisses, and the intersection of Chocolate and Cocoa avenues was the centerpiece of downtown. The headquarters for the Texas team was the Cocoa Inn, where the coaching staff was staying.

Hershey was situated a hundred miles slightly northwest of Philadelphia and two hundred miles slightly southeast of Pittsburgh. Unlike the big cities of the Commonwealth, the town ambled along unnoticed most of the time. That was before Wilt Chamberlain and the Philadelphia Warriors came to town on March 2, 1962.

That day at the Hershey Arena, Chamberlain shattered the league's scoring record with 100 points against the New York Knicks. A crowd of 4,124 fans sat on the edge of their seats, praying for the moment "the Big Dipper" would hit 100. In the final ten minutes, legendary public address announcer Dave Zinkoff, known as the "Zink," provided a running total every time Chamberlain scored. . . . *Chamberlain with 87. . . . Chamberlain with 89* . . . as the fans chanted, "Give it to Wilt! Give it to Wilt!"

The game was not televised, and only two photographers were on hand (one left after the first quarter). The only video camera in the arena was not turned on. With forty-six seconds remaining, Chamberlain hit a short jumper to reach the tridigital number. Hardly anyone noticed the Warriors had defeated the Knicks 169-147. The lucky fans who witnessed Chamberlain's extravaganza would never forget it. No one has approached the record the past fifty-one years. The closest has been Kobe Bryant's eighty-one points against the Toronto Raptors on January 22, 2006.

In spite of its size, Hershey was a good choice for the Big 33 game, founded in 1958 by local sports editor Al Clark of the *Harrisburg Patriot-News*. That first year, the game drew an elite brand of high school talent. From 1958 to 60, Pennsylvania did not allow a team of "U.S.A. All-Stars" to cross the goalline, winning all three games. In 1961, the NCAA cited illegal recruiting and banned out of-state-teams from coming to Hershey. So the Big 33 game was transformed into an in-state affair to satisfy the NCAA.

In the summer of 1961, a star emerged from Beaver Falls by the name of Joe Willie Namath. He completed 13-of-19 passes for 205 yards and rushed for 62 yards as the West all-stars won 34-0. After two more intrastate games, the NCAA relented in 1964 and allowed an out-of-state team to be invited to Hershey.

Fans all over the state were overjoyed when the Penn squad defeated the Texas braggarts 12-6. They had managed to silence the likes of Bobby Layne and to disprove the notion that Texas played the best high school football in America. With six days and counting until Round Two, the Pennsys were still beating their chests. Soon the town would be bursting at the seams with fans from all over the region.

Before the teams put on the pads and helmets and started knocking heads, the Big 33 officials in Hershey required the players to undergo rigorous physical exams.

Norm Bulaich of the Texas team felt uneasy as the players lined up in their boxer shorts at the local gymnasium. He was in the back of the line, but the doctor called his name first. Bulaich was the top-rated blue-chipper on the Texas team, and his football feats had been the subject of national headlines. If the Pennsylvania team was to win the game, they would need to find a way to stop Bulaich.

All of the Texas players knew that the Pennsylvanians would cheat to win. They had heard the stories of how they had twice scheduled the Big 33 game on the same date as the state's annual Texas North-South All-Star Game. The plan was to make sure that Texas did not bring its best players. Now that the first-string team was in town, what would the Penn promoters think up next?

As Bulaich moved to the front of the line, a thousand thoughts sprinted through his mind. *Why are they calling me first? At least five players' names are ahead of me alphabetically. Is this a setup? Do they want me to flunk my physical?*

Bulaich would have been the perfect target for such a scheme. During three years at La Marque High School, he averaged 14 yards a carry, a phenomenal average even against high school defenses.

Bulaich's hard-running reputation was known all over the state.

As a result, every coach in the Southwest Conference had beaten a path to his door. Darrell Royal's second-most-coveted player behind Bradley was Bulaich.

Defensive backs hated the sight of Bulaich thundering through the line untouched and heading their way. In 1963, a young and promising safety for the Alvin Yellowjackets, Nolan Ryan, looked up to see Bulaich bearing down on him at full speed. He braced himself for the collision but was steamrollered by the big fullback. When Bulaich crossed the goal line, Ryan was still flat on his back with his ears ringing. It was one of the last football plays he would ever participate in. Baseball scouts were already telling Ryan that he would have a bright future as a flame-throwing right-hander in the Major Leagues.

"Nolan has told me many times that I'm the reason he quit football," Bulaich said, "and I believe him. He didn't play any football after I ran over him."

As Bulaich grudgingly reached the examining table, he noticed that the doctor was eyeing him up and down.

"Hello, Doc, what's up?" Bulaich inquired.

"Just sit down on this table and we'll find out," the doctor said.

For the next few minutes, the doctor took his temperature and used a tongue depressor to provide a view of his throat. He checked his heartbeat with a stethoscope. When the halfback was told to lie on his back for an electrocardiogram, Bulaich knew something was wrong.

"Doc, why do I need a heart exam?" Bulaich asked. "I'm eighteen years old. My doctor back in Texas says I'm healthier than a horse and stronger than an ox."

The doctor frowned. "You don't look that healthy to me." Bulaich could hear his teammates laughing behind him.

"I think this doc's about to tell Bulaich he's dying," Bradley said. "Hey, Bulaich, you're looking pretty pale."

The gym thundered with laughter.

After the EKG was completed, the doctor delivered the bad news. "I knew there was something wrong with you, son. Mr. Bulaich, you have a heart murmur. Until we can find a way to fix your condition, you will *not* be playing in the Big 33 game. You might as well go on back to Texas."

Without saying a word, Bulaich converted his right forearm into a huge broom and swept every instrument off the doctor's table. When the clattering stopped, Bulaich pointed his finger at the doctor and yelled, "I heard you sorry bastards were cheaters. I don't have a damn heart murmur. You're trying to stop me from playing in the game. I'm playing in the *damn* game."

The doctor nodded his head in agreement and said, "Okay, if you say so. I can't stop you."

Over the next thirty minutes, thirty-two players took their physical exams and were quickly "passed." Not a single one was required to take an electrocardiogram. Not a single one was told that he had a heart murmur.

That night, coaches Bobby Layne and Doak Walker learned about the doctor's concern with Bulaich's heart. They insisted that he go to the local hospital to be checked out. As it turned out, Bulaich's heart was fine. As one of the doctors told him, "Son, you have a heart of a racehorse." He would be suiting up for the Big 33 game without a heart murmur, but with a chip squarely on his shoulder.

12

Soul Man

Bill Bradley and I loved each other in that man kind of way. Bill Bradley was a genuine human being.

—Jerry LeVias

The soul music of Bill Bradley's life emanated from three radio sources—WLS out of Chicago, KNOE in New Orleans, and KLIF from Dallas.

Tuning into WLS, a thousand miles to the north, or KNOE, 450 miles east, was actually a snap in 1965. At night, those stations powered up to 50,000 watts and could be heard with crystal clarity in the small East Texas town of Palestine.

Rising from the southern hills of Dallas, the KLIF tower was seventy miles from Palestine. So it was no surprise that Bradley kept his radio tuned to "Mighty 1190" for much of the day. At KLIF in the 1950s and '60s, Gordon McClendon was credited with refining the Top 40 format. Known as "the Maverick of Radio," McClendon was born in the East Texas town of Paris and lived for a few years in Palestine before attending high school in Atlanta, 150 miles to the north. He amassed a fortune in radio and, among other notable feats, called Bobby Thomson's "Shot Heard 'Round the World" on national radio in the 1951 finale of the three-game playoff between the New York Giants and the Brooklyn Dodgers.

Bobby swings, and there's a long one out to left: Going, going GONE and THE GIANTS WIN THE PENNANT! THE GIANTS WIN THE PENNANT!

McClendon, who called himself "the Old Scotsman," managed to outdo iconic broadcasters Ernie Harwell, Red Barber, and Russ Hodges with his hair-raising yell on the Liberty Radio Network. So colorful was his call that it is still frequently replayed on ESPN TV and radio.

What McClendon brought into Bradley's radio world on KLIF was the sounds of James Brown, Otis Redding, the Four Tops, the Temptations, and Bo Diddley. These were just a few of Bradley's favorites. So how is it possible that a boy growing up in a blue-collar, redneck town like Palestine could come to love Negro music?

The biggest contributor was his sister, May, named after her aunt.

May Bradley was born four years ahead of Bill and by 1961 was sprouting her own musical wings. She tried to conceal her new musical devotion from her parents, Joe and Mildred, but was quick to share it with her little brother.

As May was growing up in Palestine, she gravitated to artists like Otis Redding, Jimmy Reed, Bobby "Blue" Bland, and Bo Diddley. One of her favorite Diddley songs was "I'm a Man"—*Now I'm a man, spelled M-A-N.* Diddley sang with a tremolo in his voice and played with a tremolo in his guitar. His rhythm-and-blues guitar was drenched with rock and roll.

"I loved it all," she said, "and I listened to it every day."

According to the Rock and Roll Hall of Fame, soul music "arose out of the black experience in America through the transmutation of gospel and rhythm & blues into a form of funky, secular testifying." This did not mean it was off-limits to white people.

At the age of sixteen, May went to a private party in Kilgore, and who should show up but Chuck Berry? After hearing "Maybelline" (*Oh, Maybelline, why can't you be true*) and "Johnny B. Goode" (*Go, Johnny, Go*), she was completely hooked.

Bill Bradley reveled in the R&B records that May smuggled into the house. Not long after graduating from high school, he and Curtis Fitzgerald sold a set of wheel covers for thirty bucks and took off for Tyler to see Bo Diddley perform at the Caldwell Auditorium.

"We were the only white faces in the crowd, and that was okay because everyone was having a good time," he said. "It was one of the most fun things in my life."

Bill Bradley was not afraid to show his goodwill toward black people. His father raised him that way. When Joe Bradley said, "You don't say nigger in my house," he meant it.

"My brother learned from my father never to pass judgment on people," May Bradley said. "My daddy was kind to everyone he ever met, and he loved his friends."

One afternoon, Bradley and his friends were walking the downtown streets when they came upon the drinking fountains marked WHITE and COLORED. Bradley decided to have a little fun. He said to the boys, "Come over here. Let me show you something." He bent down and began drinking from the colored fountain.

"Now, look here, fellas," he said. "The water coming out of the faucet is clear—as clear as anything I've ever seen. It tastes good. It tastes just like the water coming out of the white fountain. So what is the big deal here? Why can't we all drink from the same water fountain? I will never understand that."

In the blink of an eye, Bradley sprinted into the restroom marked COLORED and took a whiz. Walking back outside, he said, "You know, the colored restroom is a lot cleaner than ours."

Bradley and Curtis Fitzgerald and the gang counted several black friends. It was not unusual for the majority of the Palestine Wildcats football team to fill up one section of the downtown stadium when the black team from A. M. Story played on Thursday nights. The Wildcats did not seem to mind that they were in the vast minority.

On Friday nights, the Story players came to Wildcat Stadium and cheered their lungs out for Bradley and all of the Wildcats.

"It was just too bad we couldn't have all played on the same team," Bradley said. "With their talent and our talent, we could have won state every year."

In 1965, the top 5 soul hits on *Billboard* were 1) "I Got You (I Feel Good)" by James Brown, 2) "My Girl" by the Temptations, 3) "I Can't Help Myself," 4) "Ain't That Peculiar" by the Four Tops, and 5) "Shotgun" by Junior Walker & the All Stars.

Bradley and LeVias were sitting around the farmhouse room on the second night in Hershey when Bradley pulled from his suitcase a small radio with a handmade antenna and a roll of aluminum foil. He looked across the room at his roommate relaxing on the bed.

"Jerry, I bet you a hundred dollars that I can pick up WLS out of Chicago."

"Bill, I don't gamble," LeVias said. "I'm from the Church of Christ. If the Church of Christ knew I was betting with you, they'd send me straight to hell."

Both youngsters laughed, and LeVias continued, "You know, Bill, I truly believe you can pick up that radio station with that little radio of yours. I believe that because you *are* Bill Bradley, the legend from East Texas."

Bradley grinned and said, "Now, hold on, Jerry. I've seen some pretty big headlines attached to your name. Seems the whole world sat up and took notice when you signed with SMU back in May."

"That was just a day's worth of headlines," LeVias said. "Bill Bradley, you've had a lifetime of big, bold headlines."

"Yeah, but I never averaged more than 40 yards on kick returns. How in the world did you manage that?"

"Well, I took quite a few to the house. Long touchdowns help your average. Long touchdown runs are what a colored ballplayer is supposed to do. Surely you've noticed that I'm colored."

Bradley stuck a wad of chewing tobacco between his teeth and said, "I've witnessed your speed out on the practice field. We're going to have a lot of fun with these fat dumbasses from Pennsylvania come Saturday night. I'm just going to rear back and let her fly."

(*Left to right*): Doak Walker, coach Rusty Russell, and Bobby Layne. They were together at Highland Park High School from 1942 through 1943. (*Texas Sports Hall of Fame*)

Bobby Layne (*center*) chats with Highland Park coach Rusty Russell (*right*) and Herman "Sleepy'" Morgan (*left*). (*Texas Sports Hall of Fame*)

Bobby Layne running the ball against Texas A&M,
1948. (*Texas Sports Hall of Fame*)

Bobby Layne displays a
jump pass for the Detroit
Lions. (*Texas Sports Hall
of Fame*)

(*Left to right*) Doak Walker, Norma Walker, and North Carolina All-American running back Charlie "Choo Choo" Justice. (*Texas Sports Hall of Fame*)

(*Left to right*) Bill Bradley, wingback Curtis Fitzgerald, and coach Luke Thornton in 1964 after the Palestine Wildcats erased a 23–0 deficit against the Wichita Falls Hirschi. In the final ten minutes Bradley threw a touchdown pass to Fitzgerald to win the game 28–23 with no time remaining. (*Bill Bradley collection*)

Bobby Layne punts for the Highland Park Scots in 1944. (*Texas Sports Hall of Fame*)

Bobby Layne tossing the football. (*Texas Sports Hall of Fame*)

Jerry LeVias as a sophomore at SMU, 1966. (*Texas Sports Hall of Fame*)

Texas team photo at the Big 33 game, 1965. (*Fred Cervelli*)

Bill Bradley playing defensive back for the Philadelphia Eagles, 1972. (*Bill Bradley collection*)

Bill Bradley intercepting a pass with the Philadelphia Eagles. (*Texas Sports Hall of Fame*)

Bill Bradley as a senior
with the state champion
Palestine Wildcats in
1964. (*Texas Sports Hall
of Fame*)

Bill Bradley broad-
jumping at the University
of Texas, 1966. (*Bill
Bradley collection*)

Bill Bradley at quarterback for the Texas Longhorns,
1966. (*Texas Sports Hall of Fame*)

LeVias pointed at his roomie and said, "When you threw me that pass left-handed today, all the guys were oohing and ahhing. They acted like they didn't know you were ambidextrous. Hell, I thought everybody knew that. I must have read about it fifty times."

"Here's the best part. I'm going to throw you one left-handed in the game."

"Why don't you let me throw you one left-handed?" LeVias suggested.

"What?"

"That's right, I'm ambidextrous, too."

"Does anybody know that?"

LeVias shook his head and said, "What you've got to understand is that it's not cool to be left-handed in the black community. They think you're the child of the devil. That's what my own aunt called me. When I tried to write left-handed, the kids laughed at me and said, 'You are just dumb.' It was pretty tough growing up left-handed."

"So you were born left-handed and you had to teach yourself to be right-handed."

"That's right. I taught myself to be ambidextrous. Black people don't think that's cool."

Bradley shook his head "Hell, everybody in Palestine thought it was cool that I could write with both hands. I started dunking a basketball with my right hand when I was in the ninth grade, and with my left hand when I was in the tenth grade."

Bradley walked across the room and began to attach the aluminum foil to the crude antenna. His eyes brightened. He was already sensing music in the air. LeVias moved a little closer to the radio, and his anticipation also showed.

"By my best estimation, we are seven hundred miles from Chicago," Bradley said. "It was a thousand miles from Palestine to Chicago. We have some rolling hills in East Texas just like they do up here. But somehow I wonder if the signal is going to be as strong."

LeVias said, "You're going to a lot of trouble. Just how much Negro music do you listen to?"

"A lot," Bradley said. "Maybe I've got some black in me. I think that people in my neck of the woods all have a little black in them."

During the pre–Civil War years, Palestine was a main link for the Underground Railroad, a network of secret routes and houses for slaves seeking freedom. Many Negroes came straight through Palestine en route to St. Louis and Chicago. A good percentage traveled by boat or train, but most covered about fifteen miles a day by foot. The actual railroad did not come to Palestine until the 1870s.

With the antenna properly aluminized, Bradley set the radio next to the window and turned it on. Blasting from the little speaker was the voice of James Brown singing the No. 1 soul hit of the year.

I feel good, I knew that I would now . . .
I feel nice, like sugar and spice.

Within seconds, Bradley and LeVias were up and dancing around the room, impersonating the moves of "the King of Soul."

LeVias said, "Bill Bradley, how in the world do you know the words to all of these damn songs? Hell, you know the words better than I do."

Bradley answered, "I've been listening to this stuff since I was a little boy." Then he threw back his head and laughed. "I've never danced with a black man before, though," he said. "Much less an ambidextrous one."

13

Beach Party Football

Doak Walker was so humble that when he earned All-American honors at SMU in 1947, he wrote a thank-you note to the Associated Press.

He received his thanks the following year by winning the Heisman Trophy. All he did was finish among the collegiate leaders in rushing, passing, punting, kick returns, field goals, and interceptions. So famous was "the Doaker" that the Cotton Bowl in Dallas added 20,000 seats to accommodate his fans. In the summer of 1965, Walker was Bill Bradley and Jerry LeVias rolled into one.

On a hot and humid morning, Walker stood 20 yards up the practice field and studied LeVias running pass patterns. The wide receiver position was totally unfamiliar to LeVias, who had lined up at halfback and quarterback for the Hebert Panthers.

"Looky here, Jerry," Walker said. "Plant your foot like this, then cut it back. That's right. *That's right.*"

Walker was teaching LeVias the comeback route.

"Blast out of your stance. Sprint to right here and stop. *Right here.*"

Walker pointed to a spot 15 yards from the line of scrimmage.

"Then cut it back 3 yards. Keep your eyes on the quarterback. The ball's coming fast."

Rusty Clark, a 6'3", 200-pound quarterback from Houston Westbury, cocked his arm and cranked a bullet into LeVias's chest.

Texas wide receiver Jerry LeVias with coach Doak
Walker at the Big 33 game in 1965.

—*Fred Cervelli*

"Turn and run," Walker shouted, "Show the DB your spin move. He's going to be in your hip pocket when you catch the ball. You've got to get around him."

LeVias had been taught in high school to take off at full speed and keep going. Coach Clifton Ozen prayed the quarterback's arm would be strong enough to reach him 40 or 50 yards away. Most of the time, LeVias had to slow down and wait for the ball.

Walker could not wait to change the drill to go-routes. He wanted to see which quarterback could throw the farthest. He split out James Harris of Brownwood to the left and LeVias to the right. Clark would be throwing to Harris, and Bradley to LeVias.

On the first route, Clark floated a high, arcing pass to Harris that hit him in stride. Bradley then lofted a perfectly placed pass that found LeVias in a full sprint 50 yards down the field.

They continued the drill for several more throws until Walker and Layne huddled in the middle of the field.

"Who throws the best deep ball, Doaker?" Layne asked.

"Right now, it's a tie," Walker said. "Clark has the stronger arm, but Bradley knows how to put air under the ball. Jerry has not outrun a single ball Bill's thrown."

LeVias hauled in another long ball from Bradley. As he jogged to the huddle, he reared back and fired a left-handed strike to his room-mate.

"What the hell was that?" Layne shouted. "Did I just see Jerry LeVias throw a pass left-handed?"

As he ran past Layne, LeVias said, "You sure did, Coach. You see, I'm ambidextrous just like the great Bill Bradley."

LeVias would provide the same explanation to Layne and Walker that he had given to Bradley the previous night. He was born a natural left-hander but was forced to use his right hand so he would not be called a "child of the devil."

"I can also kick field goals and extra points with both feet, just like my roomie, Bill Bradley, the legend from East Texas," LeVias said. "I'm hoping to get a tryout as your placekicker."

As he watched LeVias throw another left-handed pass, Layne's jaw dropped. A light went on in his head. He brought LeVias and Bradley together and drew up a play in the dirt.

"Jerry, you line up as the split receiver to the right," Layne said. "Then you come back to the left, and Bill's going to pitch you the ball on the reverse. You roll around left end, stop, and throw back across the field to Bill. He should be wide open."

Both players smiled. The play was executed beautifully, LeVias hit a wide-open Bradley down the right sideline.

"Touchdown!" Layne shouted. "That'll work every time."

Walker put his arm around LeVias's shoulder as they walked together back to the huddle.

"Jerry, we're going to make good use of you Saturday night," he said. "You'll outrun everybody on their defense."

Practically everyone in the Texas camp was trying to make LeVias feel at home. Walker tutored him more than any other player. Knowing LeVias would be the centerpiece of the Texas attack, Walker instructed him on every nuance of the offense.

Both Layne and Walker had grown up in a segregated culture with virtually no contact with blacks, but neither displayed racial prejudice. Both had played high school football in the wealthy, all-white suburb of Dallas known as Highland Park. Layne went off to all-white Texas, and Walker to all-white SMU. Not until they reached professional football in the late 1940s did either play with or against Negro athletes. Both adapted quickly to integration in the pros. One of Layne's best friends was fullback John Henry Johnson, a man he called "Sweet John." During the off-season, Johnson spent a lot of time at Layne's home in the West Texas town of Lubbock.

During their time together in Pittsburgh, Layne and his best friend, Ernie Stautner, hit the town virtually every night. They loved the jazz clubs on the North Side. Two of their running buddies were Johnson and Gene "Big Daddy" Lipscomb, the 300-pound defensive end traded in 1960 to the Steelers from the Colts.

"We liked to go to the black clubs with John and Big Daddy,"

Stautner remembered. "The next night, they would go to the white clubs with us. Believe me, we had a wonderful time."

During the water break, LeVias sidled up to Bradley and said, "Did Doak Walker really win the Heisman Trophy?"

"Hell yes he did," Bradley said. "He's one of the greatest players in the history of the Southwest Conference. You didn't know that?"

"Where I came from, nobody paid attention to SMU. I never thought I'd be allowed to play at an all-white school like that."

Bradley shook his head and said, "That must have seemed pretty strange knowing you had to leave the state to play college football."

"Everybody had to," LeVias said. "That's just part of life. Willie Ray Smith went off to Iowa, then Kansas. Bubba Smith took off for Michigan State. My cousin Mel Farr went to UCLA. What seems weird is that I'm going to be playing for a school in Texas that produced a Heisman Trophy winner. Maybe I can win it."

Spitting a stream of tobacco, Bradley said, "Only one Negro's ever won it, and that was Syracuse's Ernie Davis in 1961. I hate to break this news to you—he died of leukemia about a year later and never got to play pro football."

"That's terrible," LeVias said. "I felt like I was going to die with polio once. Thank the good Lord, I got over that."

The Pennsylvania players were working out on a practice field about a hundred yards away. The Texans could hear them grunting and banging helmets. They had been at it for more than two hours, having begun the morning practice just past dawn, a good hour before the Texas players came out in shorts and T-shirts.

Layne couldn't have cared less that George "Lefty" James was working his players like rented mules. The Texas coach did not plan to conduct hitting drills all week. Not once before the Saturday night game would the Texans suit up in shoulder pads and helmets. He had his reasons. Most of the Big 33 players had participated in the Texas North-South All-Star Game a few days earlier. In the week leading up to that game, they had endured two-a-day practices for five straight days. With a game already under their belts, Layne knew his players would be in hitting shape and sharp.

Just as the Texas players were watching the northerners labor through the heat and high humidity, the Pennsys were keeping close watch on the boys from the Lone Star State. From afar, it looked like the Texans didn't give a hoot about the upcoming game. Instead of calisthenics, they had warmed up with a football version of volleyball. They batted a football back and forth over one of the goalposts and actually kept score.

Quarterback Terry Hanratty, who would become an All American at Notre Dame and win a national championship in 1966, could not believe his eyes.

"While they're playing volleyball on their field, we're down there doing crab crawls across the field and breaking our fingers," Hanratty recalled. "Believe me, I wanted to be down on that other field with Bobby Layne playing volleyballl."

"Crab crawls" meant the players walked on all fours from one sideline to the other, a distance of about 60 yards. The exercise supposedly was designed to build muscle in the thighs and hamstrings. More than anything else, it caused leg cramps, especially in tired and dehydrated players.

By instructing his boys to play volleyball, Layne was promoting an appearance of nonchalance. In truth, Layne's practices were not always a stroll on the beach. He was running structured and fairly disciplined workouts that focused on teaching the players his offensive and defensive schemes. Texas would be running a complex NFL-style offense. Layne's playbook overflowed with counters, traps, keepers, reverses, and draws. He was dusting off the shotgun formation that San Francisco coach Red Hickey had reintroduced to the NFL a couple of years earlier. All of Layne's chips would be on the Texas speed. Four of his players could run the 100-yard dash in 9.8 seconds or better, and the entire backfield, with the exception of Ronnie Scoggins, covered the distance in less than 10 seconds. Scoggins had recorded a lumbering 10.1.

Layne was taking it easy on his players, but he had not lost his edge. He was still angry about the loss to Pennsylvania the previous year. He remembered walking off the field and hearing the cat-calls from the stands. How could he forget the Hershey fans blaming his kids for the assassination of President John F. Kennedy? He could still hear the public address announcer bellowing, "Hey, Texas, do you want a rematch?"

The previous day, Layne had met the press head-on at the Cocoa Inn. He told the gathering of writers, "These chicken turds from Pennsylvania cheated us last year. Furthermore, they tried to cheat us again this year. If me and the Doaker hadn't gone to the governor, we'd be back here again with the second stringers. I can tell you right now without a doubt that we are going to whip the snot out of these Yankees come Saturday night."

It would be the umpteenth time the past year that Layne had called the Pennsys "cheaters". This time, coach James decided to punch back.

"I can't believe that Bobby Layne has the gall to say some of the things that he says," James said. "We've never tried to cheat anybody. Layne is still mad that we beat them fair and square last year."

Layne read the James quote while drinking his morning coffee. His face turned beet red as the veins in his neck popped out. He yelled, "Fair and square! Fair and square!" Then he turned to Walker and said, "I'll tell you, Doaker, the only square in this town is George 'Lefty' James his own self."

The Pennsylvania coach was bald with thick glasses and a pedigree from the Ivy League, where he had coached from 1947 through 1960. He wore a pinkie ring on his right hand and was so soft-spoken that his players could barely hear him. He did not believe in bluster or fiery pep talks. In short, he was the antithesis of Bobby Layne.

What further separated Layne and James was the latter's vast coaching résumé. After ten years of high school coaching, James did his college apprenticeship at the University of North Carolina under Carl Snavely, who had coached him at Bucknell. In 1947, he replaced the impetuous Ed McKeever as the Cornell head coach and turned the program around in just one year. The Big Red's only loss in 1948 was to Army 27–6 during a season when the Cadets outscored opponents 294–89 and finished 8-0-1 with a number 6 ranking. James won the Ivy League title that year, then again in '49 and '53. Cornell tied Yale for the title in 1954. He stressed that football was a "thinking man's game" during a period when the alumni wanted to pursue big-time status and to compete with the Syracuses of the collegiate game. After a 2–8 season, he was fired at Cornell in 1960.

The next year, Pennsylvania was forced to turn the Big 33 into an in-state game. James was hired in 1961 and coached the West to victories in 1961, '62, and '63 by the combined score of 109–20.

On paper, James seemed the perfect coach to lead Pennsylvania into the series with Texas. On the field, he would have to stop an angry Layne and a roster that was far improved over the 1964 team.

Carlton Stowers of the *Lubbock Avalanche-Journal* was the second Texas sportswriter after Fred Cervelli to hit the scene in Hershey. He stepped into Bobby Layne's room at the Cocoa Inn and found Cervelli in a peculiar position—down on his hands and knees.

"Come on, double deuces," Cervelli yelled. "Baby needs new shoes."

Cervelli instead rolled a seven, and Layne grabbed his cash.

"Fred, you are the worst damn dice player I've ever seen," Layne said. "Furthermore, when it comes to picking football players, you wouldn't know a Texas blue-chipper from a fat Chinaman."

Layne filled his scotch glass and said, "Carlton, did you know that Fred here went out and found me a left-handed center? Do you know how hard it is for a quarterback to take a snap from a left-handed center?"

Taking a swig from his favorite libation, Cervelli said, "Bobby, I didn't bring you a single left-handed center. Not Terry Don Phillips, not Skippy Spruill, and not Ken Gidney."

"Gidney, he's the left-handed one," Layne squealed. "Hell, Bradley couldn't even hold on to the danged ball when Gidney snapped it."

Cervelli shook his head and said, "Gidney's not left-handed either."

"Then why was he snapping it left-handed?" Layne asked. "Anyway, roll the damn dice, Fred."

Also down on his hands and knees, waiting for his chance to roll, was defensive coach Mal Kutner, one of Layne's teammates from his collegiate days at Texas. Cervelli looked forlorn. "Bobby, I'm not as good a gambler as you are."

"That's all right, Fred," Layne said. "As long as you've got money, you can gamble with me anytime."

Stowers knew that Layne would soon try to snooker him into the game, so he walked next door to Harley Sewell's room. Sewell was an All-American linebacker at the University of Texas in the early 1950s and a first-round choice of Detroit in 1953. Moving to guard, he helped protect Layne during that second straight championship season. He played ten years in Detroit, four with Layne at quarterback.

A stout man at 230 pounds, Sewell was considered a scrapper and a street fighter in the NFL. He played with great energy, threw back whiskey with passion and, like Walker, would have done almost anything to make Layne happy.

When Stowers walked into the room, Sewell was lying bare-chested on his bunk with a Budweiser propped straight up on his chest.

After greeting the sportswriter, Sewell said, "I just got off the phone with my wife. She thinks we're all up here on one big vacation."

Stowers grinned and puffed on his pipe. He said, "After watching practice this morning with all of the volleyball, then coming to the hotel to see y'all so hard at work, I would say she is *dead* wrong."

"Very funny, Carlton," Sewell said, taking another pull off his beer.

14

Coal Crackers

While radically different in size, Texas and Pennsylvania were identical when it came to raising football players. The states were forged into football factories by the same blue-collar work ethic. Texas youngsters grew up working on the ranches and the oil derricks. During the broiling heat of summer, roughnecking and hay baling could turn your skin to leather. The Pennsylvania youngsters hardened their exterior by following their fathers into the steel mills and coal mines.

The unofficial nickname for the Pennsylvania team was the "coal crackers." It was a moniker worn with pride. A coal cracker was a tough hombre from the northeastern part of the state, one who lived among the anthracite mountains and mined coal for a living. Miners drank a lot of beer and consumed pounds of hot bologna. They also worked long hours for low wages. A good percentage of the miners died on the job.

The coal crackers wanted everyone to know they were not intimidated by the tough boys from Texas. Given their state's celebrated football lineage, why should they be? In 1965, Pennsylvania could boast four Heisman Trophy winners—quarterback Angelo Bertelli (Notre Dame, 1943), quarterback Johnny Lujack (Notre Dame, 1947), end Leon Hart (Notre Dame, 1949), and halfback Ernie Davis (Syracuse, 1961). The list of non-Heisman stars over the years was equally as impressive: Joe Namath, Johnny Unitas, Fred Biletnikoff, George

Blanda, Chuck Bednarik, Lenny Moore, Herb Adderley, Joe Schmidt, Bill George, Charley Trippi, and Mike Ditka. Even Bert Bell, the NFL commissioner from 1946 until his death in 1959, played college football at the University of Pennsylvania and led the Quakers to the 1917 Rose Bowl. Pennsylvanians also claimed Harold "Red" Grange as one of their own. "The Galloping Ghost" was born in the state but moved to Wheaton, Illinois, at age five.

Two Heisman Trophy winners came from Texas—TCU quarterback Davey O'Brien in 1938 and SMU halfback Doak Walker in 1948. Texas could brag of three times more All Americans than Pennsylvania. This was not surprising, though, since the state of Texas was five times larger.

Beating the Texas Big 33 team the previous year was a historic event for a state impassioned by football. It was further proof that Pennsylvania was the leading producer of high school talent in America. Coach Lefty James planned to keep it that way. That was why he was cracking the whip on his coal crackers.

"What we were going through that summer of 1965 was a boot camp," Penn quarterback Terry Hanratty recalled. "Lefty thought it was totally wrong that Bobby Layne was letting the Texas guys cut up and have fun. Meanwhile, we were working our butts off."

The Pennsylvania roster was filled with well-fed, muscled-up players. With 235-pound Mike Reid of Altoona lining up at fullback, the average weight of the coal crackers' offensive backfield was heavier than both of the Texas lines. Playing alongside Reid would be 205-pound Steve Edwards of Duquesne. James was planning to wear down the small, quicker Texans with big backs pounding the line.

In the mid-1960s, tight end Ted Kwalick of Montour seemed like a giant at 6'4" and 225 pounds. Penn State assistant coach Joe Paterno had spent the better part of the recruiting season pursuing Kwalick and signed him to a letter of intent in February.

"I've never seen a kid in my life catch the football like Ted Kwalick," Paterno said during the Big 33 week. "He plays as well on defense as he does on offense. Already, people are comparing him to Mike Ditka."

Ditka in 1965 was the greatest tight end in the history of the NFL. Playing at the University of Pittsburgh from 1958 through 1960, Ditka was an All American. He caught an unheard-of 56 passes his first season with the Chicago Bears in 1961 and was named Rookie of the Year. This was during an era when the tight end was just another blocker in the offensive line. Beginning in 1961, Ditka made the Pro Bowl five straight seasons, catching 284 passes during that stretch. His 59 receptions in 1963 helped lead Chicago to the 1963 league championship as the Bears defeated the New York Giants 14–10 at Wrigley Field. In 1964, he led the entire league with 75 receptions.

Was Kwalick going to be the next Ditka? Hanratty thought so. In fact, he was so intrigued with Kwalick that in the weeks leading up to the Big 33 game, he had traveled two hundred miles to Montour to work out with the big tight end. He was champing at the bit to team up with Kwalick against the Texas blue-chippers.

"He probably had the best hands I'd ever seen," Hanratty recalled. "He could catch any pass with his fingernails. The comparison that Paterno made to Ditka is very good. You could put the ball in the crowd and he would come up with it. He had hands like a vise. If you were going to shake hands with him, you'd better brace yourself. I just don't think that I ever saw him drop a pass."

With players like Kwalick on his roster, Lefty James felt certain that he could beat Texas for the second straight year. He was not worried that Texas possessed considerably more speed and that LeVias was going to stretch his defense. James knew that if he could whip his players into shape with grass drills, crab walks, and eye-openers, the coal crackers would hold an advantage over the laid-back Texans. He was planning to work his boys until their tongues hung out.

Near the end of the second morning workout, James peered toward the Texas practice field and shook his head.

"Just look at all of the crap they do," he said. "They're playing volleyball again. I wonder if they even brought shoulder pads and helmets to practice with. We'll kick their ass."

In truth, most of the coal crackers wished they were playing for Layne.

"Lefty decided he wanted to be a drill sergeant, and most of us couldn't figure it out," Hanratty recalled. "I really think he should have let us have some fun, just like the Texas guys. They were getting to do all of the socializing. They were loose because of Bobby Layne. I wish we could have had fun like that."

After each practice, the Pennsylvania players were forced to pass within about 20 yards of the Texas practice field on their way back to the locker room. On the second day in Hershey, Layne planned an ambush. He ordered all of his players to gather beneath the goalpost to play volleyball.

"Cut up and make a lot of noise," Layne told his players. "I want to piss those coal crackers off."

He pulled Bradley aside to plot a little strategy.

As the coal crackers approached, the fatigue on their faces was evident. They slowly trudged up the hill, having endured a three-hour practice that had included a lengthy, full-contact scrimmage.

With the coal crackers within earshot, Bradley yelled, "Remember the Alamo!"

A coal cracker shot back, "The Alamo was where you dumbasses got massacred."

Bradley stepped forward and shouted, "But come Saturday night, we're doing the massacring."

The Penn players stopped and stared. A few wanted to fight, but they knew that Lefty James would probably kick them off the team.

As they continued their slow march to the locker room, they could not help hearing the next voice slathered with a thick Texas drawl.

"Keep on walking, boys! After we get through with you Saturday night, your coach will be wiping your fat fannies!"

One of the coal crackers yelled, "We'll settle this on the field!"

"Hell, no," Bradley shot back. "We'll be the one settling the score this time."

—Texas Sports Hall of Fame

15

Hershey Kisses

We would tell the girls in Hershey that we were from Texas and they would just swoon. They all wanted to be with us.

—Jerry LeVias

Bobby Layne reconnoitered a bar called Martini's and chose it as the headquarters for nightly libations and football fellowship because it was a few blocks from the Cocoa Inn and provided plenty of cold beer and scotcz to cool down a bunch of burly men after a long, hard day on the practice field.

Among those who regularly gathered around the tables at Martini's were Doak Walker, Harley Sewell, Mal Kutner, Fred Cervelli, and Layne. Occasionally, University of Texas recruiting coordinator Russell Coffee dropped by, along with former UT basketball star Slater Martin, a drinking buddy of Layne's from their days in Austin. Martin, a 5'10" guard with quick hands, led the Longhorns the NCAA Semi-Finals in 1947. A member of the rai smith, he guided the Minneapolis Lakers to four NBA titles.

Legendary New York Giants All-Pro linebacker Sam Huff, who made on the cover of *Time* in 1959, also came to see Layne at Martini's. He and Layne had fought it out during their NFL careers, prompting Huff to say, "A fellow like Layne, a scrappy back-alley veteran, makes me want to play harder. He throws the challenge right at your feet and then dares you to do anything about it."

So cocky was Layne that he would say, "Hey, Huff, we're coming right at you. And the snap count is on two." Years later, they were still laughing about it over drinks at a bar on Chocolate Avenue.

Another friend of Layne's was Ray Renfro, who played twelve seasons with the Cleveland Browns and was known as "the Rabbit." Proof of his speed was a 19.6-yard average per reception. He scored a touchdown every sixth time he caught the ball. Also joining the boys at Martini's was Buddy Parker, who was Layne's coach in Detroit and Pittsburgh. Layne and Parker, along with Walker, had teamed up for two NFL championships in the Motor City in 1952 and '53.

On the second night in Hershey, Cervelli was having a drink when, out of the corner of his eye, he noticed Bill Bradley waving at him. Bradley, in fact, was standing in the middle of Martini's parking lot, waving both arms. While not a lip-reader, Cervelli could clearly see Bradley mouthing the words, "Hey, Fred, I really need to talk to you!"

Cervelli liked Bradley and was willing to help out in any way. So he strolled outside and said, "What can I do for you, Bill? I hope everything is okay."

"Fred, I need to borrow your car for a little while."

"Bill, where are you planning to go?" Cervelli asked.

"Well, we'd like to either find a casino or a Playboy Club."

"Wow! That's going to take some driving. I think the closest casino is in Las Vegas, and the nearest Playboy Club is New York City."

"Well, then we'll just tool around town and try to find some girls."

"Who's going with you?" Cervelli asked.

"Ah, nobody, really." Bradley did not want to alert Cervelli or anyone else that Jerry LeVias was going. Taking a Negro out on the town in 1965 might seem a little radical to the white grown-ups.

"What time will you be back?" Cervelli asked.

"I promise we'll be back by ten o'clock."

"Okay," Cervelli said. "Not one minute later, you hear?"

Cervelli felt a little nervous handing over the car to one of his players. He knew that Bradley was a free spirit, but he was the best football player in Texas and a bona fide star on the Big 33 team. Cervelli was just going to have to trust him.

Bradley grabbed the keys to the 1965 Buick and took off. Just around the next corner, he stopped to pick up Norm Bulaich, standing behind a tree, who swung open the front door and ducked down beneath the dashboard. A little farther up the street, LeVias jumped in the backseat and lay flat.

"Why are you guys hiding?" Bradley asked.

"Because we don't want the coaches to see us," Bulaich said.

Bradley laughed. "What the hell! If Bobby Layne knew what we were up to, he'd probably want to go. He'd probably want to meet our girls' mamas."

The Texas quarterback already had big plans for the evening. They had met three girls at Hershey Park the previous night, and Bradley had arranged a rendezvous. As they pulled into the dirt parking lot of the amusement park, LeVias said, "Bill, I don't think I want to ride that stupid roller coaster again. The beer and the roller coaster made my stomach do cartwheels." Bradley didn't know that LeVias had actually spit out his beer.

"Well, we're not drinking beer tonight—not yet, anyway," Bradley said. "Besides, the girls'll want to take a couple of spins on the roller coaster before they get in the car with us."

"Why's that?"

"Because that's how it works," Bradley said. "That way, they feel like they know us better. They can tell their mamas that three nice youngsters from Texas spent money on them. I'm sure the mamas around here are a little wary about us wildcats from Texas."

LeVias laughed and said, "You've got it all figured out, don't you, Bill. I guess it's just all part of being Bill Bradley, the legend."

"Proud to oblige, Jerry. Proud to be your friend."

"I'm proud to be your friend," LeVias said.

The girls were Mary Jane, Pam, and Sylvia. They were all pretty in their pleated miniskirts and saddle oxfords. Bradley was willing to step aside and let his teammates make their choices. That was before Mary Jane took his right hand and put it around her waist. Mary Jane was a tall brunette with dark brown eyes. Bradley felt her warmth as he pulled her closer. Pam soon was holding hands with Bulaich, and LeVias was doing the same with Sylvia.

Bradley knew that LeVias wanted to avoid the roller coaster at all costs. His roomie kept motioning with his head toward the parking lot.

"Okay, girls, let's take a vote," Bradley said. "As you know, we have a brand-new red Buick out in the parking lot. Who wants to ride the roller coaster? And who wants to go for a *ride*?"

In the blink of an eye, Mary Jane said, "We all want to go for a ride. Let's get out of here before somebody sees us."

Back at the bar, Layne was holding forth as the crowd around his table continued to burgeon. Layne was drinking scotch at an ever-quickening pace. They stopped just long enough to clink glasses.

Layne grinned and said, "Based on what I've seen of my football team, we'll beat these Yankees 30 to nothing. No, make that 50 to nothing."

Just then the surprise guest of the night was walking through Martini's front door. At 6'1" and 235 pounds, he was known as the greatest undersized tackle in the history of the NFL. Some thought he was the greatest—period. His most recognized feature was a thick, square jaw that looked like it had been molded with hot tongs, then shaped in the fiery oven of U.S. Steel. The chiseled man was Ernie Stautner, and he walked up behind Layne and wrapped his mammoth hands around his friend's neck. He whispered into Layne's ear, "If you lose this game to the coal crackers, I'm going to snap off your head."

Without turning, Layne said, "Well, if it's not the crazy Bavarian his own self. I heard you were around town or in the vicinity, raising hell, wreaking havoc, and probably drinking too much."

Layne and Stautner had played together for five years (1958–62) in the Steel City when times were tough, the players partied, and the fans booed. They would be a part of three winning season, but no one ever accused them of giving up.

After retiring, Stautner sought a career in coaching that had taken him to Washington, D.C. In the summer of 1965, he was defensive line coach of the Redskins. That was why he was in the vicinity, about thirty-five miles to the west in Carlisle, where Washington trained during the summer. Following the afternoon practice, he had decided to surprise Layne and drive into Hershey, knowing he could find his best friend after dark at a watering hole not far from the Big 33 camp.

Layne and Stautner had been inseparable from the moment the quarterback was traded from Detroit to Pittsburgh in September of 1958. Stautner was the Steelers' greatest player during the woeful years, and Layne was second best. In the era when the head slap was still legal, Stautner broke enough helmets with his hands and forearms to make Riddell a fortune. With one powerful blow to the head, he would leave their ears ringing. Hall of Fame guard Jim Parker once said, "That man ain't human. He's too strong to be human. He's the toughest guy in the league to play against because he comes headfirst. Swinging those forearms wears you down. The animal used to stick his head in my belly and drive me into the backfield so hard that when I picked myself up and looked around, there was a path chopped through the field like the farmer had run a plow over it."

Stautner had missed only six games in his fourteen-year career, having suffered three fractured ribs, a separated shoulder, two broken hands, and a fractured nose. His number 70 jersey was formally retired in 1964, the year after he left the game.

Layne and Stautner were hardly the odd couple when they hit the bars in Steel Town. They were there for one purpose: to drink. Instead of ordering one drink at a time, they ordered the entire bottle— scotch for Layne and scotch for Stautner. The circus always seemed to follow them.

That night in Hershey, so many people wanted to buy them drinks that the waitress said, "Maybe you guys should just move to Hershey and buy this bar. You could make a lot more money than we're making now."

Stautner had come armed with a lot of questions for Layne. He had read most of the newspaper accounts from last year's game and surmised that Layne was still mad as hell.

"Let me tell you something, Ernie, the people who run this Big 33 game will cheat you faster than a Vegas blackjack dealer," Layne said. "But we've got 'em this time. Wish you'd come by tomorrow and just take a look at the studs on my team."

Stautner said, "Who's your best player?"

"Clearly it's Bill Bradley, because he does everything—pass, run, catch passes, kick off, punt, kick field goals, and return kicks. Hell, he probably could coach better than me. Here's the spooky part about Bradley. He can do everything equally well left-handed or right-handed, left-footed or right-footed. I've been around this game all of my life and I've never seen anything like this kid."

"Have you got speed, or size, or both?"

"This is where we've got 'em beat," Layne said. "We're going to kill those fat boys with our speed. Jerry LeVias can fly. Hell, I never had a receiver that fast when I was quarterbacking. I threw 196 touchdown passes. I would've thrown 296 with LeVias on my team."

In the darkness of the deep woods along the Susquehanna River, the Buick's windows were fogging up. Bradley and Mary Jane were kissing in the front seat, and the other two couples were tangled up in the back.

If they had cared to look, they would have noticed the shimmering dome of the state capitol across the river in Harrisburg. The building was designed in 1902 as a Beaux-Arts style with Renaissance themes. The dome stood out like a fat green thumb on the skyline of Harrisburg.

The Susquehanna River that rolled past the Texas lovebirds was the sixteenth-largest river in the United States and was a mile wide at Harrisburg.

Bradley came up briefly for air and peeked out of the driver's side window long enough to catch a glimpse of the river.

"Y'all have got more water around here than the whole state of Texas," he said. "Other than the Mississippi River, I've never seen anything like this monster."

The smooching continued until Mary Jane said, "By the way, what time is your curfew?"

Bradley grabbed the front seat and pulled himself up, looking at the foursome in the back. "Hey, guys, what time is our curfew?"

"We don't have a curfew," LeVias said. "Bobby Layne doesn't care what time we come in so long as we make it to breakfast at seven and to the morning practice at eight."

"That's kind of strange," Mary Jane said. "The coal crackers have a nine o'clock curfew."

A silence fell over the car. With a look of surprise, Bradley rose up and said, "Now, how would y'all know what time the coal crackers are supposed to be in?"

Mary Jane smiled and said, "Because a couple of us girls in this car have boyfriends on the Pennsylvania team."

The kissing stopped, and the car grew even more quiet. The boys looked at each other and smiled. Then Bradley burst out laughing, almost uncontrollably.

"Now, that's the best news I've heard all week," he said. "We've been looking for a way to really piss off the coal crackers. Looks like we just found one. Y'all are going to be *our* girlfriends the rest of this week, you hear? And we really don't care if you tell your boyfriends that you've been kissing three big studs from the Texas team."

Bradley had worn all of the lipstick off Mary Jane's lips, so he decided to drive the sixsome back to Hershey. The girls had a midnight curfew. Bradley pulled up next to Mary Jane's car at Hershey Park as the boys enjoyed the long kiss good night. Then the Buick roared off again.

"We've still got some gas in this car," Bradley said. "Let's drive around and see if we can get ourselves in some more trouble."

Little did they know that Fred Cervelli was frantically looking for his car. He had left Martini's just past midnight and walked beneath the streetlights shaped like Hershey Kisses down Chocolate Avenue. He was hoping to find the car in the parking lot at the Cocoa Inn. Much to his chagrin, there was no Buick in sight. Bradley had promised to return it by 10:00 P.M. Cervelli was really worried. He did not like the prospect of calling parents back in Texas to say their kids were in jail.

From his room at the Cocoa Inn, Cervelli could see the entire parking lot. He paced the floor anxiously until 3:00 a.m., hoping to see headlights approaching. He finally lay down at 3:30 and fell asleep, then was tormented by nightmares until dawn, when he awoke to find the Buick back in its space. Bradley had returned at 4:00 A.M., then walked back to the farmhouse to get some sleep.

Bradley, LeVias, and Bulaich were all bright-eyed and filled with energy as they walked into the breakfast room at 7:00 A.M. They noticed that the coaches, with the exception of Harley Sewell, were glassy-eyed and dragging. Sewell, the last coach to bed at 3:00 A.M., was nowhere to be found. Cervelli was also missing.

The room was quiet except for the voice of Bradley. The other boys were still half-asleep, having logged eight hours. Bradley was still energized after two hours of smooching with Mary Jane.

"Boys, you should have seen it," he said. "We had three of the prettiest girls in all of Pennsylvania out with us last night. A couple of them happen to be girlfriends of the coal crackers. Wait till they find out what the Texans were doing with their girls last night."

At eight o'clock, following a big breakfast, the Texas players trotted onto the practice field in shorts and T-shirts. In the distance, the coal crackers were already cracking heads.

"Lefty's going to wear those boys out if he's not careful," Layne said. "Guess he doesn't know that volleyball is a great way to get a team ready."

The only Texas player to wear a helmet to practice was Bradley. A surprised Layne said, "What the hell are you doing, Bill? You didn't need to wear your bonnet to practice."

Bradley was standing close to Layne, fielding punts. He grinned and said, "Bobby, I want to show you something."

As the football flew toward him on a high arc, Bradley whipped off his helmet, held it over his head, and caught the pigskin in the center of the headgear—*thwump!*

Layne cackled and said, "Bradley, do it again!"

Bradley caught five more balls in his helmet without dropping one.

Then he said, "I've got one more thing to show you. Have you ever seen anybody throw a pass off his foot?"

"What?" Layne asked.

"Yeah, watch this, Bobby!"

On cue, LeVias took off running across the field. Bradley then punted the ball left-footed on a low spiral that looked like a pass. LeVias caught the ball shoulder-high 20 yards down the field and took off for the end zone.

Sounding like a radio announcer, the quarterback yelled, "Bradley to Levias! *Touchdown!*"

Layne giggled like a schoolkid. The laughter quickly died, though, when he spotted Sewell and Cervelli trudging across the practice field more than a half hour late.

"Where've you boys been?" Layne asked. "Practice started fifteen minutes ago, and y'all are just now dragging out of bed. Time to run some laps."

Cervelli frowned and said, "You've got to be kidding. I'm just a sportswriter."

"Don't care," Layne said. "Take off."

Sewell dropped his head, pumped his arms, then took off running without one word of protest. He knew better than to argue with Layne. Cervelli also should have known better.

"Bobby, I haven't run a lap around a football field since I was in school," Cervelli said. "I'm not sure that I can make it."

Realizing all hope was lost, Cervelli began to chug up the sideline. He was breathing hard when he approached the finish line with the players cheering him on. His punishment, however, was not yet over.

"One more lap, Fred," Layne shouted. "And get the lard out of your rear end."

Cervelli stumbled and staggered through one more lap before dropping to one knee to catch his breath. The players loved every minute of it. Bradley spoke up. "Hey, Bobby, maybe you should let Fred practice with us. We'll give him a good workout. Then he can get himself into drinking *and* football shape."

After Layne enjoyed his fun with Sewell and Cervelli, he finally started the practice. Meanwhile, the coal crackers had been banging helmets for more than an hour. This day, Bradley would line up at safety for most of the practice while Clark took 80 percent of the snaps at quarterback. Bradley wondered if the tall kid from Houston had moved ahead of him on the quarterback depth chart. In truth, Bradley did not mind playing safety. In fact, he had intercepted 11 passes his senior year while also making all-state at that position.

For Bradley, covering LeVias on the go-routes turned out to be an educational experience. He fully realized just how fast the youngster was.

"Roomie, you're wearing me out," he said. "Can I catch a break here?"

"Bill, you're just as fast as I am," LeVias said. "In fact, I bet you could beat me in a footrace."

As the practice was coming to a close, a man drove past the Texas practice field, smiled, and flipped Bobby Layne the bird. "F——you, Bobby Layne!" he yelled.

Layne ran toward the car, yelling, "F—— you back! F—— you back!" The man mashed the accelerator, and the car zoomed away.

Layne could not believe what he was seeing, or hearing. He turned to Walker and said, "Doaker, I actually recognized that guy. He bought me a drink last night at Martini's."

Walker grinned. "Well, Bobby, I guess you didn't buy him one in return."

Layne shook his head and said, "So that's how that works?"

16

Stealing Jerry LeVias

The Big 33 Football Classic was a magnet for all types—football fa-
natics, social drinkers, whiskey shooters, hangers-on, hustlers, and
pretty young women. Creating the most worrisome presence were the
college recruiters hoping to make an eleventh-hour backroom deal with
players already signed by other schools.

Nowhere in America could you find better high school talent than
in Hershey. Most college recruiters got an adrenaline rush at the mere
mention of the Big 33 week. Pennsylvania and Texas produced the
mother lode of high school football gold. Turn on the TV during the
fall and you were certain to hear a litany of accolades about Billy Bob
Smith from Itasca, Texas, or Rich Constantine of Uniontown, Pennsylvania.

That was why Chocolate Town U.S.A. was still rife with cheating.

What happened in Hershey from 1957 to 1959 was dirty business.
Rogue recruiters the big-time players and asked them to break letters
of intent already signed. The NCAA stepped in and told Big 33 officials
that the game would have to become an in-state contest. That would
reduce the number of star players and recruiters and the amount of
cheating.

That ban was lifted in 1964 when Texas was invited to Hershey to
play a series of games. The NCAA obviously did not realize that the

college recruiters would return in even larger numbers. With the Texans singing, dancing, drinking beer, and playing volleyball in Hershey, the number of college recruiters more than quadrupled.

One of those was Colorado coach Eddie Crowder, who in '64 had his eyes trained on hard-running fullback Wilmer Cooks of Dallas Madison High School. Cooks had already signed a conference agreement with UCLA, but he had not yet inked his national letter of intent, technically leaving the door open for him to switch schools. So talented was Cooks that Dan Jenkins would write in *Sports Illustrated* a year later, "He could become the best sophomore fullback in the Midwest since Jim Grabowski started for Illinois two seasons ago."

In the 1964 Big 33 game, Cooks carried 10 times for 66 yards against Pennsylvania. He gained the attention of every college coach in town. The day after the game, Crowder managed to get Cooks's signature. Cooks had come to Hershey as the property of UCLA and left as a signee of the Colorado Buffaloes.

Most coaches who came to Hershey were not there to shanghai players. Notre Dame coach Ara Parseghian dropped by in 1964 to watch the teams practice. USC's John McKay and Michigan State's Duffy Daugherty also made the trip in '64, as did Texas coach Darrell Royal, whose sole purpose was to see his six recruits play in the game. About the only elite college coach not to make an appearance was Paul "Bear" Bryant of Alabama.

After the game in 1964, Parseghian had returned to South Bend and told his coaching staff how appalled he was at the dirty recruiting going down in Hershey. The next year, he planned to play defense— literally. He dispatched defensive coordinator Johnny Ray to keep an eye on Irish signees Terry Hanratty of Pennsylvania and defensive tackle Ronnie Bell with the Texans. Likewise, Royal had sent Russell Coffee to "babysit" Texas's top recruits, including Bill Bradley, Chris Gilbert, Corby Robertson, and Danny Abbott.

Coffee came to Hershey with his game face on. Encountering a coach known for shady recruiting, he told the man, "If I see you talking to one of my players, I will personally kick your ass. In fact, I should just go ahead and kick your ass right now because I know you're a cheater."

Of all the bodyguards in Hershey, SMU assistant Chuck Curtis stood out the most. Wearing a large white Stetson, he was certainly the most intimidating. Curtis came to the Big 33 game to shoo the crooked recruiters away from one big-time blue-chipper by the name of Jerry LeVias.

At times, it seemed that Curtis was everywhere. He could be found watching practice, or standing outside the front door of the old farmhouse, or tipping a few with Layne and the boys down at Martini's. He kept tabs most of the day on his prized recruit.

On the morning of the third day at the old farmhouse, LeVias returned from practice to find a phone message from UCLA coach Tommy Prothro. He wadded it up and threw it in the trash. Then he heard the phone ringing down the hall and someone yelling his name—"Jerry LeVias, telephone!"

"Tell them I'm not here," LeVias yelled. Less than a minute later, the young female phone operator walked into his room and handed LeVias a piece of paper with "Tommy Prothro" written on it, along with a phone number.

"He said he's staying at the Holiday Inn and he'll be here all week," she said. "Mr. Prothro sounds like he really wants to talk to you."

LeVias thought his ties to Prothro had been severed by signing with SMU. Oh, he had enjoyed his trips to Los Angeles to visit the UCLA campus in Westwood, and he was always stoked to hit the town with his cousin Mel Farr. He knew the Bruins were going to have a good season in 1965.

Reading the preseason college football magazines like *Street & Smith*, LeVias noted that UCLA was ranked fourth in the preseason poll. What really stood out, and made LeVias feel a little sick, was the reference in *Sports Illustrated* to the "Dream Backfield" of Farr and quarterback Gary Beban. LeVias thought, *I could have been in that dream backfield. I worked out with those guys just a few months*

ago. Mel is my cousin. Gary is my friend. I could have been playing
for one of the best teams in the whole country.

A few hours later, LeVias and Bill Bradley were walking to the afternoon practice when Prothro came into sight.

"See that kinda tall guy over there with the horn-rimmed glasses?" LeVias asked. "That's the UCLA coach, Tommy Prothro. He recruited the heck out of me. I went to Los Angeles a couple of times. On one trip, I stayed several days. But I had to turn down UCLA when I signed with SMU. You can see Coach Prothro won't give up. He's still after me."

"What do you mean, he's still after you?"

"Well, he called me this morning. He's staying in Hershey all week, hoping I'll change my mind."

"Are you changing your mind?"

"No, I'm committed to SMU and Coach Fry."

Ten minutes later, Bradley was fielding punts before the start of practice when Bobby Layne swaggered past him.

"Hey, where's your helmet?" Layne asked. "Thought you were going to show us a few more tricks."

"Nah, Bobby, not today. But you never know what I might do tomorrow. Stay tuned."

Layne was walking away when Bradley said, "You ever heard of a guy named Tommy Prothro?"

"Yeah, he's a pretty good coach. He actually turned Oregon State from a doormat into a Rose Bowl team. This is his first year at UCLA, I think. Kind of a nutcase, I hear."

Bradley said, "Well, the nutcase is bothering my roomie. Prothro is in town trying to get Jerry to change his mind about SMU. Wants him to sign with UCLA."

Layne furrowed his brow and said, "Don't worry, Bill. I'll take care of it."

Halfway through practice, LeVias and Bradley were surprised to see Prothro working his way down the sideline toward Layne.

"He's going to get his head bit off, roomie," Bradley said. "He apparently doesn't know Bobby Layne."

LeVias and Bradley moved a little closer, hoping to overhear the conversation.

"Coach, I'm Tommy Prothro from UCLA," Prothro said. "I—"

"I know who you are," Layne said. "I heard you were in town. I can't say that I was happy to hear it."

"Well, I came all the way from Los Angeles to see Jerry LeVias. I was wondering if you could help me—"

"Absolutely no way," Layne snapped. "Jerry LeVias is already signed, sealed, and delivered to the SMU Mustangs. So you need to pack your shit and get out of Hershey."

Prothro smiled weakly and said, "Well, you know, we live in a free country, and you can't just throw me out of town. I have my rights."

"Let me tell you something, mister," Layne said. "Hayden Fry is a friend of mine, and you'd better not try to steal Jerry from him. Second of all, I want to see the color line broken in the Southwest Conference. It's about time, and based on what I've seen of this youngster the last few days, he's the perfect Negro to do it."

Prothro cleared his throat and said, "I'm just a little worried about how he's going to be treated in Dallas, that's all. On the West Coast, we've had Negroes on our rosters for decades. Jerry would be a lot happier in L.A."

Layne balled his fists like a man ready to fight. His face turned crimson. "Apparently, you don't know much about my history, mister," he said. "I was the toughest sumbuck to ever play quarterback in the NFL. If I were you, I'd start walking."

Prothro said, "You don't really scare me. I'm not leaving town until I talk to Jerry LeVias." Then he turned and walked away.

"Don't even think about talking to him, Prothro!" Layne yelled as the UCLA coach quickened his pace. "I wouldn't shit you, even though you are my favorite turd."

After practice, Layne called members of the coaching staff and Fred Cervelli together. They were huddled in the middle of the practice field when Layne said, "I want all of y'all to keep a close eye on this character Tommy Prothro. If you see him around Jerry LeVias, I want you to call the police."

As Bradley and LeVias walked together back to the old farm-house, they could see Prothro watching from the distance again. He was holding a briefcase. They wondered what he was thinking.

Lying on his bed after dinner, LeVias abruptly stood up and walked to the window. He stood there for several minutes, staring into the darkness.

"He's not out there," Bradley said. "I guarantee you that Tommy Prothro is back at his hotel, packing his bags. Bobby Layne scared the hell out of him."

LeVias laughed and shook his head. "I actually like Tommy Pro-thro. I spent some time out in L.A. and I thought Tommy was pretty cool. But now that I've made my decision, I just want him to go away."

"So why didn't you sign with UCLA?"

"I was going to. I really was, but everybody was trying to talk me out of it. My grandmother fell in love with Coach Fry, just like every-body else. My dad doesn't really trust a whole lot of white people, but even he started liking Coach Fry."

Bradley stood up from his bunk and began to walk around the room. "How did you feel about Fry?"

"At first, I didn't know what to feel. I never thought a white man would walk into the kitchen and start showing my grandmother how to cook pinto beans without giving people gas. That's just crazy. But before long, my grandmother was saying, 'There is something godly about that man.'"

Bradley threw up his hands and said, "I think people put some pressure on you."

"They did. Coach Ozen wanted me to be the first colored in the Southwest Conference. He watched all of his top players go out of state. He needed somebody to stay in Texas."

"How do you feel about being the first Negro?" Bradley asked.

"Here's the tricky part. I didn't know I *was* going to be the first. I really didn't. Hayden kept talking to me about being the next Jackie Robinson, but I didn't know I was going to be the very first Negro in the Southwest Conference."

"So when did you find out?"

"The Beaumont paper."

"How'd you feel?"

"Scared to death. I'm still scared. I just don't act like it anymore."

"Okay," Bradley said. "Somebody along the line didn't shoot straight with you. Was it Fry?"

"I can't be mad at Coach Fry, and here's why. When Coach Fry interviewed for the SMU job in '62, he told their president that he wanted to recruit black players. President Tate was surprised. But he finally realized it would good for the school to have black ball-players."

LeVias paused and Bradley could see tears gathering in the corners of his eyes.

"You will have to excuse me if I start to cry," he said, "but Hayden Fry and Willis Tate did a great thing. They cleared the way so I could become the first Negro in the Southwest Conference. At that point, it was up to me to do the right thing, and I did."

Bradley smiled and said, "That's a pretty cool story. I didn't know about any of that stuff. I had no idea what you went through."

LeVias walked to the window again and looked out. "I've done a lot of thinking the last few months. Why did they want *me* to break the color barrier? Why not Bubba Smith or Willie Smith Jr., the best high school player I've ever seen? You should have seen Willie Ray before he got hurt. He tore up his knee and they just kept riding him like a mule. They almost ruined that knee, but when he got to Kansas, they said he was still better than Gale Sayers. Now Willie Ray's out of football and he never got to show his stuff."

"You never know," Bradley said. "You might turn out to be the best one of 'em all, Jerry."

Bradley adjusted the aluminum strip on the antenna and turned on the radio. Blasting out of Chicago was the voice of James Brown.

He's doing the jerk . . . He's doing the fly . . .
Papa's got a brand-new bag.

They were singing and dancing again.

The morning practice was scheduled for Hershey Stadium. At seven thirty, the Texas players started boarding a yellow school bus for the ride across town.

"Let's go play some volleyball," Bradley yelled. "I bet those coal crackers will be beating each other up the whole day long."

Bradley and LeVias took seats next to each other on the third row. Bradley peered out the window and said, "There he is, Jerry. That sonofagun Tommy Prothro just won't go away."

LeVias's eyes widened when he saw Prothro standing about 10 feet from the bus door.

"He's going to do something crazy, Bill," LeVias said.

At that very moment, Prothro took off at a fast pace for the open door to the bus. He quickly climbed the steps and took a hard left. He walked down the aisle, his eyes searching for LeVias. When he spotted him, Prothro said, "Jerry, I really need to talk to you. Now! I came all the way from Los Angeles—"

Bradley stood up and yelled, "Shut up, old man, and get off our bus before I have to kick your ass."

From the rear came the voice of Fred Cervelli. "Don't do anything, Bill. I'm calling the police."

Then, out of nowhere, Chuck Curtis came thundering down the aisle. He looked seven feet tall wearing the white Stetson.

"Do not call the police, Fred," he said loudly. "It's time for me to handle this." Curtis wrapped his right arm around Prothro's neck and began to drag him up the aisle.

"Get your hands off of me," Prothro yelled. "I need to talk to Jerry LeVias."

"Shut up," Curtis snapped.

As Curtis pulled him down the stairs, Prothro yelled, "Jerry, if you go to SMU, they'll burn crosses. If you come to UCLA, we will treat you like a man!"

Reaching the ground, Curtis spun Prothro around and threw him into a chain-link fence. He landed a left to his jaw and a right to his midsection. Another right sent blood streaming from Prothro's nose.

"Stop, I'm going!" Prothro said.

"Going where?"

"Back to Los Angeles. I promise I won't be back."

As Prothro turned to walk away, Curtis pushed him, then kicked him in the butt with his size 13 cowboy boot.

"You bother Jerry LeVias again and I will kick your ass all the way back to Los Angeles."

The boys on the bus cheered wildly.

17

Fathers and Sons

Joe Hill Bradley was born in 1909, the year that Ty Cobb won baseball's Triple Crown. The Detroit Tigers outfielder hit .377 with 107 RBI and 9 home runs, all inside the park, thus becoming the only player to lead the league in home runs without hitting one over the fence. The Tigers reached the World Series but lost to the Honus Wagner–led Pittsburgh Pirates in seven games.

Baseball and Joe Bradley would be forever inseparable. Although he went to work for the railroad at the age of twelve, the game rarely escaped the reach of his mind. The sandlot fields of Dodge, Texas, were his heavens on earth.

The team that captured his imagination was the St. Louis Cardinals, the southernmost and westernmost team in the Major Leagues, and the only one he could pick up on his radio. Because of their location, the Cardinals would become a de facto "America's Team." They won the World Series in 1926 and '31, but the unforgettable season was 1934, when "the Gashouse Gang" led by Dizzy Dean reached the World Series against the Detroit Tigers. Dean is the last National League pitcher to win 30 games, going 30-7 with a 2.66 ERA in '34.

Dean and the Gashouse Gang became heroes of the Depression because they were hardworking and earthy. The Cardinals were the symbol of perseverance during a time when many Americans were trying to survive on the soup lines. The Gashouse Gang was so named because of their shabby appearance and rough-and-tumble style. Gas houses in that era were industrial plants that produced gas from coal for the purpose of lighting and cooking. The plants were normally found in the poorest parts of town.

Dean, from the tiny town of Lucas, Arkansas, was the kind of gritty, hardworking southerner fans gladly made a role model. As a sign of his fortitude, Dean once pitched both games of a doubleheader and won each one. Dean was also one of the first colorful characters in sports and was never afraid to make a prediction. Before the start of the 1934 season, he promised that he and his brother, Paul "Daffy" Dean, would combine for 45 wins. On September 21, Dizzy gave up 3 hits in the first game of a doubleheader against the Brooklyn Dodgers, winning his twenty-seventh game of the season by the score of 3–0. Daffy then threw a no-hitter for his eighteenth win, thus fulfilling Dizzy's forecast of 45 combined W's for the brotherhood.

After the game, Dizzy said, "If I'da knowed he was going to throw a no-hitter, I'da throwed one, too."

Few fans were as enamored of Dizzy and the Cardinals as Joe Bradley. His dream of playing Major League Baseball had slipped through his fingers, thanks to the long hours working as a railroad porter. His father was gone most of the time, peddling his wares on horseback, so Joe was left to support and run the family. He promised himself he would have a son to whom he would pass along his love of baseball. When Bill Bradley was born in January of 1947, he officially became a St. Louis Cardinals fan.

"I think the whole state of Texas was in love with the St. Louis Cardinals," Bill Bradley said. "You've got to remember that Texas didn't have Major League Baseball until the Houston Colt .45s came along in 1962. Until then, the Cardinals were *it*."

Bill Bradley was born the year before Stan Musial got his rhyming handle in 1948—"Stan the Man." Musial was to Bill Bradley what Dizzy Dean was to Joe Bradley. Musial enjoyed a sixteen-season stretch of hitting .300 or better and a seven-season run of .330-plus.

Pitcher Preacher Roe once said, "Throw him four wide ones and pick him off first."

"I loved Stan Musial," Bradley said. "He was the guy I followed all through the 1950s."

The Cardinals reached the World Series four times in a five-year stretch with Musial in the lineup. They fell short in 1945 when Musial was off to war. Musial was a god in St. Louis during his twenty-two-year career, playing for only one team. He was a symbol of hard work and consistency and a man who did not need to seek the spotlight. He was postwar Americana in a baseball uniform. He made you want to sing patriotic songs. He might have symbolized the end of the age of innocence. It was like Rockwell had painted him onto the green grass of Sportsman's Park. When he retired in 1963, Commissioner Ford Frick said, "Here stands baseball's perfect warrior. Here stands baseball's perfect knight." Frick's words would be engraved onto the Musial statue outside of St. Louis's Busch Stadium.

Men like Dizzy Dean and Stan Musial would help strengthen the bond between Joe and Bill Bradley. Father and son also shared a love of radio. In the 1940s, the '50s, and even the '60s, families sat around the radio and listened to the voices of announcers like Harry Caray and Jack Buck. Long before the Internet and ESPN, the radio brought people together. It was a glorious era when the swagger was not the thing.

Growing up deep in the Piney Woods of East Texas, Charlie LeVias barely had time for school, much less sports. He was forced to drop out of school at age thirteen because his family needed the paycheck he was drawing from the lumber mill.

The phenomenon of football was thrust upon Charlie LeVias at a time when he least expected it. He did not believe a child with polio-riddled legs could rise up and become one of the greatest high school football players in the history of Texas. Charlie had never seen a football game in his life. Because he knew nothing about the sport, he did not attend a single game during Jerry's career at Hebert High.

Leura LeVias went to one game, and that was during her son's senior season. She was not there to enjoy his performance. Rather, she had been guided by a mother's instincts to make sure her injured son did not play that night.

"She sat on the front row with her arms crossed all night," Jerry remembered. "Even though I had two sprained ankles, I was still in uniform. Coach Ozen would look into the stands and see that mad look on her face and he'd say, 'Sit down, boy. You are *not* playing football tonight.'"

Charlie LeVias finally and begrudgingly attended his first football game during his son's sophomore year at SMU. It was during a troubled time when Jerry was getting hate mail from the white racists. *If you play in the next game, I am going to shoot you.*

Charlie came to the Cotton Bowl packing a .45 beneath his overcoat.

"He was scared to death," Jerry said. "He knew that they were beating up on me, and I had told him about the letters. He was going to shoot them if they tried to take me on."

Jerry's years at SMU would be a time of great worry for the LeVias family. They knew that Jerry would face obstacles along the way, but they had no clue as to the degree of hate that would be generated by the inclusion of the first black athlete in the history of the Southwest Conference.

As he grew up in Beaumont, LeVias actually had two fathers. Clifton Ozen was his football dad. If not for Ozen, LeVias would have never played football, much less achieved greatness. He launched LeVias's career at a time when he weighed less than 120 pounds. He nurtured him, built him into a star, and led him to the top of the mountain. Most important, Ozen discovered the pioneer who would break the color barrier in the Southwest Conference.

"Clifton always carried the torch at Hebert," LeVias recalled. "He carried on the tradition year after year. He was the man. He called himself 'the Big Demon.' But he was really the man who made everything happen."

Ozen was the Bear Bryant of black Beaumont football.

"He had a way of motivating you, and it was called a trimmed down two-by-four," LeVias said. "It looked like a baseball bat. And if you didn't run fast in practice, or if you didn't play hard enough, you were going to get hit by Coach Ozen's paddle."

Unless you'd been struck in the butt by a large wooden paddle, you could never comprehend the pain felt from the top of your head to the bottom of your feet.

Ozen made good use of this tool during halftime of the Hebert games.

LeVias recalled, "He would say to one of my teammates, 'Son, we are losing this game. So don't make me take out my board. If I have to take out my board, it's going to hurt the both of us.'"

With the biggest game of their lives three days away, Jerry LeVias and Bill Bradley were lying on their bunks in the semidarkness of their room at the old farmhouse. They were talking about their fathers.

"We called my dad 'the Confucius of Soul,'" Jerry said to his roommate. "It was like he always had things figured out. He would say things like 'Work hard when you're young and play hard when you're old.' He would also say, 'Got to get things going while you can' and 'Always be nice to everybody.'"

Confucius was the Chinese philosopher born as Kong Qui in 551 B.C. During the sixth century B.C., Confucius fought against moral decline in his country by espousing a philosophy of self-discipline. One of the most famous sayings attributed to him is "By three methods we may learn wisdom; first, by reflection, which is noblest; second, by imitation, which is easiest; and third, by experience, which is the bitterest."

Another Confucius quote that Charlie LeVias often espoused was "Choose a job you love and you will never have to work a day in your life." He also said, "Our greatest glory is not in never failing, but in rising every time we fall."

Joe Bradley was also a philosopher who loved nothing better

than to spread wisdom. He was tagged by his family with the nick-name "Cepheus" after the mythical Greek king. Cepheus was the husband of the lovely Cassiopeia, and the father of Princess Andromeda. All three would be be immortalized in the names of constellations.

"My dad was a philosopher, plain and simple," Bill Bradley said. "He loved nothing better than to sit around, maybe have a few drinks, and talk about life. I learned more from that man than you could ever imagine."

Charlie LeVias loved nothing more than teaching his kids about life. He took them on a driving vacation each summer to the West Coast.

"He wanted us to know that there was more out there than just Beaumont," Jerry said. "We would go through California and Oregon. We would go to Seattle. There is no telling how much I learned."

Charlie wanted his children to know that there was life beyond the segregationist views of most Texans. They would come to learn that people were more racially friendly the farther you traveled west, or east, for that matter.

"We would have five people in one car going west on Route 66," Jerry said. "I was the smallest, so I sat on the cooler that had the soda pop and the Spam and the cake."

In Texas, the LeVias family would drive all night because they knew there was little hope of five Negroes getting a hotel room. Eating in a restaurant was also out of the question, That is why the cooler was filled with food and drink.

One night, Charlie LeVias got tired behind the wheel and decided to pull over into a gas station. He asked the proprietor if the family could sleep for a few hours on his property.

"I can't be responsible for you if something bad happens to you," the man said.

Jerry recalled, "so we took turns watching out for the bad people, Thankfully, they never came."

18

The Road Less Traveled

Two roads diverged in a yellow wood, and sorry I could not travel both . . .

—Robert Frost

No one prayed any harder than Clifton Ozen that Jerry LeVias would excel in his new role as the Jackie Robinson of the Southwest Conference. For years, the Hebert coach had watched the "black gold" of the Golden Triangle beat a path beyond the state's borders to play football at a distance of hundreds, even thousands of miles from home.

Ozen also knew that the road ahead for LeVias would be rocky. There would be landmines. To take the road less traveled in 1965 for a black man was to put one's well-being on the line.

"I had hoped that Jerry LeVias had the tools to be the first Negro in the conference," Ozen recalled during a 1976 interview. "He was honor roll and all of that stuff. He never argued with anyone. But I wondered if SMU and the Southwest Conference were too big. I wondered if they would break his heart and break him down."

In mid-August of 1965, LeVias knew that everything in his life was about to change. He had grown up deeply rooted in an all-black neighborhood of Beaumont. Everything he desired was in his own backyard. The grocery stores and the filling stations were owned and operated by Negroes. His grandmother lived next door, and his aunts, uncles, and cousins were just blocks away. All of his desires could be satisfied among friends and relatives. Negroes living in the Pear Orchard section of Beaumont insulated themselves against the slings and arrows of the white world. With the exception of the driving trips each summer, he saw little of the outside world.

LeVias would soon be leaving his comfortable nest for a burgeoning town with its bright lights, bullies, and dark underbelly. The skyline of downtown Dallas had recently added the forty-two-story Southland Life Building, the tallest west of the Mississippi. The structure not only glowered over the city, it cast a large shadow to the south. In Dallas, Negroes were restricted from buying houses north of the Trinity River, which cut a straight line east to west from the southernmost point of downtown Dallas to downtown Fort Worth. Even the black stars of the Dallas Cowboys like Bob Hayes, Mel Renfro, Don Perkins, Pettis Norman, Frank Clarke, Cornell Green, and Jethro Pugh could not live in North Dallas, where the biggest houses, along with the greenest and most affluent neighborhoods, were located.

Dallas was the financial center of the Texas oil industry and the tenth-most-populous city in America. In spite of its wealth and status, though, Dallas in that era could be hard-edged and keenly racist. The Ku Klux Klan dominated the police force. A mammoth dark cloud from the Kennedy assassination would loom over Dallas for years to come.

Before signing with SMU, LeVias knew little about the politics, attitudes, and racial views of the white people in Dallas. He did not know that when black NFL players visited the city to play against the Cowboys, they would be forced to stay in separate hotels away from their white teammates. He did not know that when the University of Oklahoma football team came to Dallas each year to play Texas, the black players would be relegated to the seedy hotels south of downtown. This had been going on since Prentice Gautt broke the color line with the Sooners in 1956.

Friends and neighbors of the LeVias family had heard about the racial tensions in Dallas and worried about Jerry getting tangled in the conflict. They wondered if he was psychologically equipped for the battles that lay head.

Hershey, on the other hand, had been a wonderful experience. His first time being around white players and coaches was going far more smoothly than expected.

"It helped that Bill and I bonded right off the bat," LeVias recalled. "As for the team, we never had any fighting about race. I really believed that if any racism had come up Bobby [Layne] would have stopped it. Nobody said, 'You white guys sit over there, and you dark guys sit over there.' There was none of that. We really were one big happy family."

Still, LeVias had questions about the future.

"Bill, what do you think my life is going to be like at SMU in the all-white Southwest Conference?" he asked.

"Jerry, that's a tough question," Bradley said. "Don't take this the wrong way, but I don't think it's going to go all that well for you. Not right off the bat, anyway."

LeVias grimaced and said, "You're kidding, aren't you? I thought that you were going to tell me just the opposite."

"Nah. There are some racist people in Texas, and they're going to be out to get you."

Bradley told LeVias the story of Abner Haynes. In 1956 at North Texas State, he became the first Negro football player for an all-white college in Texas.

"The team was on a bus going to Abner's first game, at Kilgore Junior College," Bradley said. "The Kilgore people were so mad that a Negro was coming to their stadium that they shot at the bus. A couple of bullets hit the roof. I hear the team hit the floor for thirty minutes."

Levias shook his head and said, "But that was almost ten years ago. Surely times have changed."

"No," Bradley said. "Those boys at Texas Tech and Texas A&M and TCU are going to try to bully you. Remember that a lot of these players are just rawboned country boys."

LeVias contemplated his words and said, "Won't they be just like the guys on the Big 33 team? I mean, these fellas are pretty doggone nice."

"These boys are the cream of the crop," Bradley said. "The Texas blue-chippers are a cut above. Players like Corby Robertson and Chris Gilbert and Norm Bulaich come from good families, and they're smart. You're going to be up against a bunch of real dumbasses. Just think about going into Texas A&M and facing all of those rednecks. Hell, A&M is still about 90 percent military, and they've got no girls."

"What about Arkansas?"

"Those fans are going to call you nigger and spook and monkey. They're going to yell 'Give the ball to Leeeeeeeroy!' You better get ready."

The Southwest Conference was just slightly ahead of the Southeastern Conference when it came to racial attitudes. Consider that the state of Louisiana had passed a law in 1956 forbidding black athletes from competing against whites. SEC football was integrated in 1966 when Nat Northington and Greg Page were allowed to play for the Kentucky football team. The other conference schools did not quickly follow suit. Five years would pass before every team in the SEC would have at least one Negro player.

Paul "Bear" Bryant had yet to integrate the University of Alabama football team in 1968 when LeVias was a senior at SMU. In December of 1968, LeVias was chosen to compete in the East-West Shrine Game, a college all-star game in San Francisco. Bryant, the head coach of the East team, became enamored of LeVias and his speed. The SMU All American caught 9 passes for 168 yards and scored 2 touchdowns.

After the game, Bryant put his hand on LeVias's shoulder and said, "When they let me, I'm going to get me some of y'all."

Two years later, Bryant would coach his Crimson Tide against the USC Trojans in Birmingham. It would become one of the most historic games in the history of southern football. For years, Bryant had been trying to convince university officials and fans to let him integrate his team. When USC's Sam "Bam" Cunningham ran wild, gaining 135 rushing yards and scoring 2 touchdowns, Bryant knew his wish would come true. 'Bama fans were embarrassed at the 42–21 loss, giving Bryant a reason to add Wilbur Jackson to the roster the next season, along with other black players over the coming years.

As Alabama assistant football coach Jerry Claiborne said, "Sam Cunningham did more for integration in sixty minutes than Dr. Martin Luther King did in twenty years."

19

Blue-eyed Soul Brother

The Big 66 was a collection of teenaged girls who acted as "dates" for the Texas and Pennsylvania Big 33 players.. Most of the girls were locals; a few were bused in from nearby towns. It was a high honor to be a member of the Big 66, the equivalent of being invited to a debutante ball. The girls would come in handy at the Big Dance scheduled for Thursday night at Hershey Country Club.

Bill Bradley could not wait to meet them all.

"I'm going to dance with every girl in the room," he told Jerry LeVias. "I'm going to steal those coal crackers' dates. Boy, are they going to be pissed."

LeVias laughed and said, "Bill Bradley, you are more fun than a box of Cracker Jacks."

At the end of the afternoon practice, a few hours before the dance, Layne gave his team a pep talk.

"I want you to go out there on the dance floor and do your thing," Layne said. "Dance with all of them. I don't care if some of them are the girlfriends of the coal crackers. We're not here to make anybody happy. Just go and enjoy yourself."

Bradley, LeVias, and Bulaich had had plenty of fun the previous night and did not come home until 3:00 A.M. They went out with Mary Jane, Pam, and Sylvia. Mary Jane had driven her cherry red Mustang to the old farmhouse to pick up the boys. There was no curfew since each of the three girls told her parents they were staying at a friend's house overnight. There was no reason to worry about their boyfriends since the Penns were stuck with a 9:00 P.M. curfew.

Bradley was happy to see Mary Jane again. He smiled and said, "So tell me, Mary Jane, how are the coal crackers spending their evenings? We don't see them anyplace around town."

"They're basically riding the roller coaster and going to the movies," she said. "They don't have their cars because Lefty James wouldn't allow it. Most of them are just hanging around that dumb, seedy hotel."

Pennsylvania quarterback Terry Hanratty confirmed that the coal crackers had spent the week bored to tears. "Ted Kwalick and I rode the roller coaster every night," Hanratty recalled. "Then we'd go to the movies. The only movie showing at the local theater was *Mary Poppins*. Ted and I saw it five straight nights. In the meantime, all of the Texas guys were going out and having a howling good time."

Lefty James never let up on his players. They were ordered to wear coats and ties to the dance and to be back at the hotel no later than 10:00 P.M. Layne couldn't have cared less what his players wore or what time they came home. So they all showed up at the dance at eight o'clock decked out in blue jeans, T-shirts, and cowboy boots. Some wore cowboy hats. The coal crackers could not believe their eyes, or their ears. Bradley led a parade of players into the gym singing a Manfred Mann hit.

Bradley: *There she was just a-walkin' down the street, singin'*
Players: *Do wah diddy diddy dum diddy do.*

Bradley and the boys rolled through all of the verses and three choruses without flubbing a single word. The Big 66 girls loved it. The coal crackers were mad enough to fight.

One of the Pennsylvania boys yelled, "Hey, Bradley, did you come up here to sing or to play football?"

"Both," Bradley shot back. "In fact, I do both quite well, don't you think?"

Bradley then swaggered across to the room toward Mary Jane. Right in front of her boyfriend, he said, "Well, hello, Mary Jane. Seems that I haven't see you in at least six hours. Are you going to take me for another spin in that hot little Mustang of yours tonight?"

The coal cracker reared back to take a swing but was grabbed from behind by one of the big linemen. Just then the band cranked up "Johnny B. Goode."

"Mary Jane, would you like to dance?" Bradley asked.

"Well, of course I would, Bill Bradley," she said, batting her eyelashes.

The Big 33 host committee had invited six Negro girls to the Big 66 dance. They equaled the number of Negro players on both teams. Bradley was tearing up the dance floor when he spotted Jerry LeVias dancing with one of the black girls.

"Hey, roomie, you're looking good," Bradley said.

"Not as good as you," LeVias said with a laugh.

After the band played "I Can't Help Myself" by the Four Tops, Bradley said to LeVias, "You know, roomie, it's okay to dance with the white girls. If the coal crackers say anything, we'll just whip their butts."

The Pennsylvania players were lined up on one side of the dance floor, with the Texas players on the other. This had been arranged by the host committee in hopes it would keep the boys from fighting. Most of the boys were standing with their "dates." Bradley, however, spent the better part of the night on the Pennsylvania side, hoping to pick out yet another pretty girl to dance with. He paid no mind about the tension he was causing.

By ten o'clock, though, it no longer mattered. The coal crackers were long gone back to their hotel. So the Texas boys had sixty-six girls to chose from. Before long, there were thirty-three boys on the floor dancing with sixty-six girls.

"Now, this is what I'm talking about," Bradley told LeVias. "Two at a time. This is how it should have been from the start. To hell with those coal crackers."

As the dance was winding down, Bradley and LeVias were making their choices of the girls they wanted to leave with. Mary Jane and Sophia were definite candidates. But the Texas duo had already chosen a couple of new entries—Phyllis from Harrisburg and Lillian from Pottsville. The foursome ducked out the backdoor, hoping to leave unnoticed. But they were spotted and followed by Danny Abbott, who watched them take off across the golf course.

LeVias and Bradley found a cedar bush to hide behind and pull their dates closer. LeVias felt uneasy that he was holding hands with a white girl. His expression posed the question, "Is this OK?" Bradley laughed and said, "Jerry, if you don't hurry up and kiss her, I will."

It was the right moment at a perfect place until Abbott found the mechanism that turned on the sprinkler system. As the nozzles began to spit water, the foursome took off running, but not before they were totally drenched.

Running side by side with Bradley, LeVias turned to him and said, "You know, I was wondering what you would think about me kissing a white girl."

"It's cool—and don't think I haven't kissed a black girl."

The boys stopped, and LeVias put his arm around his friend's shoulders.

"You know, Bill Bradley," he said, "you are my blue-eyed soul brother."

Bradley put his arm around his friend's shoulders and said, "I think that's the best thing anybody ever said to me."

Knowing the boys would be coming in late, Bobby Layne did not schedule a practice for Friday morning. At 8:00 A.M., he was walking past the basketball gym when he heard the backboard rumbling and the rim rattling. He stuck his head inside the door.

"Okay, Jerry, see if you can do this one," Bradley said. He dribbled toward the basket and leaped. In midair, he switched the ball from his right hand to his left and dunked—*ka-boom*!

LeVias then performed the same dunk with ease.

Layne walked onto the gym floor and shook his head.

"I know that everybody else is back at the farmhouse, sleeping," Layne said. "I also know that you two didn't exactly turn in early last night. I saw you walk past Martini's with a couple of babes in tow right before the two-o'clock last call. What time did y'all call it a night?"

"We really don't remember, Bobby," Bradley said.

"Then why the hell are you practicing your dunks this early in the morning?"

LeVias smiled and said, "Because Bill here said he could dunk better than me, and I wanted to prove it otherwise."

Layne shook his head again.

"Jerry, you are five foot nine," he said. "What are you, Bradley, five foot ten?"

"And a half," he responded.

Layne snickered and said, "You guys are the smallest—ahem, the shortest on my team. And you both can dunk?"

"Bobby, we've both been dunking since the ninth grade when we were little-bitty boys. Jerry was dunking left-handed by the tenth grade, and so was I."

LeVias took off and rattled the rim with a left-hander. Bradley did the same.

Layne walked toward the boys and put his right arm around Bradley and his left around LeVias.

"You are two of the best football players I've ever seen in my life, and I mean it," Layne said. "We're going to kick some coal cracker ass tomorrow night. Just make damn sure you don't break an arm or a leg dunking the damn basketball. I need both of you."

Layne started to walk away, then paused and turned to face the boys. "Y'all are also two of the best fellas I've ever met. Bradley, you've done a great job of making Jerry feel at home. Jerry, I couldn't be more proud of you if I'd been your own daddy. I'm going to miss both of you after tomorrow night. And I'm going to watch both of you play college and pro football every chance I get. You boys are going to be two of the best to ever hit the big time."

*   •   •

Layne was feeling frisky on the last night at Martini's before the big game. He was surrounded at the table by Doak Walker, Harley Sewell, Mal Kutner, Rooster Andrews, Russell Coffee, Fred Cervelli, and Ernie Stautner.

Layne walked up to the bar and said to the bartender, "Do you have one of those big glass jars that you use for tips? I need a really big one."

The bartender quickly found one and set it on the bar.

"Here's the deal," Layne said. "Last year, I lost over a thousand dollars betting on my own team. This year, I want to make it all back and then some. I want to make at least two thousand bucks. All of the bets are going to be clearly marked, and the money's going into envelopes."

Layne reached into his back pocket and pulled out dozens of money envelopes that he had collected from the local bank.

He looked at the bartender with a furrowed brow. "I want you to handle all of the money. Don't lose it. I'll collect it tomorrow night after the game, and I'll give you a big tip after we win."

The bartender smiled and said, "That is, *if you win*."

"We will win, dammit. You can count on it." Layne smacked the bar with the palm of his hand and smiled. "We've had a great time up here all week," he said. "You've given us great service. Here's two tickets on the 50-yard line. All you've got to do is cheer for Texas."

The bartender's eyes widened, and he said, "You can just bet that I will. Even if it means pissing off everybody I know in this state. You guys have been a lot of fun all week. God knows you're the best customers we've ever had."

A man walked up and eyed the bartender. "Can you tell me where I can find Bobby Layne?" he asked.

"He's standing right next to you," the bartender said.

Clearly, the man had been overserved.

"Well, there you are, you sonofabitch," he said. "Bobby Layne, I watched you play at Pittsburgh during your horseshit days. I watched you when the Steelers practiced here in the summer. You are the cockiest sonofabitch I've ever seen in my whole life."

Layne chuckled and said, "At least you're an honest man. You get most of your facts straight, too."

The drunk stammered and said, "I know you're a gambling man. I want to make a bet."

"I sure don't mind taking your money."

"Well, then, if you're so confident, then give me some points."

"Yessir, I've been thinking about that a lot," Layne said. "We are indeed a much better team than Pennsylvania. So I'm going to give every drunk in this place seven points. *Does everybody in this bar hear me? That means I'm giving Pennsylvania seven points on every bet. No limits.*"

Layne turned to the man and said, "That means seven points even to a drunk like you."

The man threw a fifty on the bar, and Layne matched it. Then Layne put the money in an envelope, marked the names, and handed it to the bartender.

He returned to his table. About three seconds later, there was a long line of customers holding hundreds, twenties, and tens.

"Good thing I went to the bank," Layne said. "Because it looks like there are a lot of people in this bar with the gambling spirit."

Stautner peered across the table at Layne and said, "Bobby, you really think you're going to win this game?"

Layne slapped his best buddy on the back and said, "I've got the best-looking football team that's ever been assembled. I knew that Texas high school football was good, but Fred Cervelli put together the best high school all-star team in the history of man."

Cervelli had taken his share of ribbing the past six days. He could barely believe that Layne was praising him.

"Gee, thanks, Bobby," he said.

"Don't get the big head, Fred. You still brought me a damn left-handed center."

"I, I, I didn't."

"It's okay, Fred," Stautner spoke up. "Bobby's been playing this joke for years. There's no such thing as a left-handed center. If the center is left-handed, every coach makes him snap it right-handed."

Cervelli looked to the heavens, clasped his hands in prayer, and said, "Thank you, Lord."

Layne had been waiting all day to break some news to the group. He knew there would be resistance.

"I'm *not* starting Bill Bradley at quarterback," he blurted.

Every man at the table almost swallowed his cocktail glass. Doak Walker rarely got excited, especially when it involved Layne, but his expression said, *Are you out of your mind?*

"Hold on," Layne said. "I have my reasons."

"Well, they'd better be good," Stautner said loudly enough for the whole bar to hear.

"Look," Layne began. "Bradley is going to be punting, returning punts, returning kickoffs, and starting at safety on defense. How much more can you ask of a man?"

"A lot more," Stautner said. "The recruiters say he's the best quarterback in America. He could start at quarterback at the University of Texas right now—and I mean today—and win a national championship."

"But he's not the quarterback I need," Layne said.

Silence consumed the table. Then Stautner yelled, "Hey, bartender, will you cut Bobby Layne off?"

The bar erupted in laughter.

"He's just kidding," Layne yelled. "Bring me another Scotch and everybody just keep on drinking."

With an incredulous look, Stautner said, "Explain, Bobby."

"Okay, here it is," Layne began. "I happen to like the hell out of Rusty Clark. He's perfect for the pro-set offense I'm running. He's six foot three. He's got a gun for an arm. He throws it straight over the top."

Walker rarely disagreed with Layne, but he said, "You're saying that Bradley can't sling it. Shoot, he can throw it a country mile."

"I know. I know. But I've seen him throw a few ducks this week."

"Bobby, every ball that Bradley's thrown this week has been caught by LeVias and James Harris."

Layne gritted his teeth and said, "That's just it. Harris and LeVias are two Negroes who can fly. We're going to beat Pennsylvania with the deep ball, and Clark can really chunk it."

Walker threw up his hands and said, "Bradley is the best high school football player I've ever seen."

"Hold on, Doaker. Darrell Royal's crazy about Bradley because he can run the football. They don't throw the ball much at Texas. They run the damn thing."

Stautner held up his right hand. "It's your call. Rusty Clark might be that good. Who knows? But if Bradley's the best high school football in America, Bobby, you've got to go with him."

No one spoke until Layne said, "Okay, boys, it's time to go back to the hotel. I've set a ten o'clock curfew for us. It's nine fifty-nine. We've got a big game tomorrow."

Stautner laughed loudly and said, "I've never known Bobby Layne to go to bed at ten o'clock in his entire life."

"Ernie," Layne said, "you've never in your life seen me wanting to win a game like I do this one."

With that, the party was over.

Saturday morning, Bill Bradley and Jerry LeVias sat across the table from each other at breakfast. Bradley could tell that something was troubling his roommate. Then the words came tumbling out.

"I can't believe you're not starting at quarterback," LeVias said with a pained expression. "It makes no sense."

With his normal aplomb, Bradley said, "Nothing to worry about, my friend. I've had a feeling all week that Bobby was going with one of the Houston quarterbacks. They fit his system better."

"Bobby never even gave you the courtesy of telling you," LeVias said. "He just decided to tell the press and it winds up in the Harris-burg newspaper."

"No worry at all," Bradley said. "Shoot, sometimes I think of myself more as a defensive back than a quarterback. You know what else? I think my favorite thing is punting, and my second favorite thing is returning kicks. I don't have to always play quarterback."

"But we were going to make headlines together," LeVias said. "It was going to be me and you picking up the trophy after the game."

"Hey, that can still happen," Bradley said. "The only time I'm leaving the field is when the offense is out there. And you're going to take up the slack for me."

LeVias said, "I bet you're playing quarterback by the second quarter. There's no doubt about that."

Bradley laughed and said, "Rusty Clark is a good quarterback. He's tall, and he can fire the ball. He's not good enough for the University of Texas, but he's good enough for Baylor."

"Rusty Clark might be good, but he's not Bill Bradley," LeVias said. They shared a laugh.

"You know," LeVias said, "for all of your cockiness, you sure are taking this well."

"Never worry about me," Bradley said. "I will always be all right."

"How can I *not* worry about you," LeVias said. "You are my blue-eyed soul brother."

The two shook hands across the table.

"You sure got that right," Bradley said.

Texas was not the only team making quarterbacking news. A surprising development out of the Pennsylvania camp came the previous afternoon when Lefty James announced that Bob Naponic, not Terry Hanratty, would be the starter. Naponic, out of Hempfield Area High School in Greensburg, had recently signed with the University of Illinois. The Fighting Illini had finished sixteenth in the country the previous season, but they were hardly the University of Notre Dame, where Hanratty would be playing quarterback. In 1964, the Fighting Irish had spent five weeks atop the Associated Press poll under new coach Ara Parseghian, who had revamped and totally turned around a program that had finished 2–7 the previous season. The Irish would have won the national championship if not for a controversial call by the umpire in the season finale at USC. Notre Dame led 17–0 at halftime and would have scored again early in the third quarter, but the touchdown was nullified on a phantom holding call. Left tackle Bob Meeker was flagged for holding even though he touched no one. Film of the game showed he had charged straight ahead, missing his man, then fallen on his face. It was the fatal bullet. USC roared from behind and scored the winning touchdown in the final two minutes to overtake Notre Dame by the score of 20–17.

When Notre Dame offered a scholarship, Hanratty's inner voice said yes in about two seconds. In his mind, no one else could compete with the Irish. They would provide the best shot at a national championship. In 1964, John Huarte had become the sixth Notre Dame Heisman Trophy winner and the fourth at quarterback. So Hanratty knew his chances for the Heisman would be greatly improved in South Bend.

Some considered Hanratty the best high school passer in the country, in spite of coming from a run-oriented program at Butler High School, twenty miles north of Pittsburgh. Coach Art Bernardi had turned out twelve Division I signees the last two years, including Ron and Rich Saul, who went off to Michigan State before gaining NFL fame.

So the news that a blue-chipper like Hanratty would not be starting in the Big 33 game set off a lot of grumbling among the Pennsylvania faithful.

James's decision was also unsettling to Hanratty, who had taken a good number of the quarterback repetitions at practice. On Friday, James told him, "You are the fastest player on our team, and I need you to cover LeVias. That young man is fast and dangerous."

Hanratty wanted to question his decision but had been taught all his life to respect his elders, especially when they are the head coach.

Upon hearing the news, outspoken Notre Dame defensive coordinator Johnny Ray told Hanratty, "Lefty James is an idiot. He won't be coaching the Big 33 next year if he loses this game. Don't worry, Terry. You'll be the starting quarterback at Notre Dame by the start of your sophomore season."

20

Game Time

There was rarely a cease-fire in the war of words. The Texans spent the better part of the week pissing off the coal crackers. In turn, the Pennsylvania players scolded the Texans for bragging and stealing their girlfriends. The Texans gladly confessed to both crimes.

In the meantime, Bobby Layne was guaranteeing a victory.

"We'll beat 'em with our speed," Layne told the sporting press. "I guarantee it. There's not a high school team in this country that could slow us down. I want to remind you press boys that we didn't bring our best team up here last year. This year, we'll run off and leave these fat coal crackers. I don't want to use the word 'annihilate,' but I guess I already did."

The day before the game, Lefty James told the writers, "Texas has put out a lot of excuses for losing last year. They said they didn't have their best team. Well, we'd like to beat their best team this year, and that's what we plan to do. Texas has put out a lot of propaganda that they plan to annihilate us."

Pennsylvania football had nothing to hang its head about. In 1965, the state could brag of two immensely talented and popular players making their way in pro football. Joe Namath of Beaver Falls was a rookie starting quarterback for the New York Jets, having signed the richest contract in the history of pro football, which included a

$400,000 signing bonus. Mike Ditka of Carnegie had developed into best tight end in the first forty-five years of the league, having led the Chicago Bears to the 1963 NFL championship.

Since the advent of the Big 33 game in 1958, twelve coal crackers had been drafted by either the NFL or the new American Football League. Pennsylvania had held a team of U.S. all-stars scoreless in 1958, '59, and '60 and managed to keep the Texans out of the end zone in 1964.

The storyline for the 1965 game was speed versus brawn. The Texas roster included eight kids who had run the 100-yard dash in 10 flat or less. Wide receivers James Harris and Jerry LeVias were in the 9.5 range. Not too far behind was big running back Norman Bulaich, who had won the 100-yard dash at the state AAA track meet in 9.6 seconds.

The plodding coal crackers were the antithesis of the blazing Texans. Pennsylvania coaches insisted their boys were the toughest breed on the planet. Joe Shumock, a member of James's coaching staff, espoused that message each day.

"We have real studs in Pennsylvania," said Shumock, the drill sergeant of the coal crackers' practices. "The studs get strong by bucking rivets in the mill or with a pick and shovel digging graves. Pennsylvania football is pure desire. Our players just want to get out there and hit somebody. Most studs are linemen. But when we have a running back who is really built, we just say that he's beautiful." He pronounced it "bee-yoo-ti-full."

Shumock was a no-nonsense coach and therefore not a big fan of a gasbag like Layne. He organized the team's bulletin board in the locker room and covered it with inflammatory quotes from Layne. Shumock reminded his boys to spend some quality time reading what the Texas coach was saying.

"Some of the things he's said this week should not come out of the mouth of a grown man," Shumock said. "Bobby Layne played without a face mask for so long that I think it scrambled his brain."

Indeed, Layne had gone into battle without a face mask throughout his high school, college, and pro careers. Most NFL players were using the face mask by the mid-1950s, but Layne, forever the blood-and-guts quarterback, refused to change. He made it all the way through the 1962 season without even using the single bar. The only NFL nonkicker to play longer without a face mask was Philadelphia receiver Tommy McDonald, who retired in 1968 without ever using one. McDonald also played for the Rams and Falcons, retiring from the Browns.

If anyone knew the value of toughness in football, it was Layne. During his fifteen-year career, he played with an assortment of injuries that included a torn labrum and broken ribs. He suffered a broken leg and ankle in a 1957 game against Cleveland. Like Layne, the coal crackers were fearless. They wanted to line up and bust you in the nose. Although Layne would never admit it publicly, he liked their style.

Reading over the Pennsylvania roster was like perusing the cast list of a Jimmy Cagney movie. They answered to names like Miloszewski, Constantine, Landolfi, Sebastianelli, Salerno, and Ruccio. They came from tough-sounding places like Altoona, Uniontown, Pottsville, Monongahela, and Coal Township. Even their team mascots seemed imposing—the Steamrollers, Crushers, Demons, Marauders, Red Raiders, and Crimson Tide.

Like the Texans, a large percentage of the Penn players came from either rural areas or small towns. Eighteen were from Western Pennsylvania, far from the trains, subways, and hubbub of Philadelphia. The coal crackers were big ol' country boys with a hankering to fight.

Game night in Hershey triggered a surge of electricity. The game had been a sellout for months. The streets buzzed with the energy of a championship fight. Fans moved at an ever-quickening pace toward the stadium. To some, this felt like America's biggest sporting event of 1965. They would not mind comparing the Big 33 game to the NFL championship played following the 1965 season when the Green Bay Packers defeated the Cleveland Browns 23–12.

One of the hottest rumors making the rounds was that Mickey

Mantle was coming to the game. New York had played a day game at Yankee Stadium, and Mantle was catching a private jet to Hershey to see his good friend Bobby Layne coach the Texas team.

Pennsylvania governor William Scranton had ridden from Harrisburg in the back of a long black limousine that was parked on the curb outside the press box. Scranton was accompanied by his wife and a group of six friends. The governor had "cashed" a bet with Texas governor John Connally the previous year, winning a set of silver spurs and a ten-gallon hat. This year, he had wagered 1,061 Pennsylvania apples against Connally's 2,122 Texas-sized pecans.

Just past seven o'clock, as darkness settled over Hershey, the locals were taken aback at the sight of so much female leg being exposed down on the field. The Kilgore College Rangerettes, wearing midthigh skirts, were high-kicking up a storm while showing more leg than Broadway chorus line dancers. One of the bands belted out "Deep in the Heart of Texas" as the young performers lined up shoulder to shoulder and kicked for the sky.

Bradley and LeVias were walking off the field following pregame warm-ups when the Rangerettes caught their eye. While the other Texas players headed for the locker room, they stopped to ogle the girls. Bradley turned and said, "Jerry, just look at that. I wish they'd brought those girls to Hershey a little earlier. We could've had some fun."

"No doubt," LeVias said. "You'd know all of their names by now."

"I'd know more than that," Bradley said as they shared a laugh.

Bradley pointed to the end of the line. "See that blonde, third from the end?" he asked. "I went out with her when I was in high school. Nothing like dating a college girl when you're sixteen years old. That's how you learn the ropes."

LeVias grinned and said, "Maybe you can invite her to our party tonight. Nah, invite them all."

Just then, two coal crackers walked past. The first said, "Hey, Bradley, do you do anything but chase chicks and sing songs? You even whistle at the ugly ones."

"I have discriminating tastes in women," Bradley said. "As you can see, our Rangerettes are a lot prettier than your coal crackerettes."

The other boy chuckled and said, "If you didn't like our Pennsylvania girls, then why'd you spend the whole week chasin' 'em?"

Bradley put his hand on the Penn player's shoulder. "You see, Jerry and I wanted your girls to know the pleasure of being with two Texas studs. Real studs, not coal cracker boys. Besides, it was a lot of fun pissing y'all off."

With that, the Texas duo laughed and took off for the locker room as a stream of explctives followed. "We'll kick your f—— pansy asses," the coal crackers yelled.

Bradley turned and yelled, "See you in the end zone."

It was not like Bobby Layne to feel nervous, but fifteen minutes before kickoff, he felt the onset of the same anxiety that had invaded his body a year earlier. He could not fathom losing a second straight game to the lousy coal crackers.

"Gather around, boys," he shoutcd at his team. "It's time to talk about winning this damn football game."

Layne sensed that his team was "on the bit," like a racehorse ready to break from the starting gate. They wcre standing way too close and breathing way too hard in his face.

"Back up a little, boys," he said. "Y'all are stealing my oxygen."

The nervous laughter helped calm them down.

Layne began, "You're the best-looking high school team I've ever seen in my life. I can't imagine better talent anywhere. You've showed me all week that you are the biggest studs in Texas. But now we've got to win this doggone football game. Everybody back in Texas is talking about us. I'm sure y'all know this game is being televised back in our home state. Your mamas and papas are going to be watching. They're expecting a lot of you, and so am I."

Layne paused, then said, "So for the sake of all great Texans, do not screw it up like our boys did last year."

Layne pulled a piece of paper from his back pocket to read the starting lineups.

OFFENSE
Tight end: Gilbert Ash
Tackles: Bill Cloud and
    Rolf Krueger
Guards: Ronnie Bell and
    Don King
Center: Skippy Spruill
Quarterback: Rusty Clark
Running Backs: Chris Gilbert
    and Norman Bulaich
Wide Receivers: Jerry LeVias
    and James Harris

DEFENSE
Ends: Terry Don Phillips and
    Leland Winston
Tackles: Bill Cloud and
    Rolf Krueger
Linebackers: Danny Abbott,
    Corby Robertson, and
    Ross Montgomery
Cornerbacks: James Harris and
    Wendell Housley
Safeties: Bill Bradley and
    Glenn Smith

In the home dressing room on the other side of the field, Lefty James pulled out his starting lineup and began to read it.

OFFENSE
Ends: John Miloszewski and
    Ted Kwalick
Tackles: Bill Urbanik and
    Jim Kane
Guards: Burt Waite and
    Rich Constantine
Center: Ellis Pherson
Quarterback: Bill Naponic
Halfback: Chuck Landolfi
Slotback: Skip Orszulak
Fullback: John Helton

DEFENSE
Ends: Ted Sebastianelli and
    Dave Bradley
Tackles: Dennis Woomer and
    Ron Kamzelski
Middle Guard: Jay McCune
Linebackers: Gene Salerno and
    Jerry Ruccio
Cornerbacks: Terry Hanratty
    and Steve Edwards
Safeties: Jeff Duncan and John
    Hetrick

At three minutes until eight o'clock, the western horizon was spangled with long streaks of orange and blue. The crowd of 25,893 barely noticed. They were too busy raising hell to care about anything beyond Hershey Stadium.

Pennsylvania fullback Mike Reid placed the football on the tee, wetted a finger, and held it up to gauge the wind. It was blowing slightly from the south and would not affect how the ball would travel. The temperature had dipped into the low 80s, but the high humidity was still raising a sweat.

The press box was so packed with sportswriters and college recruiters that it seemed ready to tip over. A voice pulsated from the TV booth. "Call this the biggest game of the year for football on any level. The Pennsylvania boys are ready to send those braggarts back to Texas with their heads bowed and their tails dragging."

The only real formidable Texas cheering section belonged to the Kilgore Rangerettes. They were tossing their cowboy hats into the air and causing a ruckus that might have gotten them banned from the First Baptist Church. They were singing, "The stars at night are big and bright (*clap, clap, clap, clap*) deep in the Heart of Texas!"

Texas lined up with two deep men, LeVias and Bradley. LeVias did knee bends and prayed. He had never imagined that the Penn fans could make this much noise. Bradley looked into the west stands, hoping to spot his mother and father. He saw Joe Bradley with his arm around his wife, Mildred, wearing a white corsage with her son's number 10 on it. They had driven fifteen hundred miles from Palestine, Texas, in a 1958 Oldsmobile to see their son play in the biggest game of his life.

Bradley could also see the smiling face of Darrell Royal behind his parents. Bill knew his dad and Royal would be disappointed to learn he was not the starting quarterback. But Joe Bradley was on his feet and yelling at the top of his lungs when he saw his son field the kickoff at the 1-yard line, fake right, then break two tackles. Bill sailed down the left sideline 51 yards to the Penn 48. Not even Bobby Layne could have asked for better field position.

The Texas coach was ready to unleash his pro-set offense. On the first play, Clark dropped to pass, searched the field for an open receiver, and was sacked by linebacker Mike Reid. The noise from the partisan crowd was deafening.

On second and 15, Clark handed off to Chris Gilbert, who was met by a stack of defenders for no gain. The coal crackers were clearly energized by Layne's boasts and Bradley's hot pursuit of their girl-friends. With much ground to cover for a first down, Clark set up in the pocket and was suddenly flushed to his left. His right arm was hit by a blitzing Reid, and the ball fluttered end-over-end and into the hands of Terry Hanratty.

On the sideline, Layne fired his half-spent Marlboro into the ground and stomped it. "It's already happening," he yelled. "Again!"

It was hard for the Penn fans to believe that Bob Naponic, not Terry Hanratty, was trotting onto the field to play quarterback for Pennsylvania. Naponic was under strict orders to play it safe. He handed off twice to Steve Edwards at right guard for gains of 5 and 4 yards. Pennsylvania was already past midfield at the Texas 47. Tight end Ted Kwalick ran a quick post and gained 17 yards. The Texas coaches knew that Kwalick could be their worst nightmare. The 6'4" tight end possessed such excellent hands and speed that Penn State assistant coach Joe Paterno was already comparing him to Mike Ditka.

For the next two plays, Mike Reid battered his way for 6 yards at right guard. The coal crackers faced a fourth and 1 at the 24-yard line. Layne could barely believe what he was seeing when Lefty James chose the field goal.

"Look at those chickens," Layne said. "They think they're going to beat us this year with a bunch of field goals. We're going to wear these bums out."

Reid split the uprights with the 40-yard kick for a 3–0 lead half-way through the first quarter. The Texans breathed a sigh of relief.

Clark completed two short passes and seemed to be settling into a rhythm. Layne felt certain his offense was about to gain traction. Then Clark twice underthrew a wide-open LeVias. The misery contin-ued when Clark was sacked for a second time, losing 12 yards. Layne could hear the catcalls.

"Hey, Layne, you dumbass, we thought you brought the first stringers this year!" a fan yelled from behind the Texas bench. "Hell, you played a whole lot better last year with your scrubs!"

Layne scuffed the ground with his right shoe as Texas set up to punt. Bradley boomed one 55 yards that was not returned.

As Clark ran off the field, Layne grabbed him by the shoulder pads and pulled him close.

"Did you not see LeVias open?" Layne yelled.

"Yessir, I did," Clark said. "I just don't have the time yet. Maybe I should roll out—"

"Nah," Layne said. "I've got a better idea." He turned to Harley Sewell. "Round up your offensive linemen and show those farts how to block. We're not going anywhere until Clark gets some time to throw."

The biggest enemy of the Texas offense was not the coal crackers' defense. It was their offense that controlled the clock and played keep-away, with Naponic hitting Kwalick with quick strikes. Hanratty entered the game for one play, completed a pass to Kwalick, then trotted back to the sideline. There was a low rumble across the stadium from the fans who wanted to see Hanratty play quarterback.

"Why are they not playing Hanratty more?" Layne yelled. "Lefty's not only a twit, he's about half crazy."

Much to Layne's surprise, third stringer John Waller entered the game at quarterback. Even though Waller had led powerhouse Ridley Township High School to an unbeaten season in 1964, no one expected to see him this soon.

Lefty James was running the split-T offense, which was about as outdated as the Nash Rambler. The Texas defensive line was effectively stopping the run in spite of being outweighed by twenty pounds per man. Tackles Bill Cloud and Rolf Krueger were almost immovable in the middle. Still, the coal crackers moved the ball 57 yards with Waller's dink passes to Kwalick, all the way to the Texas 34. They needed a yard on third down.

Layne yelled to the defense, "They're going to run the ball. Stack 'em up, Danny Abbott. This team's not going to try anything tricky."

As the safeties braced for the run, and Abbott shot the gap between the right guard and center, Kwalick sprinted up the middle of the field. Layne was dead wrong. The coal crackers were going for broke, and Kwalick was past the secondary in a blink of an eye. Waller lofted the pass a little too high, giving Texas safety Glenn Smith time to catch up—but the tall tight end with spring-loaded legs leaped over Smith. Reaching high with his "vise grips," Kwalick wrenched the ball away from Smith and came down with both feet in bounds. Touchdown! The thunder rising up from the grandstands could be heard almost to Harrisburg. Pennsylvania had done the unthinkable, grabbing a 10–0 lead.

On the sideline, Walker worried that Layne might blow a gasket. He approached his friend and said, "There's a lot of time left, Bobby. We've got a great offense. Just cool it for a second."

Layne's anger was not to be tempered, though. He grabbed Clark again and said, "Rusty, you've got to get it going. *Now.* We can't afford to fall behind like this."

Layne, Walker, and everyone else in the stadium could tell that Clark was nervous. Here was a talented young quarterback losing confidence with each passing down. Still, Layne wanted to be patient. So he called for a simple pass route that might provide a hit of confidence. Tight end Gilbert Ash would run a quick post as Clark delivered the ball for a short gain. Ash, however, had bigger plans. After snagging the ball, he broke the tackle of linebacker Gene Salerno and slipped through the arms of safety Jeff Duncan. He seemed on his way to the end zone until Hanratty chased him down just past midfield.

On the Texas sideline, Layne did a little dance. His confidence in Clark was on the rise, so he sent halfback Ronnie Scoggins into the game with a play called "X sideline, Y go." Harris would break to the left sideline, hoping to draw the attention of the safety, as LeVias zipped past the cornerback. Clark would take a five-step drop and loft the ball high into the Pennsylvania night sky. Instead, he was hurried again and threw off balance, the ball wobbling like a wounded bird trying to reach the tree. LeVias braked and tried to come back for the

Texas receiver Jerry LeVias at the Big 33 game.

—*Fred Cervelli*

ball, but it was too late. Cornerback Steve Edwards fielded the pass like a punt and returned it 20 yards before LeVias caught him from behind with a touchdown-saving tackle.

Layne could stand it no more. The tutoring of Rusty Clark was over. When the offense trotted back to the sideline, he yelled, "Everybody, and I mean *everybody*, gather around me."

Twenty-two players formed a circle around Layne while the other eleven lined up on defense, hoping to stop the bleeding. Layne was baffled. On paper, this was the best group of Texas all-stars to ever suit up. They were big, fast, and intelligent. Maybe he should have practiced them harder. *Did I screw this team up by talking too much to the press? Maybe I should have given the players a curfew and cracked the whip?*

No one could have imagined a worse scenario. The coal crackers held a 10–0 lead and good field position. The Pennsylvania fans were hissing at Layne and calling him horrible names. He could hardly remember a more embarrassing moment.

On the sideline, he yelled to his players, "Is there anybody on this team who can play quarterback?"

LeVias pushed forward, his eyes widening.

"I know who can play quarterback, Coach," he said. "He's my blue-eyed soul brother. There's nobody like him."

Layne said, "Jerry, what are you talking about? What do you mean 'blue-eyed soul brother'?"

"Bill Bradley," LeVias said. "He can sing and dance and play quarterback with the best of them. Put him in at quarterback and we'll win this doggone game."

Layne paused. Then he remembered all of the postpractice pass work done by Bradley and LeVias. Some days they worked together until the sun went down.

The light went on in Layne's brain. He boldly walked 10 yards out onto the field and waved at Bradley, who was lining up at safety for the next play. He ignored the referee's stop sign. He yelled, "Bill, when we get the ball back, just stay out here on the field. You're my quarter-back now."

Bradley smiled. "I knew it! Thanks, Bobby!"

On the next play, Bradley intercepted a pass and returned it 15 yards. He waited for the offensive players to make their way onto the field, then swaggered into the huddle singing a Junior Walker song: *I said, Shotgun! Shoot him 'fore he runs now . . .*

"Boys," he said. "If you think I'm worried about losing this game, think again. I've been in deeper doo-doo than this. Believe me, we can win. But we need to get rolling right now!"

No one spoke, but everyone nodded in agreement.

"Right now, I don't care what Bobby Layne thinks," Bradley said. "I want Jerry LeVias to go deep. Jerry, just take off, roomie. No fake, no nothing."

"Yessir, roomie," he said. "Just heave it like you always do."

Norm Bulaich cleared his throat. "Bill, what should the rest of us do?"

"Block," he said.

It was no secret that LeVias was the fastest receiver on the field, but he had yet to catch a single pass all night. The game was moving deeper into the second quarter, and the Texans needed a jump-start.

At the snap, the defensive backs could hear LeVias's cleats tear-ing up the grass. The green particles shot backward like chewed-up wood splinters. Bradley planted his right foot and let it fly. His pass shot straight into the sky and climbed so high that it looked more like a spiraling punt. Bradley wanted to make sure that he did not under-throw LeVias. At the top of its arc, the ball broke nose down and be-gan its descent. LeVias was running a step ahead of Hanratty, traveling at a speed that would have broken a stopwatch. He reached out, and the football came down squarely in his palms. The crowd gasped as Hanratty dived for LeVias's ankles and barely snagged the right one.

Texas wide receiver Jerry LeVias catching a
touchdown pass against Pennsylvania in the 1965 Big
33 game.

—Fred Cervelli

The only voice in the stadium that could be heard belonged to Bobby Layne. He yelled, "Yeeeee-haw! Way to go, Jerry! Way to go, my blue-eyed soul brother!"

The first Bradley-to-LeVias connection gained 49 yards. It was one of the first passes in the history of Texas high school football to be thrown by a white kid and caught by a black kid. Surely it was the most important.

As Bradley hustled up the field for the next play, he could see the fear in the coal crackers' eyes. He yelled, "There ain't a coal cracker in this stadium who can cover Jerry LeVias. Not a coal cracker on this planet who can get that done."

Defensive backs, nervous about being burned again, backed up. Bradley noted the adjustment and handed off to Bulaich for 8 yards. Gilbert gained 7 more yards around left end. Bradley then ran a bootleg and sprinted 13 yards down the right sideline to the 7-yard line. With hands on hips, the coal crackers were breathing like spent racehorses.

In the huddle, Bradley said to LeVias, "Run to the back line, then cut it back about 3 yards. Be looking for the ball all the way, *all the way, Jerry.*"

The ball was already in flight as LeVias turned and caught the perfect strike from Bradley. *Touchdown Texas!* In unison, the Penn fans sat down and shut up. LeVias kicked the extra point, and the deficit had been reduced to 10–7.

As Bradley jogged to the sideline, Layne yelled, "Way to go, my blue-eyed soul brother! I knew you could do it!"

"Then why didn't you start me?" Bradley said.

"You're in there now, baby," Layne said. "You ain't going nowhere."

The Texas defense shut down the coal crackers' offense as Naponic threw two incompletions. The boos were getting louder. Fans began to chant, "We want Hanratty! We want Hanratty!"

In the press box, sitting with the other coaches, Notre Dame's Johnny Ray said, "Lefty'd better get Hanratty in the game *now*. Bradley and LeVias are about to turn this game around."

After the Texas offense trotted back onto the field, Bradley turned to LeVias again and said, "We're going to do the same thing. Just rocket straight up the field. James Harris, I want you to run a quick cut to the sideline. Everybody else stay in and block."

Placing his hands under center, Bradley said, "We're coming at you, coal crackers. Hope y'all've got your shoelaces tied up tight and your chinstraps buckled."

Bradley dropped back only three steps this time. He knew that if one of the coal crackers broke through the line, he could scoot outside and break a long run. He was much more mobile than Rusty Clark.

Down the right side, LeVias broke past cornerback Steve Edwards. Bradley cocked and fired. The tight spiral dropped perfectly into his receiver's outstretched hands for 30 yard gain.

Bradley ran up the field and put his arm around his roommate. He then turned and addressed the coal crackers once more. "Boys, you'd better figure out a way to slow this man down."

In the stands, Darrell Royal tapped Joe Bradley on the back and said, "The Texas team looks like a bunch of Thoroughbred racehorses. The Pennsylvania boys look like they're running in concrete shoes."

With three minutes left in the first half, all of the momentum had shifted to Texas. Bradley was not about to let up. He took off around right end, then pitched to LeVias going the other direction. LeVias circled around left end at top speed. He never gave the play away. The Penn players had no idea he was about to pass. LeVias stopped suddenly, planted his left foot, and fired a left-handed strike across the field. Bradley, running down the right sideline, hauled in the pass at the Pennsylvania 20-yard line and would have scored if not for Hanratty grabbing him from behind.

As they got up, Hanratty said to Bradley, "I had no idea that Jerry LeVias could throw the ball left-handed, much less that well."

Bradley laughed and said, "Wait till you see me uncork one left-handed."

After two short bursts up the middle by Gilbert, Bradley hit Bulaich with a swing pass, and the big running back broke two tackles en route to a 12-yard gain. The Texans had reached the 3-yard line.

With the clock ticking down before halftime, Bradley rolled right and threw a perfect strike to LeVias in the corner of the end zone. In less than six minutes, Bradley-to-LeVias had changed the course of the game. They had erased a 10–0 deficit. Texas led 14–10 going into the dressing room at halftime.

Layne, head down, hustled to the locker room. The fans yelled, "We'll get you in the second half, you sorry bastard. You're going home a loser again!"

Bradley expected to see Layne laughing and cracking jokes in the locker room, but the cocky chatter had ceased. The coach restlessly paced the floor, looking like a man who needed a stiff drink.

Layne then walked into a quiet corner and waved Bradley and LeVias over. At first, he did not know what to say. His eyes studied the ceiling. Finally, he said, "Look, you guys are clicking. Jerry, you're one of the best football players I've ever seen. Bradley, I just don't how to describe you. Son, you might just be the most complete player I've ever seen. Thanks to you two, we've finally got the a lead. But if you screw this up in the second half, they'll never let us back in the state of Texas."

Bradley winked and said, "Bobby, I see no reason to fret. We're going to beat these coal crackers like a rented mule."

In spite of a 14–10 lead, Layne knew the game was far from over. He felt certain that Lefty James would promote Hanratty to quarterback. He told Doak Walker, "We're going to need to keep scoring. Hanratty is coming in, and there's no way we're going to win this game 14–10."

To the surprise of practically everyone, Hanratty did not start the second half at quarterback. The stadium turned deathly silent again as third stringer John Waller trotted back onto the field. At 5'9", he was five inches shorter than both Hanratty and Naponic.

The best thing going for Waller as he trotted onto the field was the presence of Kwalick. The big tight end was still on fire. Waller-to-Kwalick moved the coal crackers all the way to the Texas 10-yard line. From his safety position, Bradley came up with a new strategy. Before the snap on third down, he trotted over to cornerback Wendell Housley of Richardson High School. "Housley," he said, "we're going to double-team this big goose they call Kwalick. You and me, baby. I'll take him to the inside, you get him to the outside. Cover him tight. I'm going to get my hands on the ball."

As Kwalick ran a post pattern, and the pass arrived, Bradley slammed into him from the side, then leaped and batted the ball high. It squirted straight up and fell into the hands of Housley at the 13-yard line.

On the next Texas series, the Pennsylvania secondary continued to treat LeVias like the second coming of Lance Alworth. They were double-teaming and even triple-teaming him. So Bradley turned to the running game. Shifty Chris Gilbert gained 12 yards on a toss sweep, and Ronnie Scoggins followed up with a 5-yard burst at right guard.

LeVias managed to break free from three defenders as Bradley hit him squarely in the middle of the field for a 23-yard gain. The drive died near midfield as Bradley punted 40 yards to the Penn 10-yard line.

The crowd was getting restless. Their coal crackers needed only a touchdown to regain the lead, but the offense was going nowhere. Waller, not Hanratty, was taking every snap from center. The coal crackers made one first down and were forced to punt back to the Texans at their 39-yard line.

Bradley smiled and winked as he strolled into the huddle. "Well, boys, I guess we're going to have to go deep to my ol' roomie, Mr. Jerry LeVias, once again. The snap count is on two. You boys up front give me a little time."

As he approached the line of scrimmage, Bradley was ready to really stir things up.

"Y'all coal crackers'd better back up," he said.

They needed no warning. The entire Penn secondary had shifted over to LeVias's side of the field. Bradley could have checked off, but he stayed with the go-route. He kept his eyes locked on LeVias as he retreated to pass. Everyone in the stadium knew exactly where he was going.

The ball went up and came down in a cluster of four players. Three were wearing the white jerseys of Pennsylvania. One was dressed in the Texas orange—LeVias. When Jerry "the Jet" reached the apex of his jump, he was higher than Wilt Chamberlain playing above the rim. He snared the ball above six hands, then returned to earth with the ball cradled in his arms. The coal cracker faithful could not help themselves. In unison, 25,893 fans gasped, "Ooooooohhhh! Aaaaaaaaahhhh!"

The gain was 34 yards to the Penn 27-yard line. Bradley ran down the field shouting, "I told you coal crackers what was coming. I told you stupid coal crackers!"

The Pennsylvania players had reached the breaking point. "Shut up, Bradley," linebacker Jerry Ruccio said. "We're getting tired of you."

Two coal crackers bumped into Bradley, and one threw an elbow into his chest. The Texas team, led by Danny Abbott, looked like the U.S. Army coming to his rescue. Twenty-two players were suddenly trading punches in the center of the field as the officials tried to get between them. LeVias was squarely in the middle of it, trying to protect his friend. Layne and Walker sprinted onto the field and began to separate the players. There would be a ten-minute delay as the referee sorted things out, then walked to both sidelines and warned each team.

On the Pennsylvania side, Lefty James said to the referee, "You should throw Bill Bradley out of this game. He started the whole thing. He's nothing but a loudmouth."

"No," the referee said. "Bradley didn't start it. Your player did, and the next time it happens, he's going to the showers."

Across the field, Layne tried to lip-read what James was saying to the referee. When he approached the Texas sideline, Layne said, "What was that crap coming out of Lefty James's mouth?"

"Nothing, Coach," the referee said. "But consider yourself warned. The next time this happens, a lot of players from both teams are going to the showers."

Layne snickered and said, "I'll be the first one to go. Because I'm going to be kicking Lefty James's ass."

Following the delay, Bradley set his eyes strictly on business. He was going to let his feet do the talking. In the huddle, Abbott said, "Run it right over me, Bill. Let me kick their asses." On a quarterback

Texas wide receiver James Harris running for a big
gain against the Pennsylvania team.

—*Fred Cervelli*

draw right behind "the Chief," Bradley split the linebackers and sprinted 15 yards to the 12-yard line.

Before the next play, Bradley said, "Jerry, I need you to be the decoy on this play. Break it to the right sideline. James Harris, quick post. On two."

Bradley dropped two steps and threw a fastball straight over the middle to Harris at the 1-yard line. He caught it between Reid and safety John Hetrick and was tackled immediately.

"One more time to James Harris," Bradley said."Your turn, James. Jerry, you run a skinny post. This play is the 'Y reverse' we've been working on."

The play began as a sprint-out left by Bradley. The entire defense shifted to the right, hoping to punish the cocky quarterback. Just before Bradley reached the line of scrimmage, though, he pitched left-handed to Harris going the other way. The swift receiver from Brownwood hit the afterburners, and in the blink of an eye, was around right end and into the end zone. The entire Texas team circled Harris in the end zone, pounding him on the helmet and shoulder pads. The celebration was on. The officials feared that another melee might break out. Three red flags flew into the air.

"Unsportsmanlike conduct on Texas for too much celebrating," the referee said. "Texas, that will be your final warning."

This time, LeVias's extra-point kick was blocked. The lead stood at 20–10 with eight minutes to play. Even Layne breathed a deep sigh of relief.

Needing two scores, the only hope for Pennsylvania was the pass. Waller started throwing on every down. After reaching midfield, the Penn quarterback heaved a long one for Kwalick that again was intercepted by Housley, this time at the Texas 10-yard line.

Bradley was not about to let up against a slow Pennsylvania defense growing more tired by the minute.

"We got these fat boys licked," Bradley told his teammates in the huddle. "Let's beat these people bad."

Bradley fed the ball to Gilbert and Bulaich. The shortest gain was

5 yards. Then Bradley turned to Ronnie Scoggins from Garland High. He was not as publicized as Gilbert or Bulaich, but there was no question about his résumé. The last two seasons, 1963 and '64, Scoggins had led the Garland Owls to consecutive state championships in the 4A classification, the largest in Texas. In 1964, he rushed for 1,222 yards, caught 25 passes for 174 yards, and scored 27 touchdowns.

Reaching midfield, Bradley carried around end for 13 yards, then handed off to Scoggins for 6 more yards. Texas rolled mercilessly toward the end zone. The greatest pleasure for Bradley was hearing the coal crackers gasping for air.

With the ball at the Penn 30-yard line, Bradley swaggered into the huddle and grinned. "Jerry, take two steps and break it over the middle," he said. "Make it a post cut. You know what I'm gonna do."

LeVias smiled. "Yeah, Bill, I'm reading you loud and clear."

Bradley, forever the showman, rolled left, shifted the ball into his left hand, and fired a perfect left-handed strike to LeVias for a 14-yard gain. The ambidextrous quarterback had just pulled off the ultimate insult. The crowd booed lustily. On his way back to the huddle, Bradley turned and bowed to the Pennsylvania crowd. The boos grew even louder.

Bradley knew the end zone was attainable with one more carry by Scoggins. From the 15-yard line, he pitched around left end, and Scoggins zig-zagged through six defenders all the way to the end zone. For the night, Scoggins had carried the ball 16 times for 106 yards. Sixty-nine of the 80 yards came on the final drive.

Texas led 26–10, and the clock was ticking inside of one minute. The worst year of Bobby Layne's life was finally over. He could still remember walking off the field a year earlier and hearing the public address announcer yelling, "Hey, Texas, do you want a rematch?"

Much to his surprise, he now heard the PA man holler, "Hey, Pennsylvania, do we want a rematch?"

More than 25,000 fans stood and cheered as loudly as they could. It was sweet music to the ears of Robert Lawrence Layne.

At the final gun, the Texan players grabbed Layne and hoisted him onto their shoulders. The coach felt much more relief than joy. He shouted to the players, "Put me down, dammit. You should be carrying Bradley and LeVias off the field."

LeVias ran across the field and hugged Bradley. It was both a historical and symbolic embrace that ended decades of racial division in Texas football. In the coming years, sports would indeed integrate America. The Bradley-LeVias friendship was just beginning. Soon everyone would come to understand the bond between the two. Bradley and LeVias were destined to be friends for life. It had all begun when a young white man said, "My daddy doesn't allow us to say that word in our house . . . Sure, I'd be happy to room with Jerry LeVias."

Singing songs and slapping each on the back, the Texas players returned jubilantly to their locker room. As the players doused each other with Cokes in that madhouse, Bradley felt yet another song coming on. The players formed a circle around their fearless leader as he began a new version of "You Must Have Been a Beautiful Baby."

It must have been a beautiful game, baby,
'Cause, baby, look at the score!

Doak Walker approached Bradley and yelled, "Take off that jersey!"

Every player and coach stopped what they were doing as the room fell silent.

Bradley grinned. "Take off my jersey? Why, Coach?"

"Because I want to see that big red *S* on your chest."

Indeed, Bradley had played like Superman. If any mere mortal could leap tall buildings in a single bound, Bradley was that guy. At that moment, he was tagged with a nickname that would last the rest of his life—"Super Bill Bradley."

Playing less than three quarters on offense, Bradley completed 10 of 18 passes for 205 yards and carried 14 times for 74 yards. His total return yardage was 105. In all, he had produced 384 yards of total offense. That was not all. He also punted 5 times for a 47.6-yard average, the longest traveling 57 yards, and he had intercepted 1 pass. He was the unanimous selection as the game's most outstanding back. Bradley had never left the field after taking over at quarterback in the second quarter.

Asked about Bradley's performance, Pennsylvania coach Lefty James could only smile. "That was the single greatest single performance I've ever seen by a high school player," he said. "There was nothing we could do to stop Bradley or LeVias. In fact, that is the finest high school team I've ever seen."

LeVias caught 7 passes for 117 yards and 2 touchdowns. He returned 2 kicks for 46 yards. The Texas running backs could thank him for drawing double coverage and allowing them to gain 261 yards on the ground.

According to the pregame hype, the Texas linemen would be eighteen-wheeled by the big, muscled-up boys from the steel mills and the coal mines. Nothing could have been further from the truth. Not only did the Texans hammer the Penns for 261 rushing yards, they held them to 23 yards on the ground.

"The difference between this year's team and last year's team was speed and fight," Layne said afterward. "We had a real bunch of fighters. Many of these kids had never played on a losing team. You've got who was name the game's hand it to Bradley and LeVias for bringing us back. Until I put Bradley in the game, we were in big trouble. What a great comeback by Bradley and LeVias."

Wielding great power in the line and at linebacker was Danny Abbott, outstanding lineman. He opened huge holes for the running backs. Not once was a hand laid on Bradley while he was attempting to pass. Abbott also registered 18 tackles, 11 of those unassisted. Both Bradley and Abbott had taken the same awards a week earlier in the Texas North-South All-Star Game.

There were so many team and individual accomplishments that Wendell Housley's 3 interceptions were almost overlooked. In spite of the loss, Pennsylvania's Kwalick still caught 10 passes for 113 yards. Every college coach in the stadium wished they had his signature on a letter of intent.

As the teams were leaving the field, Lefty James jogged toward

Layne, extending the right hand of congratulations. Layne brushed him off.

In the locker room after the game, a reporter asked Layne why.

"I didn't travel fifteen hundred miles all the way up here to Pennsylvania to shake a man's hand," he said. "I came here to win a damn football game."

The Pennsylvania locker room was deathly silent after the game. Hanratty dressed quickly and told Kwalick, "All I want to do is get the hell out of here. I'm not staying here tonight. I'm going straight home to Butler."

Johnny Ray of Notre Dame was waiting for Hanratty outside the locker room.

"Did you say anything to Lefty about not getting to play quarterback?" Ray asked.

"Nah, I don't believe in disrespecting coaches."

"You're a better man than me. Besides, you will be the starting quarterback at Notre Dame before long, and Lefty James will no longer be the coach of the Pennsylvania Big 33 team."

As he left the stadium, Hanratty could hear the Texas players hooting and hollering in their locker room.

He said to himself, "I just wish I'd gotten a chance to play for Texas."

Back at the old farmhouse, the pecan and chocolate pies were stacked high on the tables. The boys had been bringing them back from the team banquets the last three days. They had big plans for those pies.

On the back porch, six cases of Budweiser were already iced down in three huge aluminum tubs. The water balloons were filled, and the girls were putting up streamers and signs that read, CONGRATS TO THE BEST FOOTBALL TEAM IN AMERICA and WE KNEW YOU COULD HANDLE OUR COAL CRACKERS.

More than sixty girls had arrived at the old farmhouse, ready to party. Mary Jane, Pam, and Sylvia were there, along with a few others with eyes for Bill Bradley and Jerry LeVias. Once again, the Pennsylvania football team was out of luck.

At the farmhouse, the girls were decked out in summer dresses and saddle oxfords. Some wore Weejun loafers, and others were brave enough to don miniskirts. They had been planning this evening for a week, since the handsome boys from Texas hit town and started spreading their good cheer.

Mary Jane had managed to sneak the family's hi-fi out of the house, and the Four Tops were playing at full volume.

Sugar Pie, Honeybunch, you know that I love you.
I can't help myself, I love you and nobody else.

As Levi Stubbs moved the quartet into the second verse, the Texas team burst through the back door. Sixty girls and thirty-three football players hit the dance floor. They danced to the rest of the Four Tops' *Second Album*, which included "It's the Same Old Song" and "Something About You."

The Temptations were next.

I guess you'd say, what can make me feel this way?
My girl, my girl, talkin' about my girl.

The music was hot and the beer was cold. When the Temptations finished, Jerry LeVias stood on one of the tables and said, "I'd like to propose a toast to one of the best men I've ever met. You know who I'm talking about. He's my blue-eyed soul brother, Mr. Bill Bradley."

Bradley jumped up on the table and put his arm around his roommate.

"If y'all would turn down the music just for a second, Jerry and I have been working on a song that we'd like to sing for you. This is from Martha and the Vandellas, and it's dedicated to the Pennsylvania coal crackers."

Bill: *Nowhere to run, baby.* Jerry: *Nowhere to hide.*
Bill: *Got nowhere to run, baby.* Jerry: *Nowhere to hide.*

With faux microphones in hand, Bill and Jerry began to dance and sing in falsetto. They actually sounded a little bit like Martha and the Vandellas.

By the second verse, the entire farmhouse was singing along. As a toast to each other, Bradley and LeVias tapped beer cans. Then LeVias jumped off the table, hustled to the restroom, and spit out his beer. No one would ever know he was not drinking.

The boys had grown so tired of eating chocolate and pecan pies that they found some new ways to have fun. After more dancing and singing, they began smacking each other in the face with the pies. Soon they were all gooed up from head to toe. Then the girls got into the act. They started smearing the pies on their dates, and the boys reciprocated. Before long, the water balloons were flying and everyone in the farmhouse was one big wet mess.

"Here's to Hershey," Bill Bradley yelled. "At least we found something productive to do with this stuff."

Bradley, still on the table, asked the room for silence.

"Hey, girls," he yelled. "I think it's time for some more Hershey kisses!" Soon the boys and girls were pairing off.

Back at the Cocoa Inn, some two hundred yards away, Bobby Layne, Fred Cervelli, and the coaching staff were having their own party. They could hear the roar from the farmhouse as if it were just across the street.

"Sounds like our gang knows how to throw a party," Layne said.

"Bobby," Cervelli said, "maybe we should go check on them."

"Nah," Layne said. "They played like warriors today. Besides, they're college kids now—and you know how college kids like to party."

EPILOGUE 1

The Future of the Game

A year later, a funeral wreath arrived at the Cocoa Inn on the morning of the Big 33 game in 1966. Attached was a note that turned out to be a poem about Bill Bradley. It read:

> *There was a lone ranger named Bradley,*
> *Who played a game not so badly,*
> *But now he is gone,*
> *And all over the lawn,*
> *Will be Texans beating the ground madly.*

The coal crackers wanted revenge so desperately that they had resorted to bad poetry. There was no signature on the card, but it was obvious that someone in Hershey was overjoyed that Bradley was now living in Austin, preparing to become the starting sophomore quarterback for the Texas Longhorns varsity.

Over the past year, the Penn executives had taken several steps to fix their team. Three days after the 26–10 loss to Texas, George "Lefty" James was fired. Fans around the state had blamed James for failing to utilize his talent properly. Several high school coaches had gone on the record saying he had misjudged his players. Case in point

Bobby Layne with his three quarterbacks from the
1966 Big 33 Game. Left to Right: Joe Norwood, James
Street, and Chuck Hixson.

—*Texas Sports Hall of Fame*

was Terry Hanratty, the future Notre Dame quarterback, who was in the game long enough to throw only a single pass.

Leaders of the Big 33 team hoped to rectify the coaching problem by hiring former Duke coach Bill Murray, who led the Blue Devils to victories over Nebraska (34–7) in the 1955 Orange Bowl and Arkansas (7–6) in the 1961 Cotton Bowl. They believed that the proper use of the bottomless Pennsylvania high school talent pool would serve to silence the braggart Texans.

Upon further review, some believed that 1966 would be "the Year of the Coal Crackers." Even Fred Cervelli, the leader of the Texas selection committee, admitted that it would be difficult to assemble a Texas team as talented as the 1965 group. He had written in the *Orange Leader*, "Nowhere in the state does there appear to be a quarterback in the same class as Palestine's Bill Bradley, the brilliant youngster who led the Texans past the coal crackers last year."

It was also duly noted that the 1966 team would not possess the same overall team speed as the '65 squad. Only one current player had run the 100-yard dash in under 10 seconds.

"We won't have nearly the speed we had last year," Layne told the sporting press. "But we'll have some size and some boys at quarterback who can really throw the ball."

In August of 1966, Layne had decided to change the Texans' routine from the previous two years. After the North-South All-Star Game was played in Houston, Layne held the team over for three days, and they worked out at the University of Houston's football facilities. Then they traveled to Washington, D.C., to tour the White House and to meet President Lyndon B. Johnson, the No. 1 Texan. They also saw many of the sights of the nation's capital and toured the Smithsonian Institution.

After pounding the pavement for a full day, the boys were getting antsy to reach their destination. James Street said to Cervelli, "We need to get to Pennsylvania fast. I hear we've got forty girls waiting for us."

Cervelli gave the boys ten minutes to use the bathroom before leaving. Once on the bus, Cervelli forgot to count heads.

"You have to remember that I was a sportswriter, not a tour guide," Cervelli recalled. "I should have had a clipboard to check off everybody's names."

An hour later, the team's plane landed in Harrisburg. Then the players were bused to Hershey and the old farmhouse. The girls were thrilled to see them. They were hoping to have as much summer fun with the 1966 team as they had with Bradley, LeVias, and the others. The beer was already iced down on the back porch, and the music was playing.

Cervelli returned to the Cocoa Inn, where Layne and the coaches were drinking and rolling the dice. Around midnight, Cervelli looked up to see tackle Robert Hall of Port Neches–Groves walking through the hotel's front door.

"Bobby, what are you doing walking around with all of your luggage?" Cervelli asked.

"Mr. Cervelli, you left me in Washington," he said. "I had to catch another flight."

"Oh, my God, son, I'm sorry," Cervelli said. "I thought we had everybody on the bus."

The youngster was almost in tears. That all changed when he walked into the old farmhouse and found a party going on.

While the Texans partied, the coal crackers were tucked into their beds. Once again they would adhere to a strict curfew all week while the Texans cut up and enjoyed their time with the Pennsylvania girls.

In 1966, the coal crackers were determined to neutralize the Texans' speed. The scouting staff was doubled in size with hopes of finding faster players. Appropriately, one of the first to sign was Wesley "Rocket" Garnett of Pittsburgh Westinghouse High School. Garnett, a 9.8 sprinter, had rushed for 1,638 yards, scored 25 touchdowns, and averaged 55 yards per kick return. He had turned down 130 other scholarship offers to sign with Notre Dame. Coaches and recruiters were already comparing him to Pennsylvania native Lenny "Spats" Moore, who played at Reading High School in the early 1950s, moved on to Penn State, and became an All-Pro with the Baltimore Colts. He was elected to the Pro Football Hall of Fame in 2008.

With Rocket Garnett on board, headline writers began referring to the Penn team as "Rocketmen."

So confident was Pennsylvania of a victory in 1966 that *Patriot-News* sportswriter John Travers wrote, "Okay, Texas, you can brag about your speed merchants like Warren 'Rabbit' McVea and Jerry LeVias. Let's hope that you have a couple more stashed away in Panhandle Land. This time, you're going to need them. Otherwise, it's Boot Hill." Someone should have reminded Travers that Boot Hill was located in Dodge City, Kansas.

Texas really had nothing to fear. Among the top signees for the 1966 squad was Longview quarterback James Street, headed to the University of Texas. No one knew the '66 class better than Darrell Royal, who had already signed twelve players from the squad. Six would be starters in Hershey: linebacker Glen Halsell of Odessa Permian, halfback Ted Koy of Bellville, center Forrest Wiegand of Edna, tackle Bobby Wuensch of Houston Jones, tight end Deryl Comer of Dallas Highland Park, and Street. Royal's 1966 Texas recruiting class would become the nucleus of his 1969 national championship team that defeated Arkansas 15–14 in the Big Shootout and Notre Dame 21–17 in the Cotton Bowl.

The biggest change in the 1966 Big 33 game would be the introduction of the blitz. Neither team had been allowed to rush its linebackers the previous year. Soon after he was hired, Murray found his mailbox filled with letters complaining that Bradley faced no pass rush the previous season. Murray soon called Layne in Texas to broach the subject. It would be one of his biggest mistakes.

"Coach, I think we should allow both teams to blitz this year," Murray said.

Layne responded, "I don't think there's any doubt about it, Bill. Let's make that deal right now!"

"You got it," Murray said.

Layne knew his big, swift linebackers would overwhelm the

Pennsylvania quarterbacks. From the first snap of the game, Wuensch and Halsell were turned loose on quarterback Charles Burkhart. He was sacked 7 times for minus 47 yards. To his credit, a bloodied and bruised Burkhart never left the game.

Conversely, the Texas passing game was never contained. Street and Joe Norwood, a fellow Texas recruit, threw 2 touchdown passes apiece, and Norwood ran for another. They combined for more than 300 yards passing. San Antonio Highlands quarterback Chuck Hixson, the team's best pure passer, came in late and completed 7 of 17 for 96 yards, running the team's passing total to 422.

It was never a contest as Texas overwhelmed Pennsylvania by the score of 34–2. Sportswriter Ronnie Christ wrote in the *Harrisburg Patriot-News*, "Once upon a time, Pennsylvania boasted its high school football was the best in the country. Alas, my friend, no more, no more."

After the game, Layne said, "This was the greatest exhibition of football I've ever seen in my life, and that includes my fifteen years as a pro. My kids made up their minds that they were going to win, and every one of them played their hearts out. I must say that I didn't expect what happened tonight. Pennsylvania was out for revenge after last year's loss. We were expecting the worst."

Notre Dame defensive coordinator Johnny Ray chimed in, "The Texas boys beat the tar out of the Pennsylvanians."

Beyond Street and Norwood, the biggest star of the game was little-known Lubbock High wide receiver Don Burrell, who caught 8 passes for a Big 33 record 218 yards. At 6'3" with 10.2 speed, Burrell was a tremendous athlete who ran great routes. He was open all night.

Burrell might not have made the team if he had not grown up around Layne in Lubbock. He played on the same high school team as Layne's son Robby, the quarterback for the Lubbock High Westerners. Layne did his best to follow the team without proving to be a pushy father. During the afternoon practice, he would drive his car behind the hedges adjacent to the practice field. Watching practices while standing on the sideline would have been bad form for a two-time NFL championship quarterback.

Layne would miss most of Robby's games in the fall of 1965 because he was coaching the St. Louis Cardinals quarterbacks, but he was always on hand at the Lubbock High booster club meetings on Tuesday nights to see the game film. While focusing on Robby, he also made note of Burrell's talents. Burrell was a three-sport star who scored in double figures on the basketball team and broad-jumped 22'7½".

Because he was black, Burrell was not recruited by the Southwest Conference. It seemed the conference was ready for only one black player at a time, and that would be Jerry LeVias of SMU. Big defensive end Lawrence "Tody" Smith, the brother of Bubba and the son of Willie Ray, faced the same prejudice as his brothers. At 6'6" and 278 pounds, he received seventy scholarship offers and was a member of the 1966 Big 33 team. The SWC schools never recruited him, though, and he wound up at USC by way of Michigan State.

With Texas winning the past two games by the cumulative score of 60–12, the future of the Big 33 matchup was in jeopardy. Pennsylvania was tired of losing, and rightfully so. They were also agitated by the brash, outrageous behavior of the Texans. Not only did Texas whip the coal crackers again in 1966, they humiliated them at every turn in the days leading up to the game. Street assumed the role of Bradley, singing and dancing his way all over town, whistling at girls and stealing a few. At the Big 66 dance, the Texans danced with all of the girls, including the ones who had been coupled with the Penn players. They also stole twenty golf carts from the Hershey Park golf course and drove them straight into the creek, leaving them to float on the water's surface.

What irritated Al Clark and his staff more than anything else was the Texans' aggressive public campaign to bring the game to the Lone Star State. Cervelli had been insistent that either the 1966 or '67 game be played at the brand-new Houston Astrodome, also known as "the Eighth Wonder of the World." Judge Roy Hofheinz, the man responsible for the construction of the $30 million indoor monstrosity, had released this statement: "We believe that Texas high school football players deserve the greatest showcase in the world, and we believe that we have that showcase. We know that Texas fans will show great enthusiasm for this game and everyone from Pennsylvania will learn that we have a hospitality second to none."

The Astrodome had opened on April 9, 1965, with Mickey Mantle hitting the first home run during an exhibition game. That night, Judy Garland and the Supremes performed to a capacity crowd.

The Houston Astros played the first season on painted grass. That problem would be solved in 1966 with Astroturf. The Astrodome would have been the perfect venue for the Big 33, and the offer to the Pennsylvanians was more than generous. They would be able to keep 83 percent of the gate, while the Texas team would receive the receipts from the game program. All of the profits from concessions would go to the Astrodome.

"Al Clark wouldn't even listen," Cervelli said. "Whenever I brought it up, he would start shouting at me. He wanted to keep his little game in Hershey."

Clark had been a small-town hero since launching the Big 33 game in 1958 and did not want to give up that status. Everyone called him by name when he strutted the streets of Harrisburg and Hershey. Moving the game to Texas would have cut into his glory.

In declining the Astrodome offer, Clark said, "Sometimes a fella can get a little big for his britches. The Big 33 has decided that the game should stay where it started—in Hershey."

Clark was never clear on his reasons for avoiding Texas. At first, he said the NCAA might not approve it. Then he admitted that he had not even asked for permission. He told Cervelli that he did not want to give up any of the charity money.

"We told Al Clark that he could keep all of the charity receipts," Cervelli said. "We told him that his charity money would actually double because the Astrodome was twice the size of Hershey Stadium. He wouldn't go for that, either. They were an unusual type of people up there in Pennsylvania."

Hofheinz kept pushing to host the game in Houston. He beat the tom-toms in the Houston newspapers, along with the *Harrisburg Patriot-News*. He practically dared the coal crackers to come to Texas. He pledged to fill every seat, or to pay the 83 percent of the gate if he failed to do so.

Clark wanted nothing to do with the offer. He might have been better off letting the 1967 game go to Texas. That way, he could have spared his fans the horror of watching what was coming next.

With every passing year, Cervelli and his staff had gained more expertise at choosing the right players. He knew the kind of talent that Layne was looking for. In turn, Layne was quite familiar with the formula for beating the coal crackers—speed, speed, and more speed.

The biggest gift from Cervelli to Layne would be the selection of six quarterbacks. The top prospect was Bill Montgomery of Carroll-ton Turner High School. Montgomery had turned down Alabama coach Paul "Bear" Bryant in spite of being only the second recruit to climb the steps to Bryant's practice field tower. The first had been Joe Namath. Montgomery had chosen Arkansas and Frank Broyles over Alabama and Bryant. His backup in the Big 33 game would be Eddie Phillips, headed to UT.

Against Pennsylvania on August 13, 1967, Montgomery would pass for more than 200 yards and 3 touchdowns. Steve Worster, one of the best ever produced in Texas, carried the ball 16 times for 188 yards, breaking yet another Big 33 record. The outcome was predictable. Texas won 45–14, bringing the three-year aggregate score to 105–26.

At the end of the game, Penn fans hooted and hollered at Layne, and to his credit, he smiled. They yelled, "Layne, you shithead, take your players back home and don't ever come back up here!"

Like the Philadelphians who once pelted Santa Claus with snowballs, the Penn fans could be downright crass. They were quick to blame the Texas high schoolers for the 1966 mass shooting on the University of Texas campus. Firing for ninety-six minutes from atop the 307-foot bell tower, Charles Whitman, a former marine, had killed fourteen people and wounded thirty-two others.

"All you Texans want to do is shoot and kill people," one of the fans hollered. "First you kill our president. Then Charles Whitman shoots up everybody in sight."

Layne and the players returned to the locker room for a celebration that lasted well into the night. As part of the tradition, Texas players sang, danced, and smeared pecan and chocolate pies on their dates back at the old farmhouse.

Late that night, after several drinks, Layne said to Doak Walker, "I bet we never play this game again. We've kicked their butts for three straight years, and now they're tired of us. We won't be coming back up here again."

Two weeks later, Fred Cervelli was sitting at his desk at the *Orange Leader* when he received a call from Al Clark.

Cervelli went straight into his pitch for the Astrodome. Clark cut him off.

"We're never going to play you at the Astrodome!" Clark yelled. "On top of that, Cervelli, you're *fired!*"

Cervelli gathered himself and said, "Just because you fire me doesn't mean you should end the game. We've got plenty of fellas here in Texas who can do my job. Why don't you call Carlton Stowers at the *Lubbock Avalanche-Journal.* He'll do you a fine job."

"I'm not calling anybody," Clark said and hung up.

Cervelli knew in his heart that the Texas-Pennsylvania game was over. Clark would blame the termination on Cervelli's insistence on playing at the Astrodome. Anyone who had been around the game the last four years knew differently. Pennsylvania wanted out of the game because they could not handle the talent-laden Texans. The coal crackers had beaten Layne's team the first year because Texas could not bring the first stringers. For the next three years, the coal crackers barely stayed on the same field with Texas.

In the coming weeks, Clark would announce that the Big 33 was going back to being an in-state game—East versus West. That would last for four years, until 1972, when the Pennsylvanians began playing an all-star team from Ohio. Five years later, the all-Penn game returned. Maryland high schoolers were involved in the game from 1985 to 1992. Then Ohio returned to the game from 1993 to 2012. Maryland came back into the mix in 2013.

An interesting note is that at least one Big 33 player has played in every Super Bowl. A total of 118 Big 33 players have participated in the forty-seven Super Bowls, making 173 appearances. At Super Bowl XLVII in New Orleans, the Big 33 was represented by Baltimore's Gino Gradkowski (Pennsylvania 2007). San Francisco's Big 33 players were Ted Ginn Jr. (Ohio 2004) and Nate Stupar (Pennsylvania 2007).

The only Texas Big 33 player to reach the Super Bowl was Norm Bulaich, who played in Super Bowl V for the Baltimore Colts.

EPILOGUE 2

The Rest of the Story

He never lost a game in his life. Time just ran out on him.

—Doak Walker

Bobby Layne returned to Texas as the conquering hero for winning the final three games of the Big 33 series. Still, he never received an offer to coach an NFL team. He continued to live the high life in Lubbock and often traveled with his friends and son Robby to Las Vegas for some serious drinking and gambling.

In truth, Layne did not need to go far to find high-stakes gambling. The poker games at the Lubbock Country Club were legendary. In *Heart of a Lion*, written by Bob St. John, it was estimated that Layne made between $200,000 and $700,000 annually from card games at the Lubbock Country Club.

"The poker games got to be famous," said longtime Layne friend Pete Durham. "I saw $46,000 in one pot one time. There were four big losers, and I bet those guys lost a million dollars a year. No, there was no doubt that Bobby was probably the second-biggest winner."

The games drew such a large crowd of wealthy players that Amarillo Slim stopped by the Lubbock Country Club. After playing poker for several hours one night, Slim supposedly said, "I'm getting the hell out of here. This game is too rich for my blood."

As the years passed, Layne thought little about coaching and figured the game was behind him. Leading an NFL team had been one of
his dreams, but living in Lubbock suited him just fine. He rarely talked
about coaching until someone brought up the subject one December
afternoon in 1980 as the boys were having cocktails at the country
club. The Texas Tech head coaching job had just come open with the
firing of Rex Dockery. Former Lubbock mayor Morris Turner wondered aloud if Layne might be interested in the job. He said, "Hell no,"
but soon reconsidered. In golf terms, Texas Tech was a driver and a
7-iron from his front door, and he had kept track of the Raiders through
the years. He knew they could use some help. Not once since joining
the Southwest Conference in 1960 had they represented the league
in the Cotton Bowl. After he thought about it for a couple of days, the
blood started pumping. He could see himself standing on the sideline
with a furrowed brow, preparing to call the next play. He had watched
Tom Landry, his former Texas teammate, call the plays for the Dallas
Cowboys each Sunday for twenty years. He wondered if he could be
as good as Old Stone Face himself. At age fifty-four, he was still in
pretty good shape in spite of the hard drinking and four packs a day.

Layne called Morris and told him he had changed his mind and
was definitely interested. Then he telephoned his longtime friend
Carlton Stowers at the *Dallas Morning News*.

"I really would like to have the Tech job," he told Stowers. "Any
way you could spread the word?"

Stowers wrote a lengthy story that would earn a big headline. The
fire was lit. The Blond Bomber was on the comeback trail.

Layne began to put together a coaching staff that included Doak
Walker and Harley Sewell. Old friend Ernie Stautner, the Cowboys
defensive coordinator the past thirteen years, said he would help when
he could. Even Mickey Mantle offered to help recruit players.

Over the next few weeks, Layne met individually with all nine
members of the Tech Board of Regents. The choice would come down
to him or little-known Jerry Moore, the head coach at North Texas
State. Moore was 11–11 the past two years. Insiders said that the vote

between Layne and Moore stood at 4–4 with the swing vote favoring the old quarterback. The trustee who would break the tie lived in Lubbock. He supposedly told Layne that he would vote for him.

Layne's desire to coach the Red Raiders grew with each passing day. He had already organized a playbook. He had slowed down on his drinking and stopped gambling altogether. Then came the news that Texas Tech had hired Moore.

"When he lost that job, it hurt him a lot," Stautner recalled in 1986. "I think it shortened his life. It still makes me extremely angry when I think about it."

Bobby went back to his old life of drinking and gambling. His health deteriorated, and he was in and out of the hospital. In spite of a failing liver, Layne was asked by Doak Walker to induct him into the Pro Football Hall of Fame in August of 1986. Bobby struggled to get through his speech. From the stage in Canton, Ohio, he said with a gravelly voice, "This is really like third down and 3, a real tough one for me. I've had three great things happen to me. One was winning the NFL title. The second was being elected to the Pro Football Hall of Fame. The third is inducting my friend."

Two months later, Stautner spoke with a reporter about the tragedy of Bobby Layne.

"I just wish I'd had taken the bottle away from him a long time ago," said Stautner, pacing the floor of his Valley Ranch office. "He was such a wonderful friend. I wish I'd been a better friend to him."

Then he picked up the phone and dialed Layne at the hospital in Lubbock.

"Bobby, I'm sorry," he said. "I wish I'd done something to help you. This is the saddest day of my life."

Stautner hung up the phone and turned to the reporter sitting across the desk.

"I tried to stop him from drinking," he said. "I just wish I had done more. This is just killing me."

Tears then flooded the eyes of one of the toughest men to ever play pro football.

"He is just too young to die," Stautner said.

Robert Lawrence Layne was one of the greatest football players to ever suit up on any level at any time. His Big 33 teams remain legendary. On December 1, 1986, he died of cardiac arrest at the age of fifty-nine.

I was like a human windshield. I caught all of the bugs.
                                                        —Jerry LeVias

Jerry LeVias, from 1966 through 1968, was the best receiver in the Southwest Conference, making all-conference three years and first-team All American in 1968. He was truly the Jackie Robinson of the SWC. Ironically, if he had accepted the scholarship from UCLA, LeVias would have played football at the same university as Robinson. Beginning in 1939, Robinson became the first Bruin to win four letters, in football, baseball, basketball, and track.

"I've often thought what it would have been like if I'd gone to UCLA," LeVias recalled almost fifty years later. "I know it would have been a lot easier for me out on the West Coast. But I went to SMU because of my good friend Hayden Fry and the promise that I made to him. Back in those days, I used to tell Hayden all of the time, 'I love you, Coach.' That was long before men started doing that kind of thing."

Fry, with his liberal passing philosophy, was the perfect coach for a wide receiver with LeVias's skills. His speed created a new chaos in the SWC. Before LeVias, most teams utilized only three defensive backs, but they were madly shifting to the four-man secondary when he came into the league in 1966. He would eventually be double-teamed more than any other wide receiver of his era.

However, touching the ball only 48 times as a sophmore, including only 18 receptions, was not what he had in mind. Hayden Fry wanted to break him in slowly, but LeVias knew of at least one more reason for the restraint.

Jerry catches a pass at SMU in 1968.

—*Texas Sports Hall of Fame*

"I was sitting outside of Hayden's office one night and I could hear him talking to one of SMU's big supporters," LeVias remembered. "The fat cat told Hayden, 'If you keep giving the ball to that little nigger I'm going to take all of my money out of this university.'"

LeVias did score touchdowns of 5 and 60 yards in the season opener against Illinois. That season, he averaged 23.3 yards per reception, the best in the nation, and he scored 9 touchdowns while making the All-SWC team. Interestingly, Fry took advantage of LeVias's left-handed passing as he completed 5 for 63 yards.

LeVias's collegiate experiences were both glorious and sad. Texas coach Darrell Royal had once said that LeVias was too small for the conference. After watching him catch 7 passes for 68 yards, score a touchdown, and lead the Mustangs to a 13–12 win at Memorial Stadium in Austin in 1966, Royal changed his tune. "He doesn't look very small to me right now," he quipped.

LeVias made national headlines, but his productive day against the Longhorns would hardly be categorized as "happy." The Longhorns called him every name in the book. They kicked and punched him several times in the bottom of the pile-ups. This behavior was not condoned by either Bill Bradley or Corby Robertson, his friends on the Big 33 team. LeVias, in fact, could hear Bradley yelling at his teammates on the sideline, "Stop calling him a nigger! Jerry's a good guy. I know him. Stop talking to him like that."

When the game was over, Bradley was the first to shake LeVias's hand. He said, "I'm sorry, roomie. Sometimes these guys just don't know what they're saying."

"Don't worry about me, Super Bill," LeVias said. "I'm hearing this stuff everywhere I go."

LeVias soon learned he would never have a better roomie than Bill Bradley. At SMU, he could not even keep one. His first roommate's parents threatened to pull their son out of the university. The second changed rooms after a few days, saying, "Look, Jerry, I know this isn't fair, but I've got to have a social life."

LeVias would live alone his entire time at SMU. Sometimes he just wanted to pull the covers over his head. His relationship with the student body would be chilly at best. His first day in an anthropology class, one of the students raised his hand and asked the professor, "Is it true that colored people's brains are smaller than white people's?"

During his first semester at McIntosh Hall, some of his fellow students asked LeVias to join the nightly poker game.

"They wanted to win my money, and they knew that I didn't know to gamble," he said. "The first night, I had five aces [including the joker] and they said that I didn't win that hand. I lost a lot of money that night because I didn't know what I was doing. So I went to the library and read everything I could find about poker. Then I started winning their money. Problem was that I played poker too much. I made three C's and two D's my first semester."

LeVias's grade point average was 1.75. Fry knew he needed to motivate his player. So he called him into his office and offered him two options for punishment. "Jerry, you can either meet me at the stadium every morning at five thirty to run the steps, or I can call your mother."

Without hesitation, LeVias said, "Why don't we make it 5:15, Coach?" LeVias then spent more time in the library than he did playing cards, and by his senior year he was an Academic All American.

The game that would decide the conference championship for SMU in 1966 was against Baylor. Arkansas had just been upset by Texas Tech, and the Mustangs were aware that a victory over the Bears would send them to the Cotton Bowl. The only problem was that they were trailing 22–21 with less than a minute to play. A blocked punt by SMU's Ronnye Medlin suddenly turned the game around. It was recovered at the Baylor 47-yard line. White then hit LeVias on a quick hitch pattern designed for short yardage. Instead of stepping out of bounds to stop the clock, though, he juked two defenders and started to zigzag his way down the field. Baylor did not stop LeVias until he reached the 15-yard line with only 17 seconds to play. Dennis Partee won the game with a 32-yard field goal.

Author Richard Pennington wrote in his book *Breaking the Ice* that LeVias was nowhere to be found in the locker room after the game. White and Fry finally eventually located him tucked into the corner of the equipment room, crying his eyes out. The Baylor players had punched him in the bottom of pile-ups and called him a nigger and a spook the entire day.

With LeVias making so many big plays, the Mustangs reached the Cotton Bowl for the first time in eighteen years. It hardly mattered that they lost 24–9, or that LeVias caught only 3 passes for 69 yards. SMU was back in the big time for the first time since the days of Doak Walker.

During this trying period, LeVias received support from a very famous source. Dr. Martin Luther King spoke at SMU, then made a point of offering some advice to the first Negro player in the history of the Southwest Conference.

"Dr. King told me that I always needed to keep my emotions in check," LeVias said. "I could have been radical, but I chose to turn the other cheek. I can't tell you how many times I had to do that. It's hard when people are spitting on you."

LeVias's junior year at SMU was brightened by the arrival of his best friend and former Beaumont Hebert teammate Rufus Cormier, a talented fullback/linebacker, but also a highly intelligent young man who would become a Rhodes Scholar and a graduate of Yale Law School. Ironically, Cormier, a partner in the law firm of Baker & Botts, would break down racial walls himself in 1997 as the first African American admitted into the ultraexclusive River Oaks Country Club. The club, built on old Houston money, had been all-white since its opening in 1923.

"It was great to have Rufus at SMU because he became my protector," LeVias said. "He had been my fullback at Hebert, and I knew he would take care of me at SMU." Cormier stood 6'1" and weighed 245 pounds. He became an outstanding linebacker for the Ponies.

LeVias's numbers went up in 1967, his junior year, when caught 57 passes for 734 yards. He continued to receive hate mail and bomb threats. On the other hand, he was invited to an Otis Redding concert by teammates Mike Livingston and Billy Bob Harris.

"The only reason they wanted me to go was they would be the only white faces in the crowd," LeVias said, "but I went anyway."

Livingston also took LeVias to the all-white Lark Club on East Grand Avenue in Dallas.

On the night before home games, SMU stayed at the downtown Sheraton on Commerce Street. One Saturday night, the players dined together, and then most of them took off for a downtown movie theater. LeVias tried to keep up with his teammates after they arrived at the theater, but he was left behind.

"They grabbed all of the seats up front," he said. "So I had to head for the balcony. There was only one seat left, between two white women. I grabbed it. Then their dates switched places with the women so they wouldn't have to sit next to a black man."

The soon-to-be-iconic film was *Guess Who's Coming to Dinner*, the story of a white woman (Katharine Houghton) bringing her black fiancé (Sidney Poitier) home to meet her parents (Spencer Tracy and Katharine Hepburn). This was an especially controversial storyline because seventeen states, including Texas, still outlawed interracial marriage.

LeVias's social life was limited. He was one of only a handful of black students at SMU, but he came to know several of the black players from the Dallas Cowboys, including Cornell Green, Pettis Norman, and Bob Hayes.

"They would come and get me after their games," he said. "We would go down on Lemmon Avenue and listen to some live music, and I would play those drums."

Fans across the SWC tormented LeVias, just as Bradley had predicted. At Texas A&M, they pulled out hangman's nooses and shook them, and a student unleashed several black cats onto the field. Responding to a death threat at TCU, the FBI set up a human barricade around LeVias on the sideline and placed their own snipers on top of buildings around the stadium. Everywhere he looked, LeVias could see men wearing trench coats, whispering into walkie-talkies.

Before the game, Fry informed TCU coach Abe Martin and his staff about the sniper threat. Each time that LeVias lined up on the TCU side of the field, the coaches scattered in all directions.

"It was the funniest thing," Fry remembered. "Those coaches were scared to get close to Jerry for fear of getting shot."

Death threats followed LeVias practically everywhere he went.

"Most people didn't know how many death threats I got," he said. "We were flying out of Dallas one afternoon and there was a bomb threat called in on the plane. Coach Fry told the team we would have stand out on the tarmac because of a mechanical problem. Coach Fry and I both knew that wasn't true. The reason for the delay was that federal agents and dogs were combing the plane for a bomb. The funny part is that me and Coach Fry just stood over to the side and laughed about the whole thing."

His life was never easy, but LeVias said he did not worry about being killed. "The only thing I feared in life was disappointing Hayden Fry," he remembered. "When they threatened to shoot me, I didn't care. I just wanted to play good football and make coach Fry happy."

LeVias expected to hear name-calling and heckling from the stands, but an incident at TCU's Amon Carter Stadium in 1968 sent him to into a blind rage. After LeVias caught a pass over the middle, a defensive back came up and spit right in his face. The goo ran down his right cheek. The Horned Frog player called him a nigger. LeVias thought about throwing a punch but remembered how Jackie Robinson turned the other cheek. He trotted to the SMU sideline, threw down his helmet, and yelled, "I quit." Then he retreated to the bench, where he sat with his head down for several minutes. It was the worst feeling of his life.

"I'd never allowed hate to enter my body, but I hated that man who spit in my face," he said forty-five years later. "Once you let hate in your body, it's like poison. It's like the vampire when he gets his first taste of blood."

Fry came to the bench and put his arm around LeVias. "Jerry, don't let that one dumbass whip you. If we win this game, we've got a chance to win a championship. If you quit now, they're going to think they beat you down."

Fry's long-standing advice to LeVias was "If you don't want them to get your goat, don't show 'em where it's hid."

When it was time to go back into the game, LeVias stood up and said, "Coach Fry, I'm running this punt all the way back." As LeVias lit out for the field, Fry yelled, "Jerry, aren't you forgetting something?" Then he pointed to LeVias's helmet.

Fry would recall, "I think that Jerry was so mad that he could have run that punt back without his helmet."

With the scored tied at 14–14 in the fourth quarter, LeVias fielded the ball at the SMU 11-yard line, then took off toward his wall of blockers at the right boundary. Horned Frogs all around him, LeVias zigged to the left, then zagged back. All eleven defenders touched him at least once, but no one could bring him down. When Jerry "the Jet" hit top speed at midfield, he was gone, 89 yards to the end zone. It was one of the most electrifying runs in the history of the Southwest Conference and happened to be the same distance as Billy Cannon's legendary "Halloween Night Run" against Mississippi on October 31, 1959. Cannon's run propelled No. 1 LSU to a 7–3 victory over third-ranked Ole Miss and locked up the Heisman Trophy for him.

The tapes of the two runs were almost identical. LeVias's 89-yard touchdown came on October 12, 1968, and beat TCU 21–14.

It was reported several years later that the TCU player who spat on LeVias did eventually apologize. LeVias said it never happened. In 2003, the man called him at his home in Houston, but there was no apology.

"He just wanted to make sure that I wouldn't mention his name in my induction speech for the College Football Hall of Fame," LeVias recalled. "In spite of never apologizing, I did forgive him."

During his SMU career, LeVias twice told *Dallas Times Herald* sportswriter Louis Cox that he was going to quit the team. Every time he thought about walking away, though, he remembered the early struggles of his father, Charlie LeVias, who was not allowed to finish high school.

"I couldn't afford to feel sorry for myself, because my dad wanted a man for a son," he said. "He took more abuse than I ever thought of when he was growing up. It's amazing the things he had to do so his family could survive."

Almost fifty years later, Fry was still appalled at how LeVias was treated. "I didn't know there were that many rednecks still fighting the Civil War," he said. "It was just amazing that he faced that kind of hatred for no reason at all."

It seemed impossible to Emma LeVias that her grandson, the star of the team, could be catching that kind of abuse. During a phone call with Jerry one night, she said, "Forgive them, for they know not what they do."

His grandmother would remain a rock for him throughout his college career. When Jerry signed his scholarship in 1965, Fry promised Emma LeVias that her grandson would call her before every game. Jerry held to that promise on every Saturday game except one. The Mustangs were playing at the University of Texas and were about to go out onto the field when Fry said, "Jerry, did you remember to call your grandmother?"

"No, Coach, I was rushing around this morning and didn't get it done," he said.

Instead of going onto the field with the rest of the team, Fry and LeVias searched for a pay phone underneath the stands. Fry borrowed several quarters from one of the SMU band members.

"It was one of the funniest sights you've ever seen," LeVias recalled. "Here we were calling my grandmother from underneath the stands and the game was kicking off. My grandmother was wondering what all of the yelling was about in the background."

LeVias finished his SMU career with a flourish, catching 80 passes for 1,131 yards as a senior and also breaking SWC records in both categories. Late in the year, he caught 8 passes for 208 yards against North Carolina State. In 1968, he made first team All American along with fellow Big 33 players Chris Gilbert, Terry Hanratty, and Ted Kwalick. On New Year's Eve against Oklahoma, playing before the largest indoor crowd in the history of Texas (53,543 at the Astrodome), LeVias caught 8 passes for 108 yards that included an 11-yard touchdown reception from Chuck Hixson. SMU won the Bluebonnet Bowl that New Year's Eve 28–27 when Oklahoma failed to convert a 2-point play in the final minute of the game. LeVias's career at SMU was over.

In the years ahead, Texas coach Darrell Royal said he regretted not recruiting LeVias. "We didn't know that LeVias was the caliber of player that he turned out to be," Royal said. "I don't think we tried to recruit him, but we should have."

The irony was that if LeVias had been recruited and signed by the Longhorns, he would have caught passes from his "blue-eyed soul brother," Bill Bradley. He surely would have helped Texas win more games in 1966 and '67, when the Longhorns finished 7-4 and 6-4.

During this three-year period when LeVias became a dominant force, another black SWC player participated in a few games for the Baylor Bears. In the fourth quarter of the opening game of the 1966 season, the Baylor coaches sent walk-on running back John Westbrook into a 35–12 blowout against Syracuse. Baylor started the season a week earlier than SMU, so he was indeed the first Negro to participate in an SWC play, but it would be folly to compare LeVias to Westbrook, who gained only 300 yards and scored 2 touchdowns in his career.

Two months later, after his final game at SMU, LeVias was drafted fortieth in the second round by the Houston Oilers of the American Football League. The Oilers during this period labored in the long shadow of the Dallas Cowboys. They had finished 7-7 the previous season and were hardly a Super Bowl contender. When one of Jerry's uncles learned he had been drafted by the Oilers, he said, "There goes your NFL career."

LeVias paid no attention to his uncle and made the best of his situation. In 1969, he was named Rookie of the Year in the American Football League. The next season, he accounted for almost half of the total Oilers offense. However, the physicality of the game began to wear him down. He told *Sports Illustrated*, "As the season progresses, I get lighter and faster and more afraid." His love for the game began

Left to Right: Jerry LeVias, Bill Bradley, and Bill
Enyart at the All-American All-Star game in 1968.

—*Bill Bradley collection*

to fade when he was traded to the San Diego Chargers in 1971. He retired after the '74 season.

"My mind never caught up with the professional game," he said,
"but that was my fault. I just didn't love pro football the same way that
I loved high school and college. All of the sudden, it was about making
money, and I wasn't with it. My mind had changed, and I just wasn't
giving my all."

LeVias never had children and did not marry until the summer of
2009, when he wed his girlfriend of more than twenty years. Janice
LeVias had been his "rock" for two decades as the anger from his college days began to flush out of his system. Not until 2007 did LeVias
realize that all of the hate directed at him in the 1960s had finally
taken its toll. He began to see a psychiatrist and came to terms with
his pain.

"I was so filled with anger that I couldn't even sleep in the same
bed with Janice and our dog," he said. "I was kicking and hitting at
the air. I'd to go sleep in the other room. It was at that point that I
realized that I needed to seek help. I had to talk to the doctors. It was
hard for me to seek help because, for a man, that's a sign of weak-
ness. But I soon learned that I was suffering from post-traumatic
depression."

LeVias's first job in his life after football was with Conoco, helping the company start self-service stations, along with Quick Lubes.
He also started LeVias Enterprises, which opened Celebrity Auto Rental
along with a court reporting firm.

Now in retirement, Jerry lives with Janice and their dog, Sophie,
in an upscale Houston neighborhood. LeVias does volunteer work for
the Harris County Child Protective Services.

"The idea is to give these kids self-esteem because they move
around so much," LeVias said. "I also consult for nonprofit youth orga-
nizations. When they need some consulting work on how to get money
or on how to deal with the kids, they call me. I am happy to be putting
kids on the right path. I am lucky that I had people who put me on the
right path."

Bill Bradley might just be the best football player we've seen
in this state in the last forty years.
                                        —TCU head coach Abe Martin

Bill Bradley picked up the nickname "Super Bill" from Doak Walker
after his Superman performance at the Big 33 in 1965. A sports information director at the University of Texas named Jones Ramsey sent
the message of Super Bill soaring across America.

Ramsey was known as one of America's leading hypesters. He
beat the tom-toms endlessly for Super Bill from the moment he
stepped onto the UT campus. Bradley seemed deserving since he was
named Freshman of the Year in the Southwest Conference after leading the Yearlings to a 5-0 record. He averaged 7 yards per touch and
scored 5 touchdowns. He intercepted 1 pass and managed to return it
99 yards for a touchdown.

Ramsey knew that Super Bill had All American written all over
him. He also knew that the Bill Bradley of Texas was just as talented
at the other Bill Bradley, who had just completed a terrific basketball
career at Princeton. The other Bill Bradley had led the 1965 NCAA
tournament in scoring, and was destined to be an All-Pro in the NBA.
Some said he possessed the look of a future U.S. senator.

The Super Bill of Texas was seemingly on the fast track to greatness when he became the sophomore starter at quarterback in 1966.
Headline writers loved the name "Super Bill."

Bradley said, "I heard 'Super Bill' so many times that it almost
made me sick. What it really did was put a big ol' bull's-eye right on my
back."

That everyone in Texas was also comparing him to Doak Walker
did not help, either. Walker was the only three-time All American in
the history of the SWC and the winner of the Heisman Trophy in 1948.

The fact that Texas lost 10–6 to USC in Austin on the opening
Saturday of Bradley's varsity career was not disheartening. The Longhorns were rebuilding. They had lost to Rice, SMU, and TCU in the

second half of the 1965 season, failing to reach a bowl game for the first time in eight years.

The Longhorns bounced back to beat Texas Tech in the second week of the 1966 season. On the following Saturday, en route to a 35–0 drubbing of Indiana, Bradley suffered a knee injury that would become a serious setback. The torn cartilage caused the knee to balloon with fluid, and he would miss the Oklahoma game the following week as the Longhorns lost 18–9. The next week against Arkansas, he was sacked 3 times for minus 25 yards. He did pass for 104 yards in his only 100-yard passing performance of the year as the Longhorns lost again, 12–7.

Often, one injury can lead to other damage. Bradley also suffered a hip pointer and a badly sprained ankle. Then came a shoulder dislocation. He was taped from his right ankle to his right shoulder.

"I was just a shell of myself," Bradley recalled. "I could barely even walk. The coaches really didn't want to talk about it because they didn't want the opposition to know how bad I was hurt."

Texas limped past Rice 14–6, but lost the following week to SMU 13–12 as LeVias tore up the Longhorns secondary. Bradley spent most of the day scolding his teammates for calling his friend a nigger.

Texas salvaged a 6-4 season by defeating Baylor, TCU, and A&M. Bradley's numbers were weak; he totaled barely 100 yards running and passing in those 3 wins. The only thing "Super" about his 1966 season was his 42.6 punting average, with a longest of 79 yards.

A 19–0 victory over Mississippi in the Bluebonnet Bowl did make the season seem brighter. Bradley rushed for 105 yards on 20 carries and scored 2 touchdowns. Suddenly, he was the Bill Bradley everyone had come to expect. Prospects for the 1967 season were on the rise.

When the September 11, 1967, issue of *Sports Illustrated* hit the newsstands, everyone knew he was back. No. 18 graced the cover.

Royal winced when he saw that cover. Then he grimaced when he spotted the bumper stickers going around town.

THE YEAR OF THE 'HORNS!

Expectations could not have been higher. It seemed that everyone had overlooked the fact that the Longhorns the past two seasons had gone 6–4 and 7–4 hardly the stuff of national champions.

For the opening game of the 1967 season, the Texas defense would have to stop one of the top prospects in college football. His name was O. J. Simpson, and, in spite of not playing a single down of big-time college football, he was already being touted as a Heisman Trophy candidate.

The game was to be nationally televised, with a sellout crowd at the Los Angeles Coliseum. The Trojans were the biggest sports draw in the city. Actor John Wayne, a USC tackle in the late 1920s, would be sitting on the bench.

Simpson ripped the Longhorns for 176 rushing yards as USC won 17–13. Still, there were plenty of reasons to believe the Longhorns were on the comeback road.

Bradley passed for 151 yards the following week against Texas Tech in Austin, but Texas somehow lost the game 19–13. Darrell Royal's band of detractors was growing larger by the day. Some believed that all of the hype surrounding the Longhorns had served to cripple one of the most promising programs in America.

After beating Oklahoma State 19–0, the Longhorns were 1-2 going into the Oklahoma game. With his team trailing 7–0 at halftime, Royal went on a rampage. Normally a composed man, Royal ripped into his team. "You're a disgrace to yourselves, your school, your state, and your coaches," he yelled.

The Longhorns were suddenly motivated. They promptly outgained Oklahoma 179 to 2 in the second half and won the game 9–7.

The next week, things continued to smooth out when Texas beat Arkansas 21–12 in Little Rock. The star of the game was Chris Gilbert with 38 carries for 162 yards. Gilbert could cut on a dime and roar off like a brand-new Camaro. It seemed that the Longhorns were finally reaching top speed. The following Saturday, when Bradley passed for 215 yards against Rice, Dan Jenkins wrote in *Sports Illustrated*,

"What happened was that Bradley looked like a spunky Bobby Layne down there in the cool, pleasant Austin evening."

Bradley passed for 193 yards in a 35–28 victory over SMU, then reached his collegiate peak against Baylor with 220 yards in a 24–0 victory.

Yes, Super Bill was back. The Longhorns had their eyes set on their first Southwest Conference championship since 1963. One more victory against a 2-5 TCU team and the Longhorns would be playing Texas A&M in the season finale for the SWC title and a trip to the Cotton Bowl—but the Horned Frogs upset Texas for the second time in three years, 24–17.

Super Bill reached the nadir of the roller coaster the following week against Texas A&M in College Station. His ultimate failure could have not have come at a worse time. The Aggies, with only 1 loss, were vastly improved under new coach Gene Stallings. Many already viewed Stallings as the second coming of Paul "Bear" Bryant, his former mentor and the man he played for during the "Junction Boys" days of the 1950s.

Against A&M, Bradley threw 4 interceptions, and the Longhorns lost again 10–7.

"There were a lot of circumstances that caused us to lose that game that day, and they weren't all about me," Bradley remembered. "I don't want to go into all of the circumstances. I just have to take the blame for what happened."

So happy were the Aggies at upsetting Texas and clinching the conference championship that they left the scoreboard glowing for nine months, all the way to the start of the 1968 season.

So frustrated was Royal that he turned down all bowl invitations. The Longhorns would be staying home during the postseason for the first time since the 1956 season.

Bradley went under the knife twice after the season, the first time to fix a shoulder separation.

"I could not raise my hand over my head all season because I know the shoulder would pop out of place," Bradley said. "Everybody said I couldn't throw the ball worth a damn. Well, it's pretty hard to throw a football with a separated shoulder. Believe me, if I hadn't had all of those injuries, we would have won another couple of national championships."

In the second operation, doctors cleaned out his knee and shaved away more than a quarter of his kneecap. He spent most of the off-season rehabilitating his shoulder.

For the first time in his coaching career, Royal could hear the wolves howling at his door. He was 19-12 the previous three seasons. Texas had not even won the conference since 1963. Royal was ready to make radical changes. He told offensive coordinator Emory Bellard to come up with a read-option run-oriented scheme so the Longhorns could play smashmouth football again.

In the spring and fall drills, Bellard introduced an option offense that was called the Y-formation." It was similar to the "veer offense" being run by Bill Yeoman at Houston. The difference was that Texas was lining up three running backs instead of two. The Texas offense looked like the T-formation with the fullback moving a yard forward.

Bradley knew from the moment he set eyes on the newfangled offense that he would struggle to operate it.

"I had run the sprint-out offense since junior high," he said. "I just couldn't get the handle on the wishbone."

Bradley's future as the Texas quarterback was in jeopardy. When Texas opened the 1968 season 0-1-1 with a tie against Houston and a loss to Texas Tech, Bradley was replaced as the starting quarterback. Royal called him into his office on the Sunday morning after the Tech loss and said, "We are making five changes in the starting lineup, and you're the first. You can keep your scholarship and hang around, but about the only thing I can promise is that you'll be a fifth-string receiver."

Bradley was devastated. He had failed to meet the monstrous expectations of the Longhorn Nation. He left Royal's office that morning and started walking.

"I just walked around and cried in every part of that campus," he recalled. "I called my dad in Palestine. I told him that I was thinking about turning it in and coming home. I never used the word 'quit.' But I was thinking about coming home."

Joe Hill Bradley was never going to let his son come home under those circumstances.

"Bill, you are a captain," he said. "You can't quit. Besides, you've never been a quitter in your life. How could you possibly start now?"

Bradley reconsidered his situation and decided to stick around. After all, he could always punt. That night, he cried again at a players-only meeting when he talked about being replaced by James "Rat" Street.

"Stick with Rat," he said. "Rat'll get it done."

Bradley then invited everyone to a local watering hole called the Flagon and Trencher.

"I might be a backup now, but I'm still a captain," he told his teammates. "Hell, I don't know half of you. I say let's get together tonight and drink some beer. Let's have some fun and get to know each other."

Bradley could have fractured the team if he had chosen to protest his demotion, but Street was a good friend and Bradley loved all of his teammates. To his everlasting credit, Bradley lifted everyone's spirits with his words and his upbeat demeanor.

The next afternoon, the press showed up in droves at practice to examine the team's emotional wreckage. However, Bradley left them laughing when he ran the length of the practice field with his pants pushed down around his ankles. The message came through loud and clear. *It's time to loosen up, guys. We might have all been caught with our pants down, but better days are coming.*

With Bradley on the bench, the Longhorns would launch a winning streak against Oklahoma State the next Saturday that would last until 1971. Some good things were also coming Super Bill's way. A couple of weeks later, defensive coordinator Mike Campbell moved Bradley from offense to the secondary.

Bradley's first game starting at cornerback was against Rice in the sixth week of the season. The Texas defensive backs were instructed by Campbell to lay off the Owls receivers, in hopes of not giving up any big plays. Rice responded by running short crossing patterns that moved the ball quickly down the field and created a 14–0 deficit for the Longhorns. Bradley decided to change his coverage on the slot receiver. He met him head-on at the line of scrimmage and hit him in the chest with a forearm shiver.

This tactic worked beautifully and knocked the Rice receivers out of rhythm. From the sideline, Campbell yelled, "Bradley, I don't know what the hell you are doing out there—but *keep doing it!*"

In effect, Bradley had invented bump-and-run coverage. He had shut down the Rice passing game. The Owls did not score another point that day, and Texas rolled 38–14.

After a slow start, the Longhorns had won seven straight games and climbed all the way to No. 6 in the country. The revenge showdown with Texas A&M was coming up. Bradley was ready to rid himself of that horrible memory of throwing the 4 interceptions the previous year against the Aggies. Steam was coming out of his ears as he walked to the middle of the field for the coin toss.

When Texas A&M lost the toss, the referee turned to him and said, "Captain Bradley, would Texas like to take the ball or defend one of the goals?"

Bradley blurted, "We don't give a shit!"

The referee was startled by the response. "Captain Bradley, you will have to make a choice."

"Ah, hell, we'll take the damn football."

Campbell had instructed Bradley to "play center field" against Texas A&M quarterback Edd Hargett that day, but he had much larger plans. He had pored over game film of Hargett all week and was ready to attack.

"Hargett was a really good quarterback," Bradley said, "but I had him pegged."

That day, Bradley became the answer to a challenging trivia question. Which college player threw 4 interceptions in one game, then intercepted 4 against the same team the next season?

The answer would be Super Bill Bradley.

"It was like I was in the huddle with Hargett and the Aggies all day long," Bradley said. "I always knew their next move."

More than anything else, it said that Bradley was back. After laboring with injuries and disappointing the Texas fans, he had found a home in the defensive secondary. His career had been saved, and there was every reason to believe that he would be "Super Bill" again.

What began as the most frustrating season of his life ended in total satisfaction. Bradley intercepted 2 more passes against Tennessee in a 36–13 victory at the Cotton Bowl, finishing with 6 in his final two games. The NFL was about to come knocking.

Philadelphia Eagles coach Joe Kuharich, of "Joe Must Go" fame, drafted Bradley in the third round in the 1969 draft as a punter. Bradley spent most of that first season punting and returning kicks until the Eagles faced the Dallas Cowboys at the Cotton Bowl. In the fourth quarter, Bradley was practically begging defensive coordinator Jim "Gummy" Carr to put him in the game. He finally did, and it would be Bradley's first play from scrimmage as a pro.

The Cowboys were ahead by 4 touchdowns, and backup Dan Reeves had replaced Roger Staubach at quarterback. The Eagles were in a full blitz, and Bradley knew that tight end Mike Ditka would be running a quick inside cut. He also realized that Ditka did not hear the check-off by Reeves at the line of scrimmage. So he ran to the point in the field where Ditka was supposed to be. It was too late for Reeves to adjust. He never saw Bradley coming. The Eagles rookie intercepted the pass and returned it 56 yards down the right sideline for a touchdown.

"What a way to start your career," he said.

In 1970, Bradley reinjured his right knee and missed most of the season, but in 1971, he was rested, rehabbed, and ready to go. His first year as a full-time starter, Bradley led the league with 11 interceptions. He also finished No. 1 in the interception race the next season with 9. He remains one of two players to lead the NFL in interceptions during consecutive seasons.

Lining up at safety with the Philadelphia
Eagles.

—*Texas Sports Hall of Fame*

It has often been said that greatness will emerge even on bad teams, and Bradley was the perfect example of that. He made All-Pro in 1971, '72, and '73 on an Eagles team referred to unaffectionately as "the Beagles" during an era when Philadelphia fans threw snowballs at Santa Claus. Bradley losing his starting quarterback job at Texas, and being moved to the secondary, provided the impetus to a terrific NFL career.

When Dick Vermeil was hired by the Eagles in 1976, Bradley went back to punter and kick returner. In seven seasons, though, he intercepted 34 passes and tied with Brian Dawkins and Eric Allen for the club record. Bradley was inducted into the Eagles Hall of Fame in 1993. He is also a member of the Texas Sports Hall of Fame and the University of Texas Hall of Honor.

Bradley was traded to Minnesota in 1977 and finished his career with the Bud Wilkinson–coached St. Louis Cardinals in 1978. In 1983, he became the secondary coach of the San Antonio Gunslingers of the USFL before moving to the Memphis Showboats with Pepper Rogers in 1985. Most significantly, he coached for eight years in the NFL— with Wade Phillips at Buffalo (1998–2000), with Herman Edwards at the Jets (2001–2003), and Norv Turner at San Diego (2007–8). His teams made the playoffs in seven of those eight seasons. He also was the defensive coordinator at Baylor from 2004 to 2006.

In 2012, Bradley became the defensive coordinator at Lamar University in Beaumont under Ray Woodard.

Fred Cervelli left the *Orange Leader* after the final game of the Texas-Pennsylvania Big 33 game in 1967 and worked in the purchasing office of the local DuPont factory. In 1972, he moved his family to Austin, where he became the news director of the nationwide AFL-CIO, which included more than a half-million people. In 1978, he lost his eyesight to a rare optic nerve deterioration. In spite of his blindness, Cervelli has continued to live a full life with his wife, Marie, in Austin. He listens to sporting events on the radio. One of his greatest loves is sports talk radio, and his favorite host is Craig Way on KVET in Austin. He owns a large collection of audio books. Sadly, Fred passed away on May 30, 2013. He was prepared to listen to the audiobook of *The Kids Got It Right*. If he's listening in heaven, I'm sure he will love every line.

Doak Walker had fallen in love with Colorado when his father had taken him there as a kid. He moved to Denver after his playing career and worked as a business representative for a construction company. He also started two stores in Dallas, called Doak Walker Sporting Goods, with his good friend and former Detroit Lions end Cloyce Box. In the mid-1960s, he divorced his wife, Norma, a former SMU homecoming queen, after they had drifted apart for several years. Doak stayed in Denver, while Norma took the four children—Laurie, Kris, Russell Doak, and Scott—back to Dallas. A year later, he did a promotional TV shoot for a ski wear company and, as compensation, received six skiing lessons. The ski instructor turned out to be Gladys Maxine "Skeeter" Werner, who had gained sports recognition by appearing on the cover of *Sports Illustrated* for the 1956 U.S. Winter Olympics team as an alpine skier. Skeeter and Doak eloped to Las Vegas in 1969, then moved to Steamboat Springs, where Doak also became an expert skier. He was never one to settle for the intermediate slopes, even at age seventy. On January 31, 1998, he was flying down the Rainbow Slope at Steamboat Ski Resort when he hit a change in the rolling terrain and flew 30 feet into the air. Upon hitting the ground, he tipped forward and fell on his head, severely bruising his brain stem. He spent eight months in the hospital as a quadriplegic and died on September 27, 1998.

Harley Sewell became a scout for the Los Angeles Rams after his NFL career was over. He played ten years with the Detroit Lions, starred on two NFL title teams, and made the Pro Bowl four times. He was regarded as one of the greatest linemen in the history of the University of Texas and was inducted into the College Football Hall of

Fame in 2000. One of his greatest compliments came after he was traded from Detroit to the Los Angeles Rams in 1963. That season, Sewell suffered a back injury and was carried off the field. Doctors informed him that a verterbra was pressing against his spine, thus ending his career. Feeling guilty for not fullfilling his contract, Sewell went to Rams owner Dan Reeves and asked how he could earn his keep. Sewell suggested that he work in the scouting department. Reeves later remarked, "In all of my years in the game, Harley Sewell was the only player ever to approach me with such a proposition. He's a wonderful, rare kind of person." Sewell died on December 17, 2011, leaving behind his wife, Jean, and three children, James, Janet, and Nathan.

Ella LeVias knew that her grandson Jerry was on track to graduate at SMU when she died in 1968. Not only did Jerry graduate, he made Academic All American and received the M Award as one of the top ten seniors of the year at SMU. At graduation in May of 1969, SMU president Willis Tate asked the crowd at Moody Coliscum to hold their applause until the end of the ceremony, but Jerry received a standing ovation when his name was announced. He could only wish that Ella LeVias could have been there. "She was a wonderful woman, and I don't know what I would have done without her," LeVias said in 2013. "I still miss her."

Bill Bradley and Jerry LeVias, friends for life, in February of 2013.

—*Photo by Jim Dent*

EPILOGUE
3

The Bradley Family Comeback

Five years ago, in 2008, Matthew Wright, the stepson of Bill Bradley, was rafting a river near Sacramento with a group of beer-drinking college football teammates. These were happy times for a young man playing quarterback at American River College and hoping to earn a degree.

Matt's foursome decided to stop at a local park, where they discovered something disturbing. Several young males were drinking heavily, and one was being rough with a woman. Matt exchanged words with the man, and a fight ensued. Before long, Matt's three friends were trying to hold off the rest of the group, which numbered at least ten.

"Matt was fighting with his fists and apparently doing a pretty good job of it," Bradley says. "He was beating up the guy pretty bad. He thought the fight was over. Then the man went out to his car and came back with one of those heavy metal Maglite flashlights like the cops use. He sneaked up behind Matt and swung it like a baseball bat and struck Matt in the back of the head. Then he kicked Matt in the face."

With Matt lying on the ground unconscious, the enemy group took off. Matt's friends dialed 911, and the paramedics rushed him to the head-trauma unit of the UC Davis Medical Center Hospital. Matt was bleeding so profusely from the brain that doctors had to perform a partial resection of the cerebellum to create more space for the swelling. The deeply concussive blows left him in a coma for two weeks, but doctors stabilized him, and he was care-flighted back to the Texas Neuro Rehabilitation Center, close to where Bradley and his wife, Susan—Matt's mother—were living.

At first, the doctors told the Bradleys that Matt might not live. If he did survive, his chances of ever living normally would be slim at best. Susan Bradley could barely believe her son's condition when she first saw him following the attack.

"When I looked into his eyes I could see he was still there," she recalls. "I also could see the terror in his eyes. I said to myself, 'I don't care. I know my son is still in there.'" Then she told Matt, "You are going to be okay, and we are not going to leave you."

They could barely communicate with Matt for several weeks. He would blink once for yes and twice for no. Then they began to use a letter board. Susan or Bill would point to a letter, and Matt would blink yes or no as they proceeded to spell a word.

"For him to blink was the equivalent of an eighteen-year-old running a hundred-yard dash," Bill Bradley said. "It just wore him out."

The Bradleys knew that traditional cures would never return their son to a normal life. If Matt was to recover, they would need an alternative treatment.

One of the first steps was hyperbaric dives. Hyperbaric chambers have been traditionally used for scuba divers trying to recompress. It is a well-established treatment for decompression sickness. For Matt, the hope was to keep neuron cells from going dormant while keeping them oxygenized. He would make more than two hundred dives, and there would be no insurance to pay for them. The cost for each dive was $125.

Step two was stem cell treatment. Bill learned the story of John Brodie, one of his buddies from his NFL playing days. Brodie had suffered a massive stroke in 2000 that had left him without speech or the ability to walk. Brodie had quarterbacked the San Francisco 49ers from 1957 to 1973 and was one of the best of his era. He retired as the third leading passer in NFL history and was named league MVP in

1970. He became a TV analyst on NFL games and PGA events, then embarked on a pro golf career of his own with the Seniors Tour from 1981 to 1998, winning one tournament with twelve top ten finishes.

"Brodie went over to Russia about a half-dozen times for stem cell treatment, and it helped him immensely," Bradley says. "We talked to John and his wife, Sue, a lot, and it really helped us. We decided to do the same thing with Matt."

As it turned out, the stem cell treatments returned Brodie to a healthy life. He is back on the golf course and has regained limited speech.

"John became the poster child for stem cell treatment over in Russia," Bradley says.

There are several ties between the Bradleys and Brodie. Bill's sister May so admired the 49ers quarterback that she named one of her children after him several years ago.

Matt and Susan made their first trip to Russia two years ago, along with Matt's sister, Carissa Wright. They went to a private clinic recommended by American doctors. Almost immediately, they began to see some improvement with Matt. He began to breathe better and was able to start moving around on his own. Matt was recovering from jaw reconstruction surgery and doctors told him that the healing time would be at least a year. The jaw healed in three weeks after the first stem cell treatment.

"He just started looking so much better," Susan Bradley says. "He started getting stronger. He started putting on a lot more muscle when he worked out."

Matt had been wearing sweatshirts even in the hottest part of the summer, but after stem cell treatment, his body temperature regulated on its own. The Bradleys no longer had to suction his trachea tube on a regular basis.

"Matt always had all of his cognitive skills," Bradley says. "It was his motor skills that he was missing. But he started getting those back pretty quick."

Susan, Matt, and Carissa made their second trip overseas in the

Matt Bradley works out in San Antonio as he makes his comeback from serious head injuries suffered in 2009.

—*Bill Bradley*

summer of 2012, this time to a clinic in Kazakhstan, formerly of the USSR. It is the ninth-largest country in the world. The treatment center in Kazakhstan uses stem cells manufactured by an American stem cell company, which is based in San Diego, but the stem cell treatment that Matt received is not yet approved in the United States by the Food and Drug Administration.

The greatest leap in Matt's recovery happened on the third day of his treatment in Kazakhstan.

"He started coughing stuff up out of his lungs," Susan says. "It was such a great relief for him. He still has the trach [trachea tubes] in his lungs, but things are much better now. Every time we do stem cell treatment, it accelerates his recovery."

Matt Wright no longer lies on his back and blinks his eyes to communicate. He works out five or six times a week in nearby San Antonio under the guidance of neurologist Dr. Phillip Onghal. He rides an exercise bicycle daily, does aquatic exercises, and works with a speech and physical therapist each day. One of his therapists, Dr. Handler, dedicated herself to Matt's recovery from day one.

"If we didn't have the support of these therapists, we wouldn't have made these leaps," Susan says. "If you don't make progress, the insurance companies either cut you off or the hospitals discharge you."

Asked if Matt's road to recovery should be considered a miracle, Susan says, "I think that part of it's a miracle. But I also think that Matt's determination is the most important thing. He tries every minute of the day to get better. He continues to defy the odds. He has already inspired so many people."

The work never stops. Susan drives Matt to the hospital each day in San Antonio.

"This has required a big effort," Susan says, "but I could not have done this without Bill. He has been incredible. Neither one of us is going to give up until Matt can do everything on his own. I think this has been harder on Bill than anyone. He has cried more than any of us. He will do anything for this family without ever complaining. He loves these kids like his own. He had a real difficult time when Matt got hurt. He has a real sensitive side that not many people know about."

Bradley was prepared to retire from coaching, but realizing the family needed more money to take care of Matt, he became the defensive coordinator at Lamar University in Beaumont in 2012.

Money has also come from unexpected sources. Over the last four years, tens of thousands of dollars have been donated from charity events put on by friends and, in some cases, total strangers.

Susan also credits her daughter, Carissa, for her tireless work with Matt. Carissa, twenty-three, recently graduated from San Diego State with a degree in child development. She now works with families of children who have a terminal illness. Susan Bradley says her daughter's career path began with helping Matt.

"Matt and Carissa have grown so much closer together," she says. "Because they are so much closer in age, they can talk about things that they might not want to share with their parents."

After the attack, Matt's biological father, Jay Wright, moved to Texas from California to provide support for his son. He spends a lot of time with Matt at night after working hours. He and Bill have become close friends.

"From Bill to my ex-husband, we've just had tremendous family support," Susan says. "It has made us all just a much closer family.

Bill Bradley helped raise Matt and Carissa from early childhood. Bill and Susan met in 1993 when he was the secondary coach of the Sacramento Gold Miners of the Canadian Football League South. She traveled with Bill and her two children during coaching assignments with the Toronto Argonauts of the CFL and the Buffalo Bills. They were married in 1999. Two years later, Bill became the secondary coach of the New York Jets under Herm Edwards. Matt started his football career at St. Anthony's High School on Long Island. In 2004, Bradley became the defensive coordinator of the Baylor Bears, and the family bought a house in the Hill Country at Spring Branch about forty miles north of San Antonio.

Since Matt was old enough to handle a football, he had been

playing catch with his stepdad. He grew up with the same kind of attention that Bill received from his father, Joe Hill Bradley.

"It seemed that Matt and Bill were always playing catch," Susan says. "We could be just walking down the street and they would be throwing a ball back and forth and back and forth."

Matt played quarterback his junior year at Smithson Valley High, a 5A high school in Spring Branch. Then he moved his senior year to Cornerstone Christian in San Antonio, where legendary high school coach Sonny Detmer already knew of his talents. Matt had attended two of Detmer's summer football camps, and the coach liked what he saw. Sonny compared Matt's passing ability to that of Ty Detmer, who happened to be Sonny's son and the 1990 Heisman Trophy winner at BYU.

Out of high school, Matt played college football for a year at Tarleton State in Stephenville, Texas, then transferred to American River College.

In April of 2013, Susan and Matt again traveled to Kazakhstan for his third stem cell treatments. The best news of all is that Matt is starting to talk again.

"When you talk, you exhale," says Susan Bradley. "So the breathing part has been difficult for him. He has to work very hard to breathe, and we have to listen very closely. But he never wants to stop trying, and that's why he gets better every day."

The Bradley Family: Left to Right (top), Bill and Susan
Bradley; bottom, Carissa and Matt Bradley.

—Bill Bradley

AUTHOR'S NOTE

The idea to write *The Kids Got it Right* came from several long conversations with Bill Bradley during the fall of 2011. Bradley joined me at book signings for *Courage Beyond the Game*, the inspirational story about his former teammate Freddie Steinmark, who played the entire 1969 season at the University of Texas with cancer in his left thighbone.

Bradley and several of his UT teammates from that era were good enough to join me for these events that soon turned into book parties. Bradley and I soon started talking about the Big 33 series that lasted from 1964 to 1967. That Bradley would wind up being the roommate of Jerry LeVias in 1965 intrigued me. Sports would integrate America, but in '65 college and high school teams in Texas could not have been more segregated. The Big 33 Football Classic turned out to be a Grand Experiment for the integration of the Texas high school all-star team. No one knew how it would work out, but the bonding that took place that week between Bradley and LeVias was a tribute to everything good about both young men.

I once told LeVias, "Not many friendships last fifty years like the one between you and Bradley." He corrected me by saying, "Our friendship will last a lifetime."

I thank both Bradley and LeVias for the countless hours they spent telling me their stories. I drove down twice to Bradley's country home in the small town of Spring Branch on the Guadalupe River just north of Boerne and about thirty miles from San Antonio. Curtis Wayne Fitzgerald also threw a helluva "research" party at his home in Palestine for all of the 1964 state championship Wildcats in March of 2012. Super barbecue and cool stories. The great David Dickey flew in from Atlanta, Georgia (not Texas), for the festivities.

In July of 2012, I spent more than five hours at LeVias's home in the Houston Museum District, about three miles from downtown. It was one of the most productive interviews of my forty-plus years as a writer. He opened up about his friendship with Bradley and becoming the first black scholarship athlete in the history of the Southwest Conference, which changed him forever. LeVias experienced some tough and trying times during those four years at SMU. No one stood behind him more than Bradley.

"Bill Bradley is one of the greatest men I've ever met in my life," LeVias said.

Sitting across the room, Bradley said, "Jerry, there is no one who has lived their life better than you."

Both agreed that they could spend time apart and still pick right up on the friendship with one phone call.

The friendship between Bradley and LeVias is still as strong as it was in 1965. The three of us gathered at LeVias's house in February of 2013 so I could photograph the famous duo some forty-eight years after the 1965 Big 33 game.

My favorite story about LeVias at SMU involved the Arkansas game in Little Rock in 1968. The Ponies trailed the Hogs 35–0 at the end of three quarters. During the TV commercial break, LeVias took a knee in the end zone. The fans in Memorial Stadium rained down racial epithets on him. "Give the ball to LeeeeeRoy!" they yelled.

I was sixteen years old and sitting with my mom and dad in the west stands. I said, "I just bet LeVias returns this kickoff for a touchdown." He did, going 91 yards to the end zone. Then Hixson and LeVias went to work on the Arkansas defense. LeVias caught 10 passes in the fourth quarter and scored a touchdown. With two minutes to play, SMU had cut the lead to 35–29.

All of the catcalls and racial slurs suddenly stopped. I did not hear a single fan use the n-word again. SMU was driving in the final seconds and had reached the Arkansas 4-yard line. Hixson called for a time-out and was ignored by the referee, who said he didn't hear Hixson's request. Time ran out on one of the greatest potential comebacks in the history of college football.

At the end of the game, Arkansas fans filed out of War Memorial Stadium in total silence. Finally a man just ahead of me yelled, "Let's get out of here before that damn LeVias *scores again!*" It was a moment I would never forget. I was hoping someday to play football at Arkansas, but seeing LeVias, and being swept up in the SMU emotion, changed my mind. I graduated from SMU with degrees in journalism and English in 1975.

The Kids Got It Right is my tenth book. My thanks once again to Peter J. Wolverton, my editor with St. Martin's Press and the associate publisher of Thomas Dunne Books. Somehow he understands all of my ideas that follow the road less traveled. This is my eighth book with Pete. Among my others are *The Junction Boys*, *Twelve Mighty Orphans*, and *Courage Beyond the Game*.

One of my first stops for research on this book was at the home of Fred Cervelli in Austin. Fred was the sports editor of the *Orange Leader* and the head of the Texas selection committee when the Texas-Pennsylvania series began in 1964. Fred shared all of his memories and his scrapbook. It's hard to imagine that a scrapbook could be one of the most valuable resources I've ever used, but Fred's wife, Marie, did a terrific job of gathering the newspaper clippings, photographs, programs, etc. Thanks to Fred and Marie for trusting me with their priceless property for more than a year.

"Fred was just proud of the Big 33, and I wanted to do something to keep the memory alive," Marie said. "The scrapbook is something that we are very proud of."

Conversations and e-mails from noted author Carlton Stowers

helped me to reconstruct the life of Bobby Layne. I also thank James Street, the late Ernie Stautner, Bradley, and LeVias for all of the Layne stories. Bob St. John wrote a great book about Layne titled *Heart of a Lion*, published in 1991. Once again, a terrific resource for me was a book titled *Pigskin Pulpit* written by Ty Cashion that covers the entire history of Texas high school football. I also drew upon Bill McMurray's great book, *Texas High School Football*. Richard Pennington wrote a groundbreaking book in 1994 about the integration of Texas football, *Breaking the Ice*, that is still relevant today. His best work was on LeVias.

When I was a young reporter working for the *Beaumont Enterprise* in 1976, I started a friendship with Clifton Ozen when he was the principal at Hebert High. He told me all of the stories about Jerry LeVias and the Farr brothers and all of the great Hebert teams of the 1960s when he was a coach.

"You should have been here," he said. "We had more fun than the law allowed."

The Ozen stories had been on my mind for over four decades. They were one of the biggest reasons I jumped at the chance to write the book. I just wish Clifton could have been here to read it.

Many thanks again to Steve Fallon and Jay Black of the Texas Sports Hall of Fame in Waco. Many of the great photos in this book came from Jay Black. Bill Bradley also loaned his photo archives. Many thanks also to May Bradley, Bob Stephenson, and Steve Missildine in Palestine for loaning their scrapbooks. Bascom Bentley was my valued historian in Palestine. Curtis Wayne Fitzgerald spent more than half a day laying out the Vietnam story. David Dickey was a tremendous source on just about everything.

NAME INDEX